MOVING FAMILIES

Employees of governments, companies and non-commercial organisations increasingly find themselves sent to live abroad for years at a time, uprooting their families from jobs, schools and support networks in the process. This study is a detailed exploration of how families cope both individually and as structures with the stresses of moving to a new culture: how children cope with the change of schools, friends, culture and language; how accompanying partners cope with the loss of status that comes from leaving professional lives behind; how the strains of running a household in an unfamiliar culture add to the isolation of losing day-to-day contact with established friends and family.

Through rich interviews conducted with families followed over a period of two years, Mary Haour-Knipe shows the processes of change and adjustment at work. Her findings will be of interest to students of wider issues of migration, to those who study the family under pressure and to families who are thinking of moving abroad to live in a new culture.

Dr Mary Haour-Knipe now works for the Joint United Nations Programme on HIV/AIDS within the migration health service of the International Organisation for Migration in Geneva.

FOR GEORGES,
ANNE AND PATRICK

MOVING FAMILIES

Expatriation, stress and coping

Mary Haour-Knipe

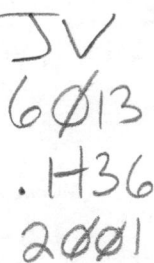

London and New York

First published 2001
by Routledge
11 New Fetter Lane, London EC4P 4EE

Simultaneously published in the USA and Canada
by Routledge
29 West 35th Street, New York, NY 10001

Routledge is an imprint of the Taylor & Francis Group

© 2001 Mary Haour-Knipe

Typeset in Baskerville by
Florence Production Ltd, Stoodleigh, Devon
Printed and bound in Great Britain by
Clays Ltd, St Ives plc

All rights reserved. No part of this book may be
reprinted or reproduced or utilised in any form or by any
electronic, mechanical, or other means, now known or hereafter
invented, including photocopying and recording, or in any
information storage or retrieval system, without
permission in writing from the publishers.

British Library Cataloguing in Publication Data
A catalogue record for this book is available from the
British Library

Library of Congress Cataloging in Publication Data
Haour-Knipe, Mary.
Moving families: expatriation, stress and coping/Mary Haour-Knipe.
p. cm.
Includes bibliographical references and index.
1. Moving, Household—Psychological aspects. 2. Emigration and
immigration—Psychological aspects. 3. Expatriation—Psychological
aspects. 4. Moving, Household—case studies. I. Title.
JV6013.H36 2001
306.85–dc21   00-030253

ISBN 1–85728–814–9 (hbk)
ISBN 1–85728–815–7 (pbk)

CONTENTS

Preface ix

1 Introduction 1

The study site 1
Theory 4
Methodology 7
How the book unfolds 10

2 Who are they, and why do they move? 14

Who are they? 15
Why do they move? 16
The relation between work and moving 18
The decision to move 28
Discussion 32

3 What is stressful about moving abroad? 51

Stress around the move itself 55
Hassles as a threat to feelings of adult competence 58
Language 60
The comfortable known-ness of things, and what is taken
    for granted 63
Not knowing the rules, threats to identity 65
Initial isolation and loneliness: 'Nobody would know if I left for
    three days' 68

4 Strains on families 71

Two careers or one? 74
Partners not 'adjusting well' 78
'Duty travel' and strains it may cover 81
Different values 90

CONTENTS

5 Coping · 96

Event and meaning, comprehensibility and manageability 96
Family sense of coherence 98
Coping with the stresses of moving to a new culture 99
Discussion 112

6 Giving and receiving social support · 116

Relationships with extended families 116
Social support over long distances 119
Support coming from the new place 121
Gaining control over social relations 123
Mobilising social support 130
Social support in Geneva and in 'hardship posts' 133

7 Social support from within the family · 138

Families operating together 138
High family 'co-ordination', meeting people and family separations 139
Low family 'co-ordination' and family members in difficulty 143
Imbalances of authority, encountering different values 145
Discussion 154

8 Effects on children · 156

School-aged children 158
Younger children 162
Adolescents and older children 164
Discussion 168

9 The effect of the move: two case studies · 170

The Foster family 170
The Wood family 180
Discussion 186

10 Families two years later · 190

Coping with issues around two careers 190
Phases of adaptation 194
Families' reflections on the effects of migration 198
Towards explaining the effects of the move on families 201

11 Summary and conclusions — 209

Summary 209
The influence of SOC and of family 'co-ordination' 215
Long-term effects? 220
Expatriation, stress, coping and families 221
Stress and families 223

References — 225
Appendix — 228
Index — 237

PREFACE

Why this book?

This book developed over almost twenty years. Around 1982 the author did a small pilot study of women who had followed their professional and executive husbands to Switzerland, attempting to investigate whether the stress of moving abroad resulted in illness. The women talked of a great many stresses (the death of a parent, for example, when one is too far away to help, or a 'surprise' pregnancy), and hassles were even more prevalent (misunderstandings with neighbours, for example, or not being able to find basic food items taken for granted at home), but *nobody* reported any illness. In fact some of the women reported being in better health than usual. I was surprised, and went back half a year later to discuss the finding with the same people. By then, some of the children had been ill, and others were experiencing adjustment problems that were worrying their mothers; some of the women were concerned about career problems their husbands were having; others talked about difficulties in relationships with extended families and friends in their home country. The women all remained in good physical health, but some described themselves as depressed, and in fact were in the midst of re-evaluating their lives.

Two major conclusions developed from that preliminary study. The first was that for the particular problem of transcultural migration it makes more sense to look at the family than to look at the individual: it is the system as a whole that reacts. The second conclusion was that a longitudinal design is necessary. What needs to be studied is a process, not a state of being: it is more valuable to examine stories as they unfold, effects as they spiral upwards or downwards. Whereas what is perceived to be an end state is by definition difficult to influence, a developing process, in contrast, may be modified through intervention from an employer, a group, a colleague or a friend.

PREFACE

Grounding

The study of families moving to a new culture comes out of, and contributes to, three different literatures. Studies of *migration* have tended to focus on refugees or economic migrants. Such migrants often have significant problems indeed, but it is difficult to pick out what may be due to the migration itself as opposed to the other factors linked with the change of location. A thorough examination of the short-term stresses involved in moving to another culture – and of coping – among relatively privileged migrants for whom 'all other things are equal' should help increase understanding of the process for all migrants. Coming at the problem from the other side, there has been a great deal of discussion in management circles of 'expatriation'. Employees have always been posted away from their home country, but the number of such postings may well increase as both business and non-government organisations (NGOs) 'go global'. Transfers of executives and professionals are expensive. They also involve a certain amount of risk since it costs a very great deal to bring an employee home early: adjustment problems of the family are often given as the reason for such failures.

From the point of view of the *stress* literature, migration with a family can be considered a moderately stressful event. Change itself is sometimes considered to be stressful, and moving involves many elements of change, but at the same time is usually chosen by people such as those who participated in this study. This raises the question of why people might actually choose to do stressful things, or as Aaron Antonovsky once beautifully put it, 'the potential glory of stressors'.

From the point of view of the *family* literature, finally, such an experience is likely to affect the family and the way it functions. Even more important, though, is that this is a study of families which generally function well. The study thus provides a rare opportunity to examine how basically healthy families cope with new experiences that can be very perplexing, and with temporary loss of the comfortable and known social structure that had surrounded and supported them. Studying the way well-functioning families handle stress can perhaps demonstrate how other families might better do so.

The study began as a doctoral thesis at the University of Geneva. The first round of interviews was initiated in May of one year in the late 1980s; the last interviews were completed by January almost three years later. Then began a long latent phase. I had in the meantime become heavily involved in an entirely different theme of migration research. The new field of work was gratifying, urgent and involved great commitment. It seemed to be taking place in vivid colour, whereas the family study was in pastels. Colleagues assumed I had completed the thesis process years ago, and the family study slid further and further down the list of things

PREFACE

to do. People started raising their eyebrows when I said I was still working on it. More than once I decided to let it go. But a large body of incomplete work is an uncomfortable thing to carry around. What made me finally get down to writing up the study was a combination of internal pressure, of commitment I had made to the people I studied, of feeling that it would be a waste to let it go, of gentle and not-so-gentle urgings from husband and mentors. Later, support and encouragement came from other friends and colleagues, including, after a while, even some of those in the HIV/AIDS world (so that I could get the thing done with and concentrate on another aspect of somewhat diverse professional fields). The thesis version of the study was defended to the Faculty of Social and Economic Sciences of the University of Geneva in September 1999.[1]

Acknowledgements

An author's personal motivation in making such a study is better stated from the beginning rather than being left to supposition. In common with a great many migration experts who have names that do not fit where they live, I grew up in a family in which ancestors had either emigrated across oceans or gone to settle at frontiers. I had a father who, as a public health physician, enjoyed moving on to new challenges, so that by the time I reached adolescence our family had moved several times between both coasts of Canada and the United States. Immediately after finishing university I transported myself to the opposite side of the North American continent, then in due course married a European and eventually moved to Switzerland.

As for this study, a project of the duration and complexity of this one builds up a large number of people to whom thanks are due. I would like especially to acknowledge the assistance of the following:

First and foremost, there are those who were interviewed. Forty-five families gave evenings and weekends, from two to a total of almost twenty hours of their time, to a stranger who said she was doing a study. For some of them, an evening at home was a rare and precious gift to give. All of them took a risk: of discussing the problems and the pleasures of moving, of letting somebody into their homes to observe them, of being misunderstood, of breaches of confidence. The obvious needs to be repeated: without the generous participation of these families there would have been no study.

Around the central core of families interviewed are a host of others who helped, listed in the following paragraphs in approximate chronological order.

[1] Pieces of this work have been presented at several conferences, as well as published in articles (Haour-Knipe, 1997 and 2000) and as a thesis (1999).

PREFACE

Although it was not yet evident at the time, transition between the pilot stress study and the family study was provided by stints at the mental health division of the World Health Organisation in Geneva. Marcus Grant commissioned a background paper about stress in international employment settings, and Norman Sartorius later widened the task by requesting an article on the effects of geographical mobility on the children of international employees.

Jean Kellerhals, as thesis director, later provided critical structure, and by his intellectual rigour helped clear up fuzzy thinking at several intervals through the years. It was also Jean Kellerhals who permitted me to go off on my own with the project, nevertheless being generously available to discuss the study when asked.

David Reiss, whose book on the family's construction of reality provided the conceptual starting point for the study, also offered some excellent pragmatic suggestions, and, more importantly, enthusiastic encouragement at the very beginning, which convinced me that the effort was worth pursuing.

Thanks are due to the several people who started 'snowballs' as interviewing began, providing names of families arriving in Geneva, and/or access to people who could do so, as well as, at a second stage, to the director of the international school, the parents committees, the three campus principals, and the secretaries who respectively gave permission and then sent lists of names of arriving students. Truly adequate sampling at a third stage was assured with the help of M-L. François and W. Hutmacher of the Geneva public education department, whose permission led to the complete listings of families who arrived during the year the study began. The Geneva Société Academique provided a small grant which helped cover some of the expenses of carrying out the study.

Even behind a highly qualitative study there hides a considerable amount of computers and statistics. Daniel Glauser deserves special thanks for writing a program macro for treating the interview data, and patiently teaching me how to use it. This technology elegantly replaced the old scissors and pile method of sorting data, and also allowed the researcher to stare fascinated at the screen as the computer did the work for a while. As for other programmes and statistics, not all visible in this text, Liz Low, especially, patiently offered explanations and assistance at various points.

Very special thanks are due to Amal King and Myriam Vandamme. Both are professionals in their own right, in transition at the time. They spent many weeks as volunteer research assistants, doing the tedious, solitary, and tiring work of coding interviews. Having each interview independently coded by three people provided a vital check, and our discussions of each family often led to valuable insights. Their generous unpaid efforts at tasks essential, but invisible in the final product, are deeply appreciated.

PREFACE

It was with Merrijoy Kelner that I originally gained experience in qualitative research, and she has been a mentor and friend ever since. Merrijoy read the first hundred pages of the first draft of this book, and asked some pertinent and courageous questions only a good friend would dare to ask. Edgar Heim and Liz Low carefully commented on a much later draft, and Barbara Hornby on one after that. Liz Low took the process innumerable small steps further, patiently nursing the manuscript through a number of subsequent revisions. Thanks are also due to the necessarily anonymous study participant who read the final manuscript to check confidentiality, and to those who helped me prepare to defend the thesis version. As for the editors, changes at Taylor & Francis – and the amount of time it took to get the study through the thesis process and into book form – meant that the manuscript was in the hands of four different editors. Comfort Jegede and Mari Shullaw were particularly important in bringing the book into being.

Two influences are all-pervasive. The first is that of Aaron Antonovsky. It is his concept of 'salutogenesis' that provides the epistemological basis for the study. It is Aaron who taught so many of us to look for what goes right, for health and growth, as well as for what goes wrong, for pathology. 'Sense of coherence' is his concept, and discussions of it in this book, including those that are critical, are shaped by the talks we had, in several different countries, at conferences, over meals, in our respective homes, and on long walks. With his support and encouragement Aaron mothered the project, especially throughout the data analysis. It was his gentle lecture about commitment that got me back to the study when I might otherwise have let it go quietly into oblivion. He patiently read and commented on the initial outline and several later versions. By the time Aaron died, suddenly and unexpectedly, the book was progressing under its own impetus, but I miss his wisdom, and I miss his friendship.

The second all-pervasive influence is, of course, that of my immediate entourage, neglected friends who have stuck by, and Madame Vidal, who has known what to do to keep our physical environment in order, and thus allowed me to steer a course more tranquil than it would otherwise have been. Finally, fundamentally, there is my family. Georges' practical support amounted to the functional equivalent of a research grant for several years, when elementary fairness would dictate that perhaps *I* should take a turn earning money, so that *he* could be free to pursue his own interests. His moral support and encouragement have been unstintingly warm, occasionally caustic, always total. As for Anne and Patrick, they grew from being just barely past needing a baby sitter at the time of the first interviews, to being 'launched', living on their own, getting on with their lives with a little less maternal attention than I might have wished, coping far more than just adequately with their studies, transforming from children to interesting young adults and even colleagues and friends.

PREFACE

Especially in recent years, when 'the family book' has had to be fitted in around other professional obligations, when it occupied literally countless evenings and weekends, my own family has been supportive, always there, far too often taken for granted. The book is dedicated to them, in heartfelt gratitude.

1
INTRODUCTION

The study site

With its large international community, Geneva is a good place to study migrants. One-third of the population is foreign, and another third consists of Swiss people from other cantons, who may well speak another language, and who often consider themselves as foreign as those from other countries. It is also a good place to make a study of relatively privileged migrants – or expatriates. Several major international organisations and several multinational corporations are based in the city, thereby also attracting the offices of numerous smaller organisations and companies. There is a university, and a cultural and artistic life surprising for a city of some 400,000 inhabitants, with, for example, an international-level orchestra, several theatres, numerous art galleries. All of this means that there is a constant movement of foreign professionals and executives, transferring with their families to take up what are usually planned to be relatively short-term assignments.

The North American family moving to Geneva is hardly isolated. The English-speaking community is large; it includes people from Great Britain and its former empire, and also from countless other countries. No less than eleven churches and two major private schools offer their services in English. English-language books, movies, and videos are easy to come by, and there are several English-speaking clubs, and a theatre group.

Some 7,000 Americans and Canadians were officially listed as living in the Geneva region the year the people studied here arrived, with others (not counted in Swiss statistics) living across the border in France, a 15-minute drive away. Thus there are available not only English-speaking, but specifically American and Canadian communities. Some of the organisations catering primarily to the North American community include the American church, community centre and library; a Women's Club; a radio station; several special interest groups such as dancing, bowling and hiking groups, and groups organised by both American political parties. Many of the American-based multinational corporations have wives' clubs, and arrange regular activities, including the celebration of traditional holidays such as Halloween.

To make an overseas posting acceptable to their employees, most multinational companies guarantee the same standard (or – more correctly – the same style) of living as they would have in North America. This means that the North American family will usually live in a house. The vast majority of Geneva's other residents, certainly including Swiss colleagues at the same socio-economic level, live in rented apartments. The real estate consequence is that there are several neighbourhoods on the outskirts of the city containing a Swiss developer's version of American-style housing. These houses are relatively expensive. Some have been bought by Swiss people, and some are occupied by foreigners from other countries, but many are owned or leased for their personnel by multinational companies. Chances are thus high in some neighbourhoods that many of the neighbours will be fellow North Americans.

Several other factors concerning the geography of Geneva affect the social relations of its sub-communities. An alliance – somewhat surprising to the non-initiated – between ecologists and the residue of a policy of national agricultural self-sufficiency left over from World War II, protects a good two-thirds of the canton's 246 square kilometres as agricultural land. Thus the centre of the city is densely urban, surrounded by a very thin zone of suburban houses and then by open fields. The suburban zone would be the norm in most North American cities. In some Geneva neighbourhoods, such as one inhabited by thousands of middle- and upper-level employees of international organisations, the landscape goes abruptly from six-floor apartment buildings to land that is used for farming.

The centre of the city is thus densely populated, with, it has been said, an automobile density the same as that of Los Angeles in a city that was laid out long before the car was invented. The public transportation system functions well, but traffic problems are monumental for those who eschew it, and the style of driving resembles that of Paris or New York more than that of the wider open spaces of most of North America.

The city of Geneva sits at the end of Lac Leman, out of which flows the River Rhone. Lake and river effectively divide the city into two halves: the possibility, or lack thereof, of getting across one of the four major bridges is a major factor determining where people choose their housing in relation to their offices, and even who they will visit during the day. Driving across the city from one end to the other may take about 20 minutes on a Sunday morning, or up to two hours at the end of a working day.

Partly because of the instability of the foreign population, who rarely plan on settling in Geneva when they arrive, partly because of the relatively sedentary nature of large segments of the local population, and partly because of the housing arrangements described above, there is relatively little social permeability between the American and the local

Geneva populations. Although exceptions abound, the myth that 'you won't meet the Genevans' is current; most Americans have been told this, and arrive expecting not to meet the locals.

Both the large international community and the North American community are made up mainly of people working for multinational companies and international organisations, and their families. The communities are thus relatively homogeneous in socio-economic status (upper middle class), age (babies may be born to these families, but there are few elderly), and life stage (young adult to middle-age families). Since most people arrive for a limited stay the communities' memberships are also constantly shifting. A proportion of these communities large enough to be dominant is made up of people who make transcultural moves very frequently, the 'Gypsy aristocrats' or the permanently rootless.

Belonging to the North American community is strictly voluntary: it is perfectly possible to avoid the North American networks altogether. Many people choose this route in hopes of integrating elsewhere. For those who wish to join in, many activities are available and, since there are invariably many other newcomers eager to meet people at any given time, someone who does wish to do so and to belong to groups can quickly and easily become very busy.

An important differentiation in the international community is that between the newcomers and the old timers, between those who have recently arrived and those who remain foreigners, but are more or less permanently settled in Geneva.[2] There is little interaction between the two sub-groups, except for certain old timers who serve as bridges, specialists in helping the newcomers adapt, some professionally as paid consultants, house-finders etc., and some as volunteers. Many of the latter are women, and pillars of such organisations as the American Women's Club.

The newcomer group thus tends to form a cohort interacting a great deal with each other, to some extent with the old timers, and very little, if at all, with the natives. The most marked characteristic of this community is that relationships remain superficial; friendly and pleasant, but not intimate. They have been described as 'fleeting friendships'. Talking about real problems is very difficult, although in certain sub-groups complaining, the '*discours misérabiliste*', is the norm. While being socially isolated under such circumstances is to some extent a question of choice, being emotionally isolated is quite another matter, as will be discussed later (Chapters 4 and 6).

---

2 In contrast with many other European countries, and with Canada and the United States, Switzerland has no policy of encouraging immigrants to become citizens. Many would say the *de facto* policy is quite the opposite, since acquiring citizenship is onerous, in terms of both effort and finances. The result is that a good many residents from other countries remain foreigners, living in the country for years, even generations, without attempting to obtain Swiss nationality.

INTRODUCTION

Theory

Theoretical underpinning for the study came mainly from the work of two authors: Aaron Antonovsky and David Reiss. The theories are briefly presented here for those who like to know where the author is 'coming from', and will be returned to in discussions throughout the book. More extensive reviews of the literature on family stress and migration, and more extensive theoretical discussions, are to be found in Haour-Knipe (1999).

The starting point for the study was in the work of David Reiss (1981). Reiss's central idea is that in the course of their development together, families develop paradigms, rich and ordered sets of beliefs about the social world. These beliefs, or shared constructs, shape the way in which families perceive the outside world and thus how they deal with it. There are three dimensions to family paradigms: 'the degree to which families delay their final decisions until they have all the evidence they can obtain', 'the family's belief that they, in fact, occupy the same experiential world, a world which operates in the same way for all of them', and finally 'a fundamental conception, by the family, that the social world in which they live is ordered by a coherent set of principles which they can discover and master through exploration and interpretation'.

The first dimension ('closure' in Reiss' terms) has to do with families' experience of novelty in the world. On one end of a continuum are families for whom all experience is reminiscent – all new events are understood with some reference to their own particular family history. For such families new situations require, at most, a modest reshuffling of past experience. At the opposite extreme are families for whom each experience is new – the past is forgotten or is not perceived as relevant. A new setting is thus experienced with a relative freshness and little preconception. The second dimension (which Reiss called 'co-ordination', but which may also be called 'family cohesion') has to do with family unity, or sense of 'us'. Those high on this dimension feel that the world perceives the family as a whole, that whatever happens to one family member affects all of them. Members of a family very low on this dimension, on the other hand, would perceive themselves as a group of individuals relatively unconnected to one another. If the first dimension has to do with a family's sense of novelty, and the second to its perception of itself as a group, the third has to do with the way in which a family perceives the structure of the outside world: this dimension is strikingly similar to a family's 'sense of coherence', which will be discussed below.

Reiss and his colleagues postulated that a family's paradigm distinctively influences the way in which it will cope with stress, particularly since a family's definitional process concerning an event is part of its *response* to the event. In other words, the way a family defines what is happening to it will shape the style of the coping that will follow. Definitions are also partly established by communities, which teach a family what attitudes to have about its experiences (Reiss and Oliveri, 1983). In the case studied here, such attitudes would be about how stressful – or fun, or gratifying, or stimulating – moving might be, as well as about such things as culture shock and hassles, for example. The community also defines an event's punctuation (the 'beginning' and 'ending'), and provides guidelines both for family coping and for community patterns of assistance. In other words, Reiss would propose that it is partly the community which determines at what point a family should reasonably be expected to cope on its own with the strains of a recent move, and when it can reasonably expect to receive help.

As for Antonovsky's work on 'sense of coherence', it developed out of quite another area of research. It was during an Israeli study of menopause that he and his colleagues (Datan, Antonovsky, Maoz, 1981) noticed that a certain number of the women they were studying had been through one of the most stressful experiences imaginable, that of having been incarcerated in concentration camps, yet many years later had nevertheless maintained good physical and mental health. While a great many studies had concentrated on the sometimes catastrophic consequences of such experiences, or more generally on what makes people ill, Antonovsky's research began to focus on what allows people to remain healthy. Among a number of psychological, social, and cultural 'generalized resistance resources' appeared a way of making sense of the world that, over the following years, developed into the concept of the sense of coherence (SOC) (Antonovsky, 1979, 1987):

> The sense of coherence is a global orientation that expresses the extent to which one has a pervasive, enduring though dynamic feeling of confidence that (1) the stimuli deriving from one's internal and external environments in the course of living are structured, predictable, and explicable; (2) the resources are available to one to meet the demands posed by these stimuli; and (3) these demands are challenges, worthy of investment and engagement.
> (Antonovsky, 1987)

As implied, the sense of coherence has three interrelated components, of which the first is:

> *comprehensibility*: the extent to which one perceives the stimuli that confront one, deriving from the internal and external environments, as making cognitive sense, as information that is ordered, consistent, structured, and clear, rather than as noise – chaotic, disordered, random, accidental, inexplicable.

In other words the individual feels it is possible to understand the outside world: the stimuli to be encountered in the future will be predictable, or if they do come as surprises, they can be put in order and are explicable. Bad things such as death, war, or failure, may happen, but one can at least make sense of them.

The second component of the SOC is:

> *manageability*: the extent to which one perceives that there are resources at one's disposal which are adequate to meet the demands posed by the stimuli that bombard one.

The person feels there is 'a high probability that things will work out as well as can reasonably be expected'. Life events are seen as experiences that can be coped with, as challenges that can be met. At worst, events or their consequences are bearable. The contrary is the attitude 'it always happens to me', that bad things always just seem to happen to one, and this will continue to be the case in life. With a high sense of manageability one will not feel victimised by events or consider that life treats one unfairly: 'untoward things do happen, but one will be able to cope and not grieve endlessly'.

The final component is:

> *meaningfulness*: the extent to which one feels that life makes sense emotionally, that at least some of the problems and demands posed by living are worth investing energy in, are worthy of commitment and engagement, are challenges that are 'welcome' rather than burdens that one would much rather do without.

In other words there is *something* one cares about, very much, things in life worthy of emotional investment and commitment. The opposite is the feeling that nothing in life really matters particularly. One or another aspect of life might be important, but only in the sense that it imposes wearisome burdens, unwelcome demands. Of the three components, meaningfulness is central, but again, the three components are most definitely interrelated.

Antonovsky convincingly argued that people with a strong sense of coherence will tend to seek to impose structure on and to accept the challenge of a situation, are more likely to confront stress with appropriate coping responses, and, in the end, will remain in good health in the face of stress. Moving to a new culture contains numerous elements requiring coping and adaptation: it seemed from the outset of the study that the aptitude to make sense out of external events, the feeling of being to some degree in control of and responsible for events, and an orientation regarding situations as challenges worthy of commitment and engagement rather than as burdens, would make a crucial difference in facilitating such an adjustment.

The pertinence of these two theories for a study of family migration to a new culture should be obvious. Dealing with a great deal of change, with goodly doses of the unknown, families' views of the world affect in fundamental ways how they cope with the new experiences. The theories of Antonovsky and Reiss guided the choice of many of the questions for the interviews, and of some of the instruments used, but were then deliberately put aside after interviewing began, only to come back late in the process of analysis, after the interviewing was finished. In other words I consciously went into the study with a fairly open mind as to what I would be finding. The process used is important for understanding the basic stance as well as the *how* of the study, and is described in the next section.

Methodology

A hopeless level of generality results when studies of expatriation or of migrants mix culture of origin, social class, reasons for relocating and a host of other variables. Such studies leave readers perplexed as to how, if at all, the conclusions might be applied to specific populations or cases. This study leans resolutely in the opposite direction, choosing specificity, aiming at depth, in hopes that the specific can then become general. In order to control the number of variables in operation, the sample was limited to one life stage, that of families with school-aged children. For similar reasons the study was also limited to families of one culture of origin, North American,[3] who moved to one site, Geneva, Switzerland, during one calendar year in the late 1980s. The fact that the researcher was of the same language and culture as those studied, and had been through some of the same experiences, was not insignificant, and considerably facilitated the first contact, especially.

Potential study participants were first identified through networking and snowball (in other words explaining the study and asking for names of recently arrived families, or of people who might know of recently arrived families) then later through lists provided by the international school and

---

3 One of the first problems that arose once the interviewing began was how to define 'North American'. Both the United States and Canada are countries of immigration, and the very first people I interviewed had grown up in another culture. They considered themselves North American, however, and it was this subjective definition that was adopted for the rest of the study. If the several study participants born in other countries considered themselves American or Canadian, they were included. One couple, who had emigrated to the United States some years before but who did not consider themselves American were thus eliminated. On the other hand, another family, technically at least partly American, but none of whose members had ever lived on the North American continent, was also eliminated.

the Geneva public education department. With the latter list of all Canadian and American children who had arrived during the calendar year, and who attended any of the schools in Geneva, I was sure of having the names of the entire population of families who met sample limitations.

Potential study participants were first contacted by letter, then by telephone a few days later. A little over 80 per cent of the families who met sample limitations agreed to participate in the study. Forty-five families were seen for the first round of interviews, 30 for a second, 26 for a third. Four families were seen for additional interviews. Several families were eliminated from most of the analysis presented here. Five of these were single mothers who moved with their children: the difficulties they experienced in moving abroad are quite different from those of dual-parent families, and would merit a specific study. Other families did not fit sample limitations, and one withdrew after a first interview. Five families (for example, those of professors on sabbatical years) had left by the time the second round of interviews began, and four more left by the next wave of interviewing, some two years after they moved. Such rates of attrition are to be expected among highly mobile families such as those studied here. The main body of the analysis for the study thus concerns 28 families, those with two parents who stayed in Geneva for the full two years of the study.

Open-ended interviews were conducted in peoples' homes, generally in the evening, occasionally on weekends. The first interview took place, on the average, three to four months after the family's arrival. Seeing families soon after their arrival proved to be less neutral, more intense, than foreseen, and themes emerged that had not been anticipated when the initial interview guide was planned. Some of those who participated in the study were lonely and fragile, newly arrived in a place where they did not yet know anybody, and I was on occasion the first person to whom they talked about their feelings about moving. It was interviewing people in crisis that prompted a shift towards depth, towards trying to understand as fully as possible, at least with some of the research participants, the effects of relocation on families. The study thus shifted towards working with, not on, the research subjects.

The change in emphasis was reflected in the introductory speech for the second round of interviews, which started about one year after the first. The second interview started with a short summary of some of the main discoveries from the first phase. I then listed a number of themes that had come up, such as phases of adaptation families may go through, how living abroad may affect the way individuals develop over the long term, or physically and psychologically feeling comfortable and at home in the new place as opposed to feeling uneasy and as though one is being criticised by strangers. Asked to comment on any of the above themes, interviewees invariably responded with interest and rarely needed more than the occasional reminder to then cover at length the themes proposed during the two or more hours the interview normally lasted. The third interview began in the same way as the second, with a brief summary of the study so far, a question as to events of the past year, and a minimally structured interview. The last interviews were completed almost three years after the study began.

A number of questionnaires were also used. One was Antonovsky's sense of coherence questionnaire (1987), which consists of 29 items to be rated on a scale of 1 to 7, such as: 'Life is: full of interest . . . completely routine' (a meaningfulness item); 'When you face a difficult problem, the choice of a solution is: always confusing and hard to find . . . always completely clear' (a comprehensibility item); or 'What best describes how you see life: one can always find a solution to painful things in life . . . there is no solution to painful things in life' (a manageability item). Other questionnaires used were a 'network inventory' of people important to the respondent, a checklist of stressful and positive aspects of living abroad, and an inventory concerning various aspects of marriage (Fitzpatrick, 1988).

Both spouses were almost always seen together. Husband and wife often completed each other's sentences, waited with obvious interest to hear what the other was about to say, added complementary bits of information, disagreed. Any differences of opinion between husbands and wives were usually hinted at sufficiently to make the interviewer well aware of them, and most often were frankly discussed. Especially in the latter interviews the tape recorder captured – in the full knowledge of the participants – some fairly striking arguments and tense conjugal moments. The only exception was for the families in trouble: in two instances husband and wife asked to be interviewed separately after the second interview. In both cases they were tense and reserved when together, but discussed their difficulties more freely in the other's absence.

Children were occasionally present, and sometimes interviewed, although not systematically. In two or three families the children participated actively in the interviews, and their observations added greatly to what their parents were saying, but parents attempts to call children in to talk with me in their presence in the middle of an interview were rarely successful. If the children had not naturally been present throughout, being called in and put on the spot, so to speak, usually yielded minimally enlightening 'yesses' and 'nos'.

Except for one done in a restaurant and another in a study participant's office, the 110 interviews were taped, then transcribed. The tape recordings later helped bring back the particular feel of an interview and of a home: clocks chiming, cups and glasses being put down, telephones being answered, dogs snoring. Transcriptions of the 110 interviews, or 160 hours of tape, resulted in more than a thousand pages of raw data to then be analysed.

Analyses were performed family by family and theme by theme. Some themes had guided the research from the beginning, others emerged as the interviews were performed and transcribed. As each theme was analysed, more abstract themes and connections emerged, hypotheses suggested themselves, groupings were made, and patterns emerged. Some of this process took place as interviews were going on, and many of the analyses were discussed with study participants. These discussions helped considerably in gaining clarification, and some led to further insights. Several study participants offered observations, suggestions and hypotheses.

With all but one or two of the families, the interviews yielded more and more information as we got to know one another. Some feelings could be formulated only once the worst was past, as with one family who refused to be interviewed about the stress of moving to a new culture until their feelings of distress had practically disappeared. Some people did not wish to talk about their hopes for a stay, for a job, or for their children, until what they had been hoping for had come to pass. Stories sometimes changed over time because those approached for the study had no particular reason to trust a stranger, and presented an idealised image of themselves when I first saw them. As we got to know one other, and as I passed tests about maintaining confidentiality, several respondents were more forthcoming. Such shifts and changes became part of the material to be analysed. The final section of this chapter sketches the way the book is organised.

How the book unfolds

The next chapter describes the families who participated in the study, then discusses why people move: how various factors are weighed when the decision is made, and what people do to prepare. The various stresses experienced are then discussed in two separate chapters, one focusing on individuals and the other on the specific strains undergone by families. These chapters are organised around Antonovsky's theory of sense of coherence, with 'meaningfulness', 'manageability', and 'comprehensibility' providing the framework for presentation and discussion. SOC affects coping, and it is to this that the following chapters are devoted. Chapter 5 discusses coping, and Chapter 6 the social support that comes from outside the family. The following chapter discusses the social support that may come from within the family, factoring in Reiss's element of family 'co-ordination', or the degree to which families operate *together* to face the challenges of adapting to a new culture. Throughout, the policy is to let the interviewees do as much of the talking as possible, with extensive quotations from the interviews. The aim is to let those studied give a feeling for 'what it is like'.

INTRODUCTION

Three last descriptive chapters discuss the effect of the move on the families studied. It proved extremely difficult to 'pin down' the results of a complex process which invariably included a mix of positive and negative aspects. How to classify, for example, the family for whom the move clearly led to disruption, to divorce and to psychiatric problems for all family members, but about which the wife said at the end that the experience had been extremely positive because of what she had learned from it? How to classify, also, a very well functioning family whose members may have been able to travel a bit, and to discover something about a new culture, but for whom nothing really changed in the way family members functioned together or viewed the world? Chapter 8 discusses effects on children. There are some surprises in this chapter, as children did not necessarily react the way the literature would have them do. Chapters 9 and 10 bring the focus back to the families. Contrasting case studies are presented first: the 'Foster' family is discussed in some detail, as is the way in which the strains of a move contributed to the family's disintegration. The 'Wood' family, who appear at several intervals throughout the book, then illustrate the opposite process, the way in which the strains of a move may promote growth and mastery among family members. Chapter 10 discusses how families coped with issues around two careers, then the outcomes of the move for the 28 families who make up the main body of the study. The chapter goes on to discuss the factors that may – or may not – have contributed to explaining such effects, picking up one of the theoretical constructs sketched above, the rapidity with which they draw conclusions about their environment. Chapter 11 summarises and raises the question of the possible long-term effects of moving.

Some technical observations are in order before turning to who the study participants are and why they moved.

Maintaining confidentiality

The Geneva North American expatriate community is small, with many overlapping networks, and a major problem for this study is to preserve confidentiality. Many of the people interviewed knew each other. I had explained that I was seeing all families with school-aged children who arrived during the same year, and on several occasions during an interview people would ask, either testing or naively, if I had already talked with a particular family. I always refused to say, of course, but on more than one occasion heard an interviewee refer to me by name to someone who happened to telephone while I was present, and quite often we all knew that a particular discussion was referring to someone with whom I had already spoken. Confidentiality is also a problem outside Geneva circles. Some of the people interviewed would be recognisable to anyone working in the same field, even from abroad. I discussed the problem with those who participated in the study: some were perfectly unconcerned, while one – although only one – was concerned to the point of withdrawing after the first interview.

Especially in the institutions it hosts, Geneva has too many particularities that affect the life of the families studied to make it possible to pass it off as 'a large European' or even 'Swiss' city. But I have attempted, wherever possible, to hide traces that would allow readers to identify the study participants. Thus I have deliberately been vague about the exact year the families arrived. The fact that quite some time has gone by since the study was made should blur some of the details by which families might otherwise have been recognised. The names used in the book have of course been made up, and details, such as where the family last lived, have been shifted, although I have attempted to preserve the underlying elements of importance.[4]

One of the most important elements that had to be edited out was the culture of origin of the quarter of the study participants who were born elsewhere than in North America. For similar reasons, the text does not differentiate between Canadians and Americans. Seen from North America the differences between the two countries are significant, sometimes highly so. Seen from Europe they are perhaps less so, but the reason to merge both into 'North American' in the text is to help preserve the confidentiality of the 10 per cent of participants in the study who were Canadian.

An important factor in the analysis will be the type of work place that brought the family to Geneva. At the expense of losing some important differences such as that between the Canadian and the American governments, between selling services and selling heavy machinery, and between international work dealing with intellectual property and that dealing with refugees, I have grouped the work places into three main categories, with a residual category of people who moved independently. These are:

> *'The company'* (14 of the families retained, 17 from the entire sample): refers to the business world. Multinational corporations are included in this category (8 families), as are smaller European outposts of North American businesses (4 families), and local banking, or trading firms (2 families).
>
> *'The government'* (4 families retained, 5 from the entire sample): as the name implies, refers to the people who work for the

---

4 Confidentiality was checked by one of the study participants, whose position in the community put her in potential contact with many of the others: she read the longer thesis version of the final manuscript, and recognised her own family, but none of the others.

Canadian or the American government. They may be diplomats, or administrative and support staff.

'*The organisation*' (7 families retained, 10 from the entire sample): is a somewhat heterogeneous category, referring to international organisations such as the United Nations and its specialised agencies, humanitarian non-government organisations, and also international scientific and regulatory agencies.

'*The independents*' (3 families retained, 7 from the entire sample): liberal professions, professors or artists.

Editing of text

While preserving, obviously, the sense of what is being said, and trying to conserve the feeling of the interview, I have edited the interview quotations. There are two reasons for this: editing out accents helps preserve confidentiality, and also increases readability. Many people are repetitious, saying the same thing two or three different ways before they feel they have got it right and can move on to the next thought. As for grammatical mistakes, which we all make, they do service to nobody and make for irritating reading. They have been edited out.

Families are referred to by letter or by name, and the interview number given in each case: for example (Allen/1) refers to the first interview with the Allen family. Citations are made in a standard format: H, W, C and M refer respectively to comments by a husband, a wife, a child, or the researcher. 'North America' has systematically been substituted when interviewees have referred to 'the United States' or 'Canada'. Letters were assigned to families in the order in which they were interviewed. These were later replaced by pseudonyms assigned to the 28 families who are the object of the bulk of the analysis for this book, as well as to some of their children. The book can be read without keeping in mind the identities of each of the families who participated in the study, but for readers who wish to do so, data about each are summarised in Box 2.1 at the end of the next chapter.

2

WHO ARE THEY, AND WHY DO THEY MOVE?

Moving abroad, even for a short-term stay, reflects a complicated decision. Reasons people give for doing so vary enormously: for some it is work that predominates, for others the move is really made for the family. Some feel they are getting too comfortable where they are living – it is simply time to move on. Some are coming towards things by moving, others are fleeing. Some have always cherished a dream of living abroad, others have never thought about it. Some have already lived in several different cultures, others have never left the region where they were born. For some, feeling rooted or attached to a particular community is extremely important, others do not seem to need roots, carry portable roots around the world with them, or feel rooted elsewhere, such as in strongly held religious beliefs. Some hesitate, some discuss the decision at length and prepare every imaginable detail, others simply say yes, phone the moving company, and walk out the door. For some couples, moving because of the career of one spouse means the other has to give up professional ambitions, for others dual careers are not a significant factor. And transporting children of different ages means quite different things: the opinions they have about moving, and their degree of participation in the decision-making process, will obviously be quite different at different ages.

The 'why' of the move was the major subject of the first interview, and a constant theme in subsequent discussions as people elaborated, and in some cases corrected, what they had already divulged, and as events in their lives unfolded. This chapter discusses the reasons behind the decision to move to a new culture. It covers the factors that either pushed or pulled families to relocate, then what the move meant for families attached to the three major employment settings: 'the government', 'the organisation' and 'the company'. The last segment of the chapter discusses some of the factors that surrounded the decision: the degree of difficulty, just who in the family was seen to be responsible for making it, then what they did to prepare before they moved. First, however, the chapter describes the families who participated in the study.

Who are they?

As discussed in the previous chapter, 40 couples, and five female-headed households, were interviewed at the beginning of the study. Except where otherwise indicated, the discussion here concerns a core of 28 of these families, the dual-parent North American families who moved to Geneva with school-aged children, and who remained long enough to be interviewed two to three years later. Box 2.1 at the end of the chapter lists key elements concerning each of these families, and Tables A.1 to A.3 in the Appendix present in detail the demographic characteristics sketched below.

The families had an average of two or three children (minimum one, maximum six). By definition, all had school-aged children living with them in Geneva, although the family life stage of 'having school-aged children' proved to cover quite a wide range. In the youngest families the eldest child was just beginning kindergarten. At the other end of the continuum were families whose youngest child was just completing school, the others already living independently. Some of these already had children of their own. The average age of the men who participated in the study was 42, that of the women 38 (Table A.1). All of those among the 28 core families considered themselves North American, although about one in five had been born on another continent. Almost one-third of the marriages were between people originating from different cultures. Those who participated in the study were relatively experienced with moving: in only one of the families had none of the members ever moved before, and some had done so extensively. Most expected to stay for three to five years, but ten of the families studied thought they would be staying longer, some perhaps to settle permanently (Table A.2). With perhaps one or two exceptions, the families belonged to what is commonly termed the 'upper middle class' – all but three of the men had graduated from university, and half had obtained advanced degrees. Half of the women had graduated from university, and five had obtained advanced degrees (Table A.3).

By definition the families who participated in this study all made a decision that distinguishes them from most other families: they decided to move away from their home culture for at least a few years. It may well be that at least one member is more ambitious than the norm, or more idealistic, and it would seem safe to venture that they are more adventurous than those who are more sedentary. There is, unfortunately, no control group for the study: it was not possible to carry out a similar set of interviews on a matched sample of families, interviewing for example, 28 families with children of the same ages and who worked in similar positions for similar employers, to whom a move abroad may have been proposed, but who declined the offer for some reason. What is known is that when compared with 700 'normal' American couples who volunteered to participate in a study of marital interaction (Fitzpatrick, 1988), the couples who participated in the Geneva study differed in several ways. They were far more likely to describe theirs as a 'traditional' type of marriage (as opposed to 'independent' or 'separate' marriages). They were thus more likely than their co-nationals to hold conventional values about relationships, to emphasise stability, to stress traditional customs, and to value interdependence and a high degree of sharing, harmony and companionship in their marriages. Husband and wife, moreover, were far more likely to define their marriage the same way: in other words 'his marriage' was the same as 'her marriage' (Haour-Knipe, 1999). In a word, they may well have been 'closer' than most families in the society from which they came. We turn now to what made them decide to move overseas.

Why do they move?

The families studied here were clearly pulled rather than pushed in their decision to move to a new culture (Table A.4). Most mentioned nothing they were especially glad to be leaving. Some of those who *did* mention 'push factors' talked of drugs and crime, but mainly they spoke of a less alarming urge simply to change lifestyle. Among the former was a family – who moved for a brief stay – who said that among their reasons for coming was to remove a child from undesirable peers. Along similar lines, a minority mentioned getting away from drugs and crime, as well as perhaps from some troublesome relationships:

> W (wife): ... getting the children away from TV, drugs, not being able to let your kids walk outdoors without being afraid of being picked up by some weirdo. You hear so much about abductions, with posters on store fronts, in supermarkets. I know most of them are family problems, but the whole philosophy in North America now seems to be to teach your children that they can't talk to anybody, can't ever meet anybody. We lived in a pretty nice neighbourhood, but a block away from us there was a place where hoodlums hung out, and drugs were getting down to the elementary school.
> ... Also, we felt like we were devoting all our time to the extended family and not enough to our children. With the children in their formative years this would be a good way to be just the [nuclear family].
>
> (Foster/1)

A more common push factor among those who were to be moving for longer periods of time was a vague, global, dislike of the previous place of residence or style of life:

W: We needed the change from [where we had last been living]. We felt so out of place there. We couldn't find a lot of people who could share our interests. Everybody else's goal was to have a nice house, raise a family, have a comfortable life. We were looking for adventure. We love to travel. Every time we went back to our apartment after a vacation we would wish we were somewhere else.

(Ogbourne/1)

Somewhat similar, or perhaps a mirror image of wanting to leave a particular place, was the feeling that one was getting too comfortable, that it was time to move on to a new challenge. The challenge could be professional, or it may simply have been time to move to a new place:

W: After three years it's time to move on.

(Hill/1)

The feeling could be more existential:

H (husband): The transfer was sudden. At dinner one night a friend asked if we would like to come. I thought 'why not' . . .
W: I was a bored, suburban housewife . . . We were both nearing 40. You start questioning: do we want life to go on like this, or do we want to have a last hurrah before we settle down? . . . It was sort of a challenge . . . an opportunity, to have a rich experience . . .
H: It's good to stretch your brain.
W: I wanted to see what grey cells were left after being a housewife.

(Zelig/1)

As for 'pull factors', besides the new job, most families cited such broadening aspects as travelling, experiencing another culture, and learning a language. This was especially the case for the families who were coming for only brief stays, but was also spontaneously mentioned by a goodly proportion of those who planned to move for longer periods. Others mentioned personal growth, or the possibility of making Swiss friends. In contrast to those who felt it was time to move on, three families said at the first interview that they hoped to settle down with this move, perhaps to integrate:

W: I would hope that we would be able to grow some roots here, to find friends.

(Thomas/1)

Several people mentioned the extended family as a pull factor in moving: this could be the possibility of having family members come and visit, or in some cases of being near or getting to know extended family living in Europe. Some people hoped to make contact with the European branches of families who had migrated to North America, perhaps several generations ago.

Almost everybody listed several hopes for their children, and in fact quite often cited more hopes for their children than for themselves. These included discovering other cultures, acquiring a sense of geography and an international perspective on the world, overcoming provincialism, acquiring tolerance, learning French, benefiting from a good educational system, learning to live anywhere, or, more generally, personal growth, becoming more well rounded, or becoming more independent. Whatever the underlying rationale, however, it was around work that the move was organised. This is the subject of the next section.

The relation between work and moving

Moving and careers were inextricably related in this study. For some, the profession had been chosen as a tool to allow the family to fulfil a long-held wish to live in a series of different cultures. For most, it was a job opportunity offered one member of a family that brought the whole group. For virtually all of the families studied, moving was considered to be a normal part of the career trajectory. In the North American business world a promotion often entails leaving not only a position but also a place, in order to take up a higher post afresh. As for work in international organisations, almost by definition such positions require living, at least for some time, in countries other than one's own. The next section discusses the factors taken into account by families in whom one of the members worked in the different employment settings: 'the government', 'the organisation' and 'the company'.

Moving with 'the government'

In four of the families who moved to Geneva the year the study was initiated (Quincy, Gibbs, Jackson, Kennedy) at least one spouse worked for 'the government'. Examples are the Jackson and the Gibbs families.

The Jackson family

The family moved to Geneva so that Mr Jackson could take a senior administrative position with 'the government'. He was born in North America, she in Europe. Both had always loved to travel, and had done so extensively, both before they met and after:

> M (the researcher): How did [he] get into working for the government?
> H: I wanted to go to Europe, maybe partly because I have an aunt who left North America right after the war and married a European. Or from reading Hemingway – expatriate life. ... I'd graduated from university and was looking for a job that would provide me with an income for going on to graduate school. I went to government offices looking for a part-time job – they said they didn't have any part-time jobs because of security, but they did have a vacancy for a diplomatic courier. And that's how I got into it: my responsibility was to travel around the world. Who could have resisted that! (laugh)
> M: So what happened to graduate school?
> H: Probably what would have happened anyway: I'm not an academic.
> M: What about [Mrs Jackson]?
> W: I was very lucky. When I was a young girl I always dreamed of travelling ... I had a father who realised that living in my country the biggest asset you could give your children was to know Europe and know languages, so very early on he sent us abroad during summer vacations.
>
> (Jackson/3)

Since they married, the Jacksons had lived in developing countries as well as in several European cities. Just before moving to Geneva they had been living in North America. They said they had moved to Europe in search of a certain style of life. Their main hopes for their stay, in addition to enjoying local culture, making Swiss friends, travelling, and having guests, was to keep a strong family atmosphere. They thought Geneva would provide a good environment for their adolescent child, and said quality of life was more important to them than the career itself. In the first interview they asserted, as did other 'government' interviewees, that Geneva was not a glamour post:

> H: For me this is not a post that stands out in one's career ... It's the good life, not 'he survived that'. An appointment to Geneva is not going to make or break a career.
>
> (Jackson/1)

They agreed with my formulation at the next interview that they had taken an unambitious job so as to be able to live in Europe:

> W: Not only Europe, but specifically Geneva. It's a first-class education. There's the freedom of being in the city, of learning.

WHO ARE THEY, AND WHY DO THEY MOVE?

> It's so different from North America. North America for somebody our child's age is just school, TV, junk food, going to the mall. Here it's quality of life.
> M: You have a certain amount of choice in the countries in which you will live?
> Both: Yes, a certain amount.
> H: When the time comes for a transfer we look at the choices. We read post reports and talk to people who have been there, and decide ... There's always a certain amount of anxiety: what I want to do is not necessarily what the government wants me to do. Or there may be twenty other people who want to do the same thing, so there's competition ... I've been very lucky to be able to go where I want to go, but I've worked at it, calling friends and that sort of thing. We all do.
> (Jackson/2)

The Gibbs family

Another family who also worked for 'the government' might not quite agree. Mr Gibbs was a technical specialist. The couple had listed Geneva as their first choice of places they would like to live when they first joined government staff and, after several tours in 'hardship posts', thought they may have been assigned to the city as a reward. Their reasoning was not as highly elaborated as that of the previous couple, however:

> H: We did want to come to this part of the world for the experience.
> W: I always thought of Switzerland as a beautiful country. There's snow. We'd seen Switzerland in movies and books, like Heidi.
> (Gibbs/2)

The Gibbs had not formulated any particular hopes for the stay in Geneva when they first arrived:

> W: I hadn't given it much thought (long pause) ... when you come to a place you just set up home and start living like anywhere else. It's just day by day living, that's the way I look at it.
> (Gibbs/1)

Although the family had moved a great deal, living in three different developing countries, with stays in North America in between, neither adult felt the early strong desire to travel, or the urge to move on after a few years, that several of the other families mentioned. Mr Gibbs had practically never moved during his childhood, but Mrs Gibbs, who came from a military family, had done so several times:

> W: I can remember I hated moving around. I hated going to new schools, meeting new people.
>
> (Gibbs/2)

The family came to their present style of life through economic necessity: Mr Gibbs took a first job with 'the government' after he finished school because the salary was sufficient to allow his wife to stay home when the children were babies. The children had long since ceased to be babies, but once the Gibbs had started in a government career, they just sort of went along. They did not, however, in contrast with the Jacksons, talk about having actively influenced where they were to live because of family factors:

> H: With the government you do what you're told . . . you do your job OK and you advance.
> M: Do you feel you have any choice about moving?
> H: We can extend one year in a post but that's all. When your time is up you get a list of available posts and apply for what you want most.
> W: . . . They don't let you stay in one place more than three to four years . . .
> M: Can you imagine yourselves settling down?
> W: Yes I can, I'm looking forward to it.
>
> (Gibbs/2)

The move for the 'government' families

For three of the four families who moved with 'the government' the move was a fairly routine affair in a series of stays in several countries. Geneva was said to be not a very difficult or exciting posting. As the Quincys, who were both career diplomats, put it:

> H: In our racket it's difficult to think of a fantastic job here.
> W: But I'm sure for some of these bankers and things there are fantastic jobs here.
> M: Some people have a chance to put ideas to work on a global level when they move to Geneva.
> H and W (in turn): There are fantastic jobs here, but it would probably be a small minority of anybody in foreign service . . . The action for us is elsewhere, when it's quite clear that the top officials are waiting for that cable you're working on . . . But here real crises are few and far between.
>
> (Quincy/2)

These families chose Geneva – to the extent that they did choose the next place they were to live – for what they thought would be a pleasant style of life, or because the city was felt to be a good place to raise a family, or, in the case of the Quincys, simply because it was where they could both get a suitable job. 'Government' families had signed on for the mobile style of life quite some time ago: the decision to move from the last place was thus not one about which they particularly had to think a great deal, although some of them did attempt to influence the choice as to just where the next post would take them. Although they were not all as subdued as Mrs Gibbs, who just wanted to 'set up living', their hopes for their sojourn in Geneva tended to be relatively modest, to see some of the country, to get to know the local culture. As Mr Jackson put it:

> H: We don't go out and be sociologists about it, but we'd like to absorb what's available, maybe to make some Swiss friends.
> (Jackson/1)

The family may well be taken into consideration in deciding whether or where to move, but, in contrast to many of those involved with 'the company', discussed below, 'the experience for the children' was not listed as a major reason to move. First, however, the families linked to 'the organisation'.

Moving with 'the organisation'

Seven families (Foster, Kent, Davidson, Friedson, Hummell, Madison, Nathanson) moved to Geneva because one of their members was to work with 'the organisation'. For five of these, coming to work at the headquarters of an international or non-government organisation was seen to be a rather heady opportunity to work internationally, a chance to apply ideas on a world level. Examples are the Davidson and the Madison families.

The Davidson family

The Davidsons moved to Geneva so that Mr Davidson could take an administrative position in 'the organisation' after many years of work in the field. The family had lived for three to four years at a time in several different developing countries as Mr Davidson, a scientist, became responsible for expanding geographical areas. They planned to settle in Geneva for at least ten years, until Mr Davidson retired:

> H: This move is a promotion. I was at the top of my career where we were before.

W: ... and getting too comfortable.
H: This was an opportunity to develop some programmes that I'd been developing on a regional level to a global level. Plus a challenge to learn a new culture and a new language.
(Davidson/1)

The couple had six children, three of whom moved with them. Having been talking to families with far fewer children, and who seemed to have far more difficulty with just one move, I asked how they managed:

M: How did you do this? You're the 30th family I've interviewed, and *nobody* has moved around with six children.
H: It's no different from moving with two or three. You just take a few more bags ... We have an adventurous attitude – bloom where you're planted. We have always tried to make the best of where we were. We like to explore the country, camp, see the territory. My work takes me to interesting places and often I take the family later.
W: It's an educational opportunity.
(Davidson/1)

The Madison family

The new job was also the summit of his career for Mr Madison. A technical specialist with 'the organisation', he came from a North American regional office for a temporary assignment in Geneva. Almost immediately the people for whom he was working started proposing a more permanent position. Mr Madison, especially, had travelled and stayed abroad extensively, but the rest of the family had never moved before, so they came at their own expense to spend a summer in a sublet flat in Geneva to see if they would like it. They did. They returned to North America to sell the house and pack, and moved three months later. When I first interviewed them they were talking about staying 'for two years', 'indefinitely', or even 'permanently'.

H: This is a dream position ... I have access to all the top people worldwide ... (he describes the natural progression from his last job). I was getting stale after 10 years: it was a natural for me to come here.
(Madison/1)

Mr Madison, for whom religion had been extremely important at one point in his life, described his studies abroad and work in developing countries. His hopes for the stay were job-related, and also perhaps to settle down:

> H: I think the best way to describe it is I'm basically an idealist. I hope I can have an impact. I may not be able to change the world, but I can make *some* changes. When I first went to [a developing country] I didn't join the volunteer work force because I didn't feel I had any skills that could be of use. I wanted to go back. Now I do have skills 'the organisation' can use... Another hope is to become acclimated enough here that we will want to stay. I would like to make Switzerland home.
>
> (Madison/1)

Both talked about learning several languages, travel, acquiring a broader view of the world, getting in contact with family roots. The family was coming to a professional situation which Mr Madison found highly gratifying, and both parents were culturally comfortable living in Europe. Mrs Madison, though, complained about her husband's extraordinarily long working hours in Geneva, and also made a point of mentioning several things she had given up by leaving North America, such as their house and car, the pleasant weather of the place they had been living, but also her stressful job and 'the world of crime'. Mr and Mrs Madison did not hide that for both of them an additional, and non-negligible, factor in leaving North America was that by moving they were also distancing themselves from a very troublesome family situation.

The move for the 'organisation' families

For the majority of the families who moved with 'the organisation', it was the chance to work internationally that was described as being of primary importance, not the particular place. They moved to Geneva only because the city houses many international organisations, not because of any ideas about a certain style of life, as with several of the families who moved with 'the government' for example. Since the move involved a chance to promote ideas to the world level, an implicit corollary was that the new job was an end of a career trajectory:

> H: The decision to come here is a kind of normal consequence of what we did in North America. In a way there was not much choice ... We worked on the local level, then were called upon to work in the regional context, then to the national level. And after that where do you go, if not international?
>
> (Nathanson/3)

Those working with 'the organisation' arrived for unlimited or long-term stays. Describing their hopes for their stay, they typically listed mainly job-related pull factors, in contrast with other families, who more often talked about travel, learning languages, or general personal enrichment.

The third large employment category is that of 'the company'.

Moving with 'the company'

Fourteen families in the study came to Geneva so that one of their members could work for a company (Allen, Cady, Elm, Graham, Hill, Newton, Renton, Vance, Wood, Zelig, Bateson, Collins, Rodgers, Smithers). The Grahams and the Smithers are examples.

The Graham family

For Mr Graham, coming to Geneva was a good professional opportunity, a promotion to an important job in a multinational firm. If he did well there was a good chance that when he went back to headquarters he would be promoted to the highest levels of management. He insisted, however, and his wife agreed, that: first, not accepting the job in Geneva would not have damaged his career; second, he would be perfectly happy not to work, to retire in a couple of years and devote full-time attention to his hobby of breeding and raising pedigree dogs; and third, he would never have accepted the job if the family had not unanimously agreed. Mrs Graham was trained as a teacher, and had taught from time to time over the years, but career considerations were not particularly important to her. She was quite happy to be a wife and mother, to raise the dogs, and to do handicrafts and volunteer work. At the first interview:

M: Tell me about the move.
W: Well, we have three children. Two would have to stay back in North America. We sat down and talked about it as soon as we knew it was a possibility ... The kids were all for it: they said we would be crazy not to ...
H: Ten years ago we lived in Europe for five years. We knew what we were getting into. I had the opportunity to say no without jeopardising my career ... In fact the company was surprised I said yes since we have the dog-breeding farm ... I'm looking forward to the interchange with different cultures, to see places we couldn't before because the children were young, to skiing. I have already worked with many of the people I work with now, so it's like a homecoming, a happy one. I can renew meaningful friendships. There are not too many negatives except for leaving the children ...
W: I wanted to come back. I'm not so tied down now that the children are older. I like the slower pace of life, it's not as

intensive. Yet I'm leaving a lot too: the dogs, two children, sports activities, our parents in their late seventies. If we hadn't had the total support of the kids we probably wouldn't have done it. The two older ones realised it was time they were more independent.

M: What are your hopes for the stay?

W: For us, to travel. For the children, that they have international experiences. In the type of town we lived in it's easy to forget there's another part of the world. It's important to see, and to do as much as you can. And jobwise ...

H: ... to help the company of course. But this will also have a significant influence on where I'll ultimately end up in the company ... I am competing with six people for a top job. If I'm as successful as I hope to be in the job here it could give me a competitive advantage over those other people. It's a challenge, an opportunity. The visibility is greater. So that's why I wanted to do it, plus ski!

(Graham/1)

The Smithers family

Quite different was the reasoning of the Smithers family, who moved to Geneva with three small children. If some of the families had never thought about living abroad, and others, such as the Grahams, were moving towards professional challenges, practically the first thing the Smithers told me was that they had always been interested in living abroad. Both grew up in provincial areas of North America, but had long had the urge to travel. Mrs Smithers had been very marked by a trip to Europe to visit relatives at the age of 13, and Mr Smithers had spent a year of university in Europe. The couple had lived in Europe for a year shortly after they were married. One of the reasons Mr Smithers later began working for 'the company' was precisely the fact that it was a *multinational* company, thus offering the possibility of being transferred abroad.

W: We have a family joke. If he were ever given the opportunity of living abroad my husband would: say yes, then ask where, then maybe talk to his wife about whether the spot was OK! (laughs)

(Smithers/1)

So there was not much hesitation when the company offered Mr Smithers a job in Geneva, although he did have some reservations about what the move might mean for his career (and he did consult his wife before he said 'yes'!). His section of the company was in the midst of restructuring, and at the first interview he mentioned that as far as his career is concerned this move involved some element of risk, and even that it may not have been particularly wise or well timed.

They both loved the language and culture of Italy ('going to an Italian-speaking country is like going into a candy store') and Mrs Smithers had in fact been teaching Italian in North America. Although they had never been much attracted by the French language or culture, they considered the move to a French-speaking region to be an opportunity to get over a prejudice and learn another culture. Geneva in fact fitted well with their backgrounds and interests, but they said they would have accepted any foreign posting, and mentioned other jobs that might have been coming up in Singapore, Malaysia and Brazil. Curiously, however, they had some trouble with my question about their hopes for their stay:

> M: What are your hopes for your stay?
>
> ... (pause) ...
>
> H: We haven't really sat down and discussed that, what we must be sure to do, and that sort of thing.
>
> W: To travel a lot, see everything we can, show the kids enough so they'll remember something, do things here you can't do when you are travelling, improve my French, maybe even enough to teach it when we go back ...
>
> (I probe for more)
>
> H: Have broadminded kids, travel, ski. Have the kids get to know our Italian relatives.
>
> (Smithers/1)

Their list of hopes was similar to that of many of the other families, but they were exceptional in their hesitation, in not having hopes clearly formulated and immediately spelled out. This was just a bit paradoxical since they had wanted so much to live abroad. It seemed to be a sort of global experience they were seeking, perhaps almost at any cost.

The move for the 'company' families

Most of those working for 'the company' talked about the move in terms of their careers. Although a sojourn abroad entails a risk of being 'out of sight, out of mind' as far as company headquarters is concerned, those who are to rise to positions of power, especially, may be expected to spend some time 'seeing how the rest of the world does business'. Several people, in addition, such as those cited above, described coming to high-risk jobs, where, if they succeeded in performing difficult tasks, they might be highly rewarded. Professionally, the rewards are of two kinds: a potential for promotion or for advancement in the company, and financial. Neither is something one necessarily talks about with strangers, and most of those in the study only hinted at such things in the first interview, even when asked directly if the new job meant a promotion. Some talked about their ambition at later interviews. A few talked about financial rewards, although usually indirectly, speaking in general, or about other people.

An additional reason for making the move given by many of the families working for 'the company' was to have the experience of living in a different culture. Most said that a significant factor was also that living in a foreign culture would be good for their children. For all of these families this was to be a sojourn: they moved for limited stays of two to five years, and only one envisaged a longer stay. All had in mind that they would be returning to North America.

The previous section discussed the push and pull factors behind the decision to move abroad, and the complex relation between the employment setting and a family move. The second part of the chapter steps back from the employer to discuss the degree of difficulty involved in the decision, and introduces one of the major problems for many families such as those studied, what to do when there are two careers in the family but when only one career can be transported. What families did to prepare before they moved is then sketched.

The decision to move

This was a cohort of people with a good deal in common: they all made the same decision, and arrived at the same place at the same time. They were all at the same life stage, from the same culture, of similar socio-economic status. This is a privileged group of families: the move was a decidedly voluntary one. Nine of the 28 families actively worked to make it come about, and most of the others maintained that they could easily have refused to move had they wanted to. Yet behind this apparent homogeneity lies a great deal of variation, and also complexity. Of the same event, definitions turned out to have been quite different, as the examples above have made clear. Some of the characteristics of the decision to move are whether or not it was difficult (and why), who in the family decides, and what families did to prepare (see also Table A.5).

A difficult decision?

The decision to move had been difficult for almost half of the core families in the study. This was particularly the case when there were dual careers to be considered: moving would mean that one spouse would have to put a career on hold for the interim, or perhaps drop it altogether. Mrs Renton, for example, had left 'a wonderful job' and major executive responsibilities in a multinational company. She talked about combining profession and motherhood:

> W: I am part of the generation of women who had to do everything. We took six weeks off work to have our babies, then went back with a full schedule.
>
> (Renton/1)

With the support of her husband she had very actively pursued her career, regularly changing companies as she advanced, working 70-hour weeks, and had just acquired enough status to get down to 40-hour weeks: 'I put in my time to get to the good times'. But:

> W: [My husband] had always wanted an international move, and the job was getting harder for me. The company was giving me international responsibilities. In the year before we moved I had travelled to Brazil, England, Germany, and Spain. It was very difficult being away from the family for ten days at a time, and the company wanted to increase the international travel. They never forced me to travel, but I knew at some point they would want me to do more, and it was going to get harder. It's physically more demanding when the kids are little, but emotionally more demanding when they get older. They get social lives, Scouts, being driven to friends and so forth, and you can't leave a ten-year-old on his own.
>
> (Renton/1)

We returned to the subject at some length a year later, as Mrs Renton struggled to explain how the situation in their couple differed from the stereotypical one in which a family moves because the husband's career predominates:

> W: It's really very different ... [My husband] was exceptionally supportive of my career. If I was really struggling with something, if I was up at 1:00 in the morning, it would not be unusual for him to get up and offer to help, to bounce ideas around with me. He felt no reservations about leaving work and picking up the children if I had to stay late. We'd compare schedules and the one with the most time would do it. If you have a vision of what you think a corporate wife should be, I'm pretty far from that (laugh). He's accepted all of that very easily.

M: Yet the fact of it is you've given up your career to come here.
W: Yes. We talked for a long time about it. It was a very hard decision. He really wanted the move, there was no question of that. I was always the one to talk about the pluses and the minuses.
H: I had a hard time seeing the minuses ...
W: And I felt if I was going to jump to the next step on my career I would have to compromise something on the family side ... I certainly could not have made a decision to be away from my children 15 per cent of the year ...
M: One person told me her first reaction was 'you go, I stay', then she thought about it and saw it as a decision between career and marriage, and when she put it in those terms the decision was easier.
W: I never got to that point.
H: If [my wife] had said she would not under any circumstances go, I would not have taken the job.
W: And I would never get to the point where I would say you go ahead and go and I'll stay. Because I could not handle the children and my job anyway! ... But it does go up and down. There were days when it wasn't clear to me what I was doing, why I was agonising over things.

(Renton/2)

For a few other families, although dual careers were not a consideration, the decision to move was difficult because the wife, especially, had been feeling happy and comfortable where she was, and dreaded uprooting, even temporarily. Two of these families had been having difficulty with geographical mobility itself: they felt they had made too many moves in too short a time, and/or that they had made a mistake in their last move. Several felt a sense of pressure in making the decision, although this was an entirely subjective impression.

The decision was easy for the other half. In a few cases there was no real decision to be made, usually since it was basically the employer that made this particular decision. For some families, such as that of the Davidsons cited above, the decision to make the current move was easy in relation to other much more difficult ones, such as one to a place where there were no schools and they would have to educate their children themselves. For others, the new job and/or the new place was simply very attractive, and there were few conflicting factors to take into account. For one or two families, finally, such as the Smithers, the decision may have been easy because they really did not think very much about the details of what living in a different culture might entail.

Who decides?

In most cases husband and wife said the decision to move to Geneva had been a joint one. The decision was clearly the husband's responsibility in a few families, however, most of which were linked with 'the company'. In these families the decision was felt to be basically that of the breadwinner because 'it's his career'. None of the wives in these families had active careers at the time the decision was to be made. They did, however, feel they had a say in the matter:

> W: It was a hard decision. It was something he really wanted to do, and I would not have liked to have been the cause of keeping him from going. If I really hadn't wanted to go, he wouldn't have taken the job, though. When we [made a previous move] I hadn't wanted to go either, but it turned out to have been good for all of us.
>
> (Allen/1)

In all cases, the decision had been discussed by the couple, usually extensively. The extent to which children participated depended foremost on their ages: in the families who described the decision as having been a truly joint family one the children were all at least pre-adolescents. In two instances, in contrast (one family on sabbatical and one of the 28 core families) the family moved – together – in spite of very strong opposition by an adolescent.

Preparing for the move

Several families who had already lived in Europe found it unnecessary to prepare for the move, but all of the others did so, some extensively:

> M: Did you do anything to prepare for the move?
> W: We did so much to prepare we were exhausted! The company sent the whole family to a four-day course about living abroad ... We bought an enormous amount of groceries so that we could save money and also so the kids could acclimatise to different foods here more slowly ... and all our clothes for two seasons because we'd heard that it's outrageously expensive here ...
> H: ... major appliances ...
> W: Berlitz total immersion French – an extravaganza.
> H: We talked to a lot of people before we accepted, made a list of questions and asked them. We got as much evidence as we could ... I deliberately sought people out at work to ask them

questions ... I literally camped on a guy's doorstep to understand the tax programme: I forced him to go over things until I understood.
M: It sounds as though you went into it very thoroughly.
W: I think we're that kind of people. We don't just glide into things. I don't know if we belabour the issue or not, but I think you can only enjoy something if you know a lot about it.

(Elm/1)

Few were as thorough about it as Mr and Mrs Elm, on their first trip abroad, but most talked to other people who had lived in another country or sought out others who had already lived in Geneva. Most read in preparation for the move – about the city, about Switzerland, or about Europe. Such reading included practical information such as that available in post reports prepared by consulates or in handbooks prepared by multinational corporations, and some also read European history, encyclopedias or *National Geographic* magazines. The next most common method of preparation involved stocking up on items known to be either more expensive or difficult to come by in the new place. The family just cited was far from being the only one to arrive accompanied by large amounts of food and stocks of clothing from home. Someone in about one-third of the core families began to study French before they moved, in efforts which ranged from buying some language tapes to taking total immersion courses.

Almost one-third of the families were able to make a visit to Geneva, sometimes even to find housing and choose schools. Some multinational companies arrange for a couple to visit before they make a final decision, and although families attached to 'the organisation' do not have such advantages, some were able to scout while in the city for professional reasons. Here, too, some prepared thoroughly, as epitomised by the Madison family who came for a summer at their own expense before they decided to make what might prove to be a permanent move. In another instance, the Thomases, all of the family members started corresponding with people living in the new place before they actually moved, thus giving the school-aged children, especially, the feeling that they already had friends when they arrived. On a somewhat different track, several people reported using the move as an occasion to sort their possessions and eliminate, and two families, the Fosters and the Madisons, reported putting their affairs in order by having their wills made before they moved.

Discussion

We begin already to discern the threads introduced in the theoretical discussion of Chapter 1. The sense of coherence elements of meaningfulness, of manageability and of comprehensibility underlie the answers to the question 'why move?'. Some families portrayed a sense of taking a particular action for a specific reason, whether because one of them might thus have a better chance to become vice-president of a corporation, or because they wished to experience what life is like in another part of the world. There was *something* about which most of those interviewed for this study cared very much, whether it be promoting an idea, giving their children the experience of seeing another culture, or simply advancing in their own careers. Some families portrayed a sense of control over what happens to them, in this instance over whether they were to move or not, and over where they would go. They described attempts to influence whatever elements of their lives they had determined they could influence. Others basically followed what someone else, in this instance the employer, decided for them. Some took active charge in preparing for a new event. The families interviewed varied in how much information they would need about living in the new place (some had already lived in Europe, and a few already spoke French), but what is important here is that some simply took it for granted that the world is comprehensible: faced with something, in this instance a new culture, that they did not necessarily understand, they would be able to define what they needed to know and take the steps required to learn what they needed.

Three of the six families who have served as examples in this chapter rate high on sense of coherence, the Jacksons, the Davidsons and the Grahams, whereas SOC questionnaire scores are low for the other three, the Gibbs, the Madisons and the Smithers (SOC scores are to be found in Table A.8, and the concept of SOC will be discussed in more detail in Chapter 5). The factors to be taken into account in making the decision to move abroad differ according to whether one works for 'the government', 'the organisation' or 'the company', but across the three employment settings the couples with a high sense of coherence (Jackson, Davidson and Graham) all portray the impression of having thought out their priorities: moving required giving up certain things, but the choices had been clearly thought through. The high SOC families transmitted an impression of doing, at least to some extent, what they wanted to do, of feeling relatively in charge of what happens to them. They all rather strikingly talked about 'challenge'. The families with a low sense of coherence (Gibbs, Madison and Smithers) in contrast, portrayed a more passive stance in moving. The Gibbs were the most obvious of the three families to fail to portray the feeling of mastery and control portrayed by the high SOC families: they simply followed the course the employer set for them, talking with wistful regret about how they wished they could settle down. In the case of the Smithers (who shared with the high sense of coherence Jacksons the urge to travel) they jumped at an opportunity to live abroad, but seemed to have curiously failed to think through the ramifications of what they were doing. They failed to take complexity into account. The case of the Madisons is a little more ambiguous: certainly Mr Madison cared deeply about his humanitarian work (meaningfulness), and the family did go to the extraordinary length of trying living in the new place before they decided to move for the long term (manageability and comprehensibility). But the caring was perhaps mainly his, and they also talked at unusual length of what they were getting away from in moving.

A large number of opportunities for tension and for conflict can be read between the lines. The Madisons introduced some of them, as did the Rentons with their discussion of managing dual careers. We will return to these and other sources of strain for families in Chapter 4, but first turn to what the families said was stressful about moving abroad.

WHO ARE THEY, AND WHY DO THEY MOVE?

	Box 2.1 SKETCHES OF THE FAMILIES INTERVIEWED	
All names are pseudonyms. Box 2.1 excludes one family which withdrew from study after first interview.		
Family*	**Brief history**	**Quoted†**
Allen 15 12 (Benjamin) 11 baby, year 1 Company (outpost, N Am) Projected stay: 2–3 years	Mr and Mrs Allen both grew up in Europe, moving to North America when the children were very small and coming to feel this was their home. Mr Allen, who worked for a North American firm, had been asked to help establish his company's operations in Europe. He felt this was probably a good career move. Mrs Allen, a housewife, was not particularly enthusiastic about moving to Switzerland, but the last move had worked out well, and 'it probably broadens your mind'. The Allens had thought at length about what moving would mean for the children. They were particularly concerned about the eldest since they had heard that moving is especially difficult for adolescents. The children attended the International School. The baby, apparently a surprise, was conceived during the move. Mrs Allen knew that she would not have the welcoming support available to women whose husbands worked for a multinational company, so was actively attending activities to meet other North Americans. She was also enjoying studying French. The family lived in a neighbourhood with many other North Americans, in a house about which they complained at length. They had numerous small complaints about Switzerland and Swiss people.	2 3 4 7 8 10
AA	Children aged 11, 8, 3. Short stay.	
B	Children aged 17 (in Geneva) and 19 (in North America). Single mother.	
Bateson 14 (Karen) Company (multi- national) Projected stay: 2–3 years	The Bateson family had spent their entire lives in one city in North America. They felt, though, that moving to Switzerland meant coming back to their roots since ancestors had moved from Switzerland to North America several generations ago. Mr Bateson's job with a multinational company was a significant promotion but to a very difficult job. He was under high stress, but could hope for another significant promotion if he handled the task in Geneva well. Mrs Bateson was a devoted teacher. Referring to giving up her work to move to Geneva she talked of feeling stripped of identity and useless to society, as well as of the risk of not finding	4 5 6 7 8

*Column 1 includes details of children's ages (and names of children discussed in text).
†Column 3 gives chapter where quoted (bold indicates more extensive citations).

WHO ARE THEY, AND WHY DO THEY MOVE?

	Box 2.1 *cont.*	
Family*	**Brief history**	**Quoted**†
	another position when the family returned to North America. But the stay was a chance to perhaps discover other professional options, to see Europe, and also to give their child a global perspective.	
	Karen was helped by another adolescent from the Bateson's home town from her first day at the International School, and assimilated very quickly.	
	They lived in a house which they all liked.	
	The whole family was trying to find ways to help Mr Bateson deal with his job stress: one was by making sure weekends were used for pleasant family trips to explore the region.	
	They were not avoiding other North Americans, but not rushing into the networks of co-nationals either, since they wanted to meet people from other countries.	
Cady 12 9 7	Coming to Europe was a promotion for Mr Cady, who came to a position in marketing for a multinational corporation.	3 4 6 8
	Mrs Cady, a secretary, had not worked since the children were born.	
Company (multi-national)	Mr and Mrs Cady both grew up in the same small town. They said the move to Geneva was mainly for the experience: they hoped to travel, to expose the children to a 'dramatically different perspective on people and the world', and to learn French.	
Projected stay: 3–5 years	The children attended the International School.	
	They had hoped to live in an urban environment, but said an advantage of their suburban Geneva house was having friendly and helpful neighbours from many countries.	
Collins 15 Company (outpost, N Am)	Mr Collins was very ambitious. He had moved several times across three continents as he changed jobs. Each was an advancement, all leading to the present job, for which he had been training and preparing for years. He had a specific task to perform, after which he hoped to semi-retire and trade in antiques.	5
Projected stay: 3–5 years	Mrs Collins agreed that the term 'two person single career' described their couple well: her job had been packing and unpacking and assisting her husband in a very significant way as his career ascended.	
	Living with them for the first time was Mr Collins' daughter by a first marriage. The adolescent had been having troubles in her mother's new family, and everyone concerned agreed it might be	

	Box 2.1 cont.	
Family*	**Brief history**	**Quoted†**
	a good change for her to try living with the Collins for a time. Mrs Collins was both apprehensive about starting her career as a parent and eagerly looking forward to it.	
	Mr and Mrs Collins described themselves as each other's best friend. They said they did not need many people besides each other, but nevertheless had a wide circle of friends, and extensive experience setting up new social networks after a move. They did not expect adaptation problems in Geneva.	
D	Children aged 5, 3. Short stay.	
Davidson 23 21 19 15 11 9 Organisation (international) Projected stay: 5+ years	Mr Davidson's work in agricultural development had taken the family to live in a number of developing countries on four continents. The move to Geneva was the summit of his career, a challenging opportunity to work on a global level. He planned to stay until he retired, then return to the family's home in North America. Mrs Davidson had not been professionally active, although she stressed that she had maintained her physical therapist's licence over the years. Establishing and maintaining a stable home over numerous relocations with a growing family had kept her quite busy enough, especially in developing countries where they had always insisted on doing things for themselves rather than hiring the help that was always available. Only three of the family's children had come with them this time: the others were travelling, studying or having children of their own or in North America. Religious beliefs permeated the family's life, and were an important source of emotional and social support. Church-related networks helped them find an unusual and very conveniently located house. Friends had explained how to relate to their Swiss and international neighbours without making cultural mistakes. After extensive family discussion the three Davidson children in Geneva had chosen to attend local schools. They expected the adjustment to be difficult at first, especially since they did not speak French, but had set up family mechanisms to deal with the extra stress.	2 3 6 7 8 10 11
EE	Children aged 12 (in Geneva), 22, 19 (in North America). Did not meet sample limitations.	

WHO ARE THEY, AND WHY DO THEY MOVE?

	Box 2.1 *cont.*	
Family*	**Brief history**	**Quoted†**
Elm 7 5 Company (multi-national) Projected stay: 3–5 years	Both Mr and Mrs Elm had always wanted to travel, and for years had been looking forward to the overseas stint that would be a normal step in Mr Elm's rise in marketing for a major multinational corporation. Mrs Elm had been a teacher for several years before 'working as a mother' and planned to resume when the children were a bit older. They had seriously considered putting the children in the local schools before eventually enrolling them in International School, about which Mrs Elm had a number of criticisms. They chose their house in Geneva for the fact that there were children in the neighbourhood, and that it was not an 'American ghetto'. They were determined to learn French, and explore and learn as much as possible during their time abroad.	2 6 7
Foster 9 (Sam) 7 6 4 3 Organisation (inter-national) Projected stay: Forever?	Mr Foster had been the author of an idea in North America that had revolutionised an entire industry, and the job in Geneva offered the possibility of applying his idea on a wider scale. Mrs Foster had worked in the same industry as her husband before the children started coming. She had been eager to resume her career, but moving to Geneva meant postponing her plans. Three of the children attended an International school. Socially the Fosters were fairly isolated, partly by choice, partly because they felt overwhelmed with children. They had many complaints about 'the Swiss'. Mr Foster's salary in Geneva had seemed high before they moved, but they were now wondering if they were headed for financial difficulties. They had hoped to live in an urban setting, but could not find an apartment big enough. They lived in a house in a subdivision far from the city. They were not quite unpacked when interviewed six months after they arrived.	2 3 6 8 9
Friedson 9 6 Organisation (inter-national)	The move to Geneva was in part a stopgap measure as the Friedson family waited for an opportunity to open up in North America. Mr Friedson was a highly qualified technician and worked with an international organisation where he was on loan from the multinational company that was paying his salary. Mrs Friedson's professional background was in the same field: in fact she was somewhat more qualified than her husband.	3 4 5 8

Family*	Brief history	Quoted†
Projected stay: 2–3 years	She had been told that it would not be possible for her to work in Geneva, but did not really believe it since people in her field are always in high demand.	
	Mrs Friedson's parents had left their native country when their children were adolescents in order to provide them with better educational opportunities, and it was in large part to do something similar for their own children that the Friedsons were now coming to sojourn in Europe. They wanted their children to experience the advantages of both Swiss and North American ways of education. The children attended a private school in French.	
	The family lived outside the city in a house that was better than they had expected, and were friendly with the neighbours. They were lonely after they first moved, however, and had several unpleasant experiences that coloured their feelings about living in Geneva.	
Gibbs 22? 17 (Nancy) Government Projected stay: 3–5 years	The transfer to Geneva was just one in a series with Mr Gibbs' government job as a technical specialist. In his line of work one expects to be moved around every couple of years, and the family had already lived on three continents.	2 3 5 8
	Mrs Gibbs had done office work in the last post, and was also doing so in Geneva.	
	The elder child had been on her own for several years already. Nancy, the younger, had had a rather tumultuous time over the past move or two, and did not want to move to Geneva. She expected to start university in North America next year.	
	Neither Mr nor Mrs Gibbs had any specific hopes for the stay in Geneva other than simply setting up a home and starting day-to-day living just as anywhere. There were several aspects they found very frustrating, however, including learning some French.	
	They lived in a detached house outside the city and were friendly with the Swiss neighbours, with whom they shared small services.	
Graham 22 21 18 Company (multi-national)	The Grahams moved to Geneva when Mr Graham accepted a significant promotion with a major multinational corporation. He described the new job as a challenge, a chance to try new ideas, but added that he had hesitated: refusing would not have jeopardised his career, and the move meant having to leave the pedigree dogs he and his wife raised.	2 4 5 6
	Mrs Graham, a teacher, had worked some throughout the years, but this was not a serious career: she was happy raising dogs,	

WHO ARE THEY, AND WHY DO THEY MOVE?

	Box 2.1 *cont.*	
Family*	**Brief history**	**Quoted†**
Projected stay: 3–5 years	doing needlework, and being active in a number of women's clubs.	
	With them was their youngest child. She had just finished secondary school, and instead of starting university right away in North America had decided to attend the International School in Geneva for an additional year in order to broaden her horizons. The two older children had remained in North America.	
	The Grahams had fond memories of the four years they lived in Europe a decade ago, and were looking forward to renewing contacts and to 'the challenge of working your way through cultural differences to make friends'.	
	They lived in an old house with a garden big enough for the large family dog who had moved with them.	
Hill 9 6 Company (multi-national) Projected stay: 3–5 years	Mrs Hill spent her childhood 'bouncing around' two continents, and had come to feel that after three years in one place it is time to move on. The family had already lived in four places in North America when Mr Hill, an engineer with a multinational corporation, was offered the opportunity to create a new job in Geneva.	2 4 6 8
	Mrs Hill had pursued advanced studies, but stopped when she first got pregnant. Over the past couple of years she had been writing a novel.	
	The Hills considered the stay in Geneva to be an educational experience for the entire family.	
	The two children attended the International School. The Hills had deliberately chosen a house with a small swimming pool in a neighbourhood with plenty of children in hopes of making friends with neighbours from Switzerland and many other countries.	
Hummell 23 21 14 Organisation NGO Projected stay: 5+ years	Both Mr and Mrs Hummell were European, although Mr Hummell had lived in Africa for a time as he was growing up. The Hummell family had lived on five continents, but their home had very much become North America.	5 6
	Mr Hummell had worked in both business and development. The offer of the job in Geneva came as a surprise and as a significant change: the position as head of an NGO represented an opportunity to serve, to live up to dreams of his youth.	
	Mrs Hummell had both taught and volunteered in several of the places the family had lived. In Geneva she worked as a volunteer in her husband's office.	

WHO ARE THEY, AND WHY DO THEY MOVE?

	Box 2.1 *cont.*	
Family*	**Brief history**	**Quoted**†
	Family members shared religious values that were felt to transcend individual factors. Decisions to move were always made with full family consensus: some moves had been highly inconvenient.	
	Two older children had stayed in North America. The youngest attended the International School in Geneva.	
	Religious networks were important sources of social, emotional and practical support. The Hummells were meeting people of all nationalities through work, neighbours, and several other activities.	
	They did not particularly like their modern Geneva row (terraced) house, but it was conveniently located.	
I	Children aged 5, 3. Single mother.	
J	Children aged 11, 7. Short stay.	
Jackson 12 (Beth) Government Projected stay: 3–5 years	The Jackson family chose with great deliberation when they moved to Geneva. The family had lived in several other European cities, as well as in Mumbai (Bombay) and in the capital of their own country. They had just been living in North America, a stay that had not worked out as they had hoped. Things had changed in the years they had been away: they could not afford to live the way they wanted to, and they wanted to travel, and to see Europe again. Mr Jackson held a staff position in a government office in Geneva. This was not a post that would stand out in his career, but a place chosen for quality of life, good educational possibilities for Beth as she neared high school age, and because the whole family felt equally comfortable living in Europe and in North America. Mrs Jackson, who grew up in Europe, was a trained teacher and had taught in several countries before she was married. She was unable to do so as the family moved around afterwards, but was quite happy with the secretarial jobs she had usually been able to find in government offices wherever the family was living. Beth attended the International School, where she was having some trouble making friends. In the meantime her parents encouraged her to keep contact with former friends by telephone. The first apartment the Jacksons found turned out to be unsuitable. Searching for another was stressful and frustrating,	2 5 6 7 8

Family*	Brief history	Quoted†
	Box 2.1 *cont.*	
	and delayed getting settled, but they eventually moved into an urban apartment they liked.	
Kennedy 8 6 Government Projected stay: 3–5 years	The job in Geneva was an unexpected turn and a new direction to Mr Kennedy's government career in international development, a chance to live in the first world for an interim before resuming a series of postings to developing countries. Mr Kennedy had lived on three different continents as a child. Mrs Kennedy had grown up in one place in North America, but like her husband, had always wanted to travel. The couple had chosen Mr Kennedy's career for its travel aspects, and the family had already lived in two developing countries on two different continents. Mrs Kennedy was not 'professionally minded', and felt strongly that mothering, providing a stable point at home for the children, is a full-time job when a family is overseas. The move to Geneva had been somewhat sudden, many of the arrangements made by the office. They had a great many complaints about the way they were treated when they first came. The children had been enrolled in the International School, and were happy, but Mr and Mrs Kennedy had some doubts and intended to look into alternatives for the next year. The family lived in a house provided by the government, a detached house with large garden near the centre of the city. They were delighted, having been living in infinitely less comfortable places in other postings. They almost immediately made plenty of acquaintances, but also enjoyed evenings alone at home. A Swiss neighbour had taken them in hand to introduce them to some of the region's sights.	3 4 5 6 7 8
Kent 19 15 Organisation (international) Projected stay: 5+ years	Mr Kent had moved extensively before he was married, and the pattern continued. The family had lived happily in Vienna for several years, but decided it was time for their adolescents to touch home base, and moved back to North America. They had trouble readjusting, and came to feel they had made a mistake. The staff position Mr Kent found in Geneva allowed most of the family to return to live in Europe. Mr Kent's job had always involved spending much time away from home, and he once again found himself working well into most evenings. Mrs Kent, who had long since learned to cope with her husband's absences, had worked as an accountant just	4

WHO ARE THEY, AND WHY DO THEY MOVE?

	Box 2.1 *cont.*	
Family*	**Brief history**	**Quoted**†
	before coming, and had found a similar job in Geneva. She did not like women's groups, volunteer activities, etc.	
	The older child had successfully started university in North America. The younger came to Geneva and attended the International School.	
	The family deliberately chose an urban apartment which they liked very much. They explored the region extensively.	
L	Children aged 15, 12. Short stay.	
LL	Child aged 8. Short stay.	
M	Children aged 15, 12, 1. Short stay.	
Madison 12 9 Organisation NGO Projected stay: Forever?	Mr Madison came to Geneva for a temporary assignment with a large NGO, but very soon thereafter was asked to consider staying permanently. At his own expense he brought the family to live for a summer to see how they would like living in Europe. They did, and after returning to North America to sell the house and pack they moved to Geneva, perhaps permanently. Mr Madison considered his new job the summit of his career, and was acutely enjoying it. He worked long hours, including from home during evenings and weekends. His work was quite present in the family's life, and he talked with great pride of the children's involvement in it. Friends tended to be colleagues, and colleagues from other countries very often came home for meals or lodging during trips to Geneva. Mrs Madison had been working before the family moved, but mainly to pay for the children's education in private schools. Juggling work and family had been stressful, and she was glad not to have to do both in Geneva. The children were becoming a bit difficult, and Mrs Madison was hoping they would be happier with her at home more. They attended the International School. The family lived in the same apartment complex as during their test sojourn in Geneva. The neighbours were mainly other international employees, and helped one another. The Madisons arrived with debts, and were having financial difficulties in Geneva: they could not have a car, or many of the things most of the others in their community took for granted.	2 3 7

WHO ARE THEY, AND WHY DO THEY MOVE?

	Box 2.1 *cont.*	
Family*	**Brief history**	**Quoted**[†]
Nathanson 25 23 19 10 Organisation NGO Projected stay: 5+ years	Mr Nathanson grew up in a Latin American country at war. He studied abroad, where he met Mrs Nathanson, a European. The couple returned to live in Mr Nathanson's country, where they were both politically very active. They stayed as long as they could before fleeing with their children to seek asylum in North America.	2 3 5 8 10
	They both became very active in peace efforts in their new country, taking on ever-widening responsibilities. Mr Nathanson's nomination to head of an NGO based in Geneva represented a chance to take activities to a world level.	
	Mrs Nathanson had always worked with her husband, both as a salaried professional and as a volunteer, as she was doing in Geneva.	
	This was the first separation for a family that had always stayed together, even at some personal risk. Only the youngest child had accompanied them. The separation was very difficult, but Mr and Mrs Nathanson felt their mission was more important than personal wishes. They were proud of their children's involvement in numerous community projects.	
	The family lived in an urban apartment, and were quite happy with it. Mrs Nathanson had gone out of her way to develop relations with the Swiss neighbours.	
	The Nathanson child attended the local school 'because it's better to learn where he is'. He spoke very little French, and the adjustment was difficult, but not as difficult as expected.	
	Friends were always made through professional contacts, and the Nathansons anticipated having no difficulty developing new relationships.	
	Both Mr and Mrs Nathanson were perfectly at ease in French, as in several other languages.	
	They had numerous complaints about practical aspects of living in Geneva.	
Newton 22 14 12 8 Company (local)	Mr Newton was European, Mrs Newton North American. Mr Newton's career had taken the family to numerous destinations over three continents, including to four very different places in the past four years. They were worried about the effects of permanent rootlessness on their children.	3 4 6 7
	The family's most recent move had been back to Mrs Newton's home, and was a shock: they found people provincial, relationships superficial, and divorces and poorly supervised	

WHO ARE THEY, AND WHY DO THEY MOVE?

	Box 2.1 *cont.*	
Family*	**Brief history**	**Quoted†**
Projected stay: 5+ years	children far too prevalent. They felt they would be more at home in Europe. Mr Newton's new position would allow them to settle more permanently, but the most recent move had nevertheless been extremely stressful. Mrs Newton, especially, felt hardly able to handle yet one more disruption.	
	The eldest child lived in North America. The three in Geneva attended the International School since their parents felt they would be different from the local children, and would fit in better with those from many other countries.	
	The Newtons were happy with their subdivision house: the neighbours from North America and many other countries helped the family considerably by quickly making them feel integrated.	
	The Newton's fondest hope was to settle down, to get away from the expatriate life style, and to *belong* somewhere.	
O	Children aged 13 (in Geneva), 27, 25, 22 (in North America). Single mother.	
Ogbourne 3 baby, year 2 Independent Projected stay: Forever?	Mr Ogbourne travelled extensively between university and marriage, earning his way as a freelance musician. Mrs Ogbourne, who grew up in Eastern Europe, fled her country under dramatic circumstances. She ended up in North America where she met Mr Ogbourne. She was also a musician, but had only worked occasionally since the first child was born. The young couple had not been comfortable in the medium-sized North American city where they had been living.	2 6 8
	The job in Geneva was adequate, but the main criterion for where the family was to live now was location, and quality of life. They had expected a difficult adjustment period after they moved, but it never happened: the Ogbournes immediately felt comfortable.	
	The three-year-old child was described as an 'easy baby'. She attended nursery school in Geneva.	
	The young couple lived in an urban apartment, which they liked very much. It was the least expensive apartment they had seen, but they still had to struggle to pay the rent.	
	They had become good friends with European neighbours, had old friends in Geneva, and had also made many new friends of all nationalities through common interests.	

WHO ARE THEY, AND WHY DO THEY MOVE?

	Box 2.1 *cont.*	
Family*	**Brief history**	**Quoted†**
P	Children aged 11, 8, 4. Single mother.	
PP	Children aged 13, 10, 6. Did not meet sample limitations.	
QQ	Children aged 12, 9. Short stay.	
Quincy 7 2 Government Projected stay: 2–3 years	Mr and Mrs Quincy, a dual-career couple of government employees, moved to Geneva only because that was where there was a job for both of them. They had been fascinated by their last post, India, and had extended as long as they could. Mr Quincy's particular field of expertise was no longer thought to be of much use by the government, and he was looking forward to retiring in a few years. They both considered Mrs Quincy's career as the more interesting one at the moment, although for this particular move they had accepted a relaxed and unchallenging posting in order to have more time with their small children. The older child attended the International School. The children's nanny had not yet been given permission to enter Switzerland, and her absence was acutely felt since both parents worked full time. Three months after they arrived their possessions had not arrived either. The Quincy family was living in their unfurnished house with a few pieces of borrowed furniture, but were quite unbothered by the situation.	2
Renton 7 4 Company (multi-national) Projected stay: 3–5 years	Mr Renton, a lawyer for a large multinational firm, very much wanted the job in Geneva. It was a chance to change, an opportunity and a challenge. Just before they left, Mrs Renton's rapidly rising career had involved high stress, more and more travel, and the possibility of a transfer to a city several hours away from Mr Renton's job. Her company might possibly have some work for her in Europe, but for the moment she just wanted to enjoy being with the children and having some leisure. Mr and Mrs Renton had immediately loved the house they chose. The location was inconvenient, though, across town both from the International School and from Mr Renton's office. For the moment Mrs Renton was spending three hours a day driving the children back and forth. Both wanted to use the time abroad to do more with the family, although the extensive travel Mr Renton's work required was a	2 3 4 5 8

WHO ARE THEY, AND WHY DO THEY MOVE?

	Box 2.1 *cont.*	
Family*	**Brief history**	**Quoted**[†]
	problem. Mrs Renton could not imagine herself joining company-related wives networks, but hoped to make friends with people from many countries.	
Rodgers 7 3 Company (outpost, N Am) Projected stay: 3–5 years	The Rodgers moved to Geneva when Mr Rodgers accepted a position in marketing at the small European office of a major North American company. He thought the experience would be good for his career. Neither Mr nor Mrs Rodgers had ever travelled much. They had never thought about even visiting Europe. They had treated the job proposal as a joke at first, but the idea had gradually grown, especially since their parents urged them to accept. Mrs Rodgers was a housewife. The elder child attended the International School. They were not quite sure how they felt about the school. The younger child was to go to the neighbourhood nursery school from time to time, in French. The family lived in a house outside Geneva in which they had immediately felt comfortable. They had minimal contact with neighbours, but were at ease with such reserve.	3 4 8
S	Child aged 13. Single mother.	
Smithers 8 5 2 Company (multi-national) Projected stay: 3–5 years	Mr and Mrs Smithers both grew up in rural North America, but adolescent visits to Europe had given both the urge to travel. The couple had lived briefly in Italy shortly after they were married, and were fascinated by everything Italian. One of the reasons Mr Smithers worked for a major multinational company was to perhaps one day be offered the possibility of a transfer abroad, so there was little hesitation when he received a job offer in Geneva. There was some career risk involved, however: the company was restructuring, and Mr Smithers' new job was not well defined. Mrs Smithers had taught Italian. She hoped to improve her French to the point of being able to teach it also when they returned. The couple considered putting the children in local schools but the eldest had some trouble reading, and they thought switching to French would be too difficult for him. He and the second child attended the International School. The eldest and youngest children had always been attention seeking and demanding.	2 4 5 8

	Box 2.1 *cont.*	
Family*	**Brief history**	**Quoted†**
	The middle one had been very easygoing until about a month after the move, when he also became difficult.	
	The Smithers had been unable to find the house 'with European character' they had imagined, and ruled out living in an apartment with three noisy children. They lived in a house they did not particularly like in a neighbourhood with many other North Americans.	
	They would have liked to integrate into Swiss society, but knew integration was difficult. They were actively attempting to meet people, deliberately trying to recreate wide and active social circles they had known in North America.	
Thomas 10 7 Independent Projected stay: 5+ years	Mr and Mrs Thomas were both professionals in a field in which it is the norm to change locations every few years. They had always imagined they might one day sojourn in Geneva. Since it is easier for a woman to find a position in their field, they accepted a job offered Mr Thomas. There had been several job possibilities for Mrs Thomas in Geneva, although some had already fallen through. She was finding the enforced lack of professional activity stressful and depressing. The family lived in an urban apartment. They liked the neighbourhood, but were having to learn to live in much less space than before. The children, who spoke some French, attended the local school. This was for financial reasons, and also because the family wanted to integrate as much as possible. Mr and Mrs Thomas had both compliments and criticisms for the school, but felt they would be better able to judge once they became more fluent in French. Their apartment attracted many guests both from the Geneva international community and from home. All family members also participated in a large number of community activities.	2 3 4 5 6 8
U	Children aged 18, 15, 13. Did not meet sample limitations.	
Vance 19 18 (Stephen) 10	The Vance family had never questioned their several transfers to different regions of North America: being transferred was simply part of working for a company, and 'you just treat it as an adventure'. They had never been outside North America, but with the move to Europe hoped to travel, to become less insular, to 'learn to handle things we never thought we could'.	3 6 7 8 9

WHO ARE THEY, AND WHY DO THEY MOVE?

	Box 2.1 *cont.*	
Family*	**Brief history**	**Quoted†**
Company (outpost, N Am) Projected stay: 3–5 years	Mr Vance's job was with a small European outpost of a large North American company. Mrs Vance, a health educator, had stopped working several months ago in order to help guide the family through the move. The eldest child remained in North America, where she had just started university. Stephen, the second, had agreed to try Geneva for six months, after which he would be allowed to go back to finish at his old school if he still wished. He and his younger sibling attended the International School. The family lived in a house near the centre of the city. It was more expensive than most of the others they had seen, but they liked it, and also liked the fact that it was on bus routes: the children could thus be more independent.	
Wood 10 (Paul) 6 Company (multi-national) Projected stay: 3–5 years	The trip to look for a house in Geneva was the first time either Mr or Mrs Wood had been outside North America. Mr Wood had accepted an overseas posting as a junior manager with a multinational company because 'it puts more arrows in my quiver'. Mrs Wood had been a secretary before the children were born, a homemaker since then. The family lived in a brand new row house. They were pleased with it: everyone was equally new to the neighbourhood so naturally met one another. The children attended the International School. The youngest had just started school for the first time. The first interview with the Woods was tearful and difficult. Mrs Wood, especially, was lonely and having a great deal of difficulty adapting.	3 4 6 9 10
EX 6 3 Independent Projected stay: 2–3 years	The Exons were the only entirely French-speaking family in the study. Mrs Exon was Swiss, and they moved to Geneva when a family-owned apartment was made available to them. The idea was that Mr Exon, a musician, would make contact with the European music world. The children, who had been used to living in a house in the country, were having to adapt to living in a more confined urban space. The elder child attended the local public school. They were in frequent contact with Mrs Exon's family, and also with several old friends in the area.	–

WHO ARE THEY, AND WHY DO THEY MOVE?

	Box 2.1 *cont.*	
Family*	**Brief history**	**Quoted**[†]
Y	Children aged 11, 6. Short stay.	
Zelig 8 5 Company (local) Projected stay: 5+ years	Mr Zelig had moved to North America as a student during a political crisis in his country. Mrs Zelig had lived most of her life in the same region of North America. They had decided practically on the spur of the moment to move to Geneva. The job proposed ideally suited Mr Zelig's background, qualifications and talents. Mrs Zelig, who had been a nurse, but not worked outside the home since the children were born, was becoming a bit bored as a suburban housewife. She thought the sojourn in Geneva would be a good antidote to impending middle age, a challenge, and opportunity which would benefit the children in the future. The family chose a detached house surrounded by hedges. Mrs Zelig liked the American feel of the neighbourhood. The older child was adapting with ease to a very significant change of style at the International School. The younger attended kindergarten at the local school, but had a great deal of difficulty and stopped after a few weeks. Mrs Zelig was having a great deal of difficulty adapting to customs and routines of living in Geneva, and was extremely uncomfortable. A great deal of tension could be sensed between husband and wife, but was not discussed.	2 3 4 7 10

3

WHAT IS STRESSFUL ABOUT MOVING ABROAD?

Stress, or a stressor, is any environmental, social, or internal demand which requires the individual to readjust his/her usual behaviour patterns (Holmes and Rahe, 1967). If moving was generally a very positive affair in the previous chapter, if pull factors outweighed push, this same move does most decidedly require readjustment of usual behaviour patterns, and feelings of stress can be intense. This chapter reports on how respondents evaluated the stressful aspects of moving to a new culture. A few months after they had moved, and also after about two years, they rated what is stressful about moving abroad, and just how stressful each aspect was felt to be (they also rated positive aspects of moving abroad: results of both may be found in the Appendix, Tables A.6 and A.7). On the whole, adjusting to living in a new culture was rated as being 'moderately stressful': on a scale of 0 to 3 (from 'not at all' to 'very' stressful) husbands gave the experience a rating of 1.9 and wives 1.8.

Language was judged to be the major source of stress, or bother, followed by housing and shopping for everyday necessities. A second group of sources of unease in moving abroad concerned contacts with other people: difficulties getting to know the local population; being far away from family and close friends, and loneliness. Practical items such as problems with schools, work and finances, were rated as being 'a little bit stressful'. It is also interesting to note items that respondents felt were *not* particularly stressful: these include a group of items centring around the theme of alienation (rootlessness, encountering different moral values in the community, and lack of roles in the community). Finally, few people were much bothered by feeling they had too little control over the decision to move, or by not having their own possessions around them. And whatever else it may be, moving abroad was certainly not felt to be boring, especially by the men.

If they were relatively positive about the stressful aspects of moving when responding to a questionnaire, as when talking about their reasons for having moved in the first place, those who participated in the study were not always so sanguine in face-to-face interviews. At the final interview respondents almost unanimously evaluated moving as having been stressful, or extremely stressful, at least in the short run. The stresses they discussed are difficult or even impossible to evaluate on a pre-structured questionnaire: these ranged from acute but short-term hassles around the move itself, about which in fact people often forgot afterwards, to disorientation and threats to self-image. These are the object of the present chapter. The interviewees do most of the talking. They discuss the 'hassles' involved in changing cultures (hassles are the mini-events which require small behavioural readjustments during the course of a day, such as traffic jams or car trouble. Their opposites are uplifts, such as an unexpected visit from friends or having a good meal). They then discuss the stresses of mastering (or not mastering) a new language, loneliness, being away from the comfortable 'known-ness' of tangible things and of rules, and the feeling that one is not quite in control of what is happening around one. As an introduction, a family not yet met, the Woods, talk about most of these themes, starting with the observation that the opportunity to move to a new culture may not necessarily come at the most auspicious moment.

An example: the Wood family

Mr Wood's employer offered him a job abroad just as Mrs Wood returned from the hospital after relatively major surgery:

> H: We found out six days after the surgery.
> W: He looked at me ... he had this look in his eye ... I knew something was up, and it was that we had an opportunity to live in Switzerland. I was so ill that I wasn't happy or sad. I was just struck with a little bit of fear and a little bit of happiness. I don't know what I felt.
> M: I should think it would also have been 'I can't cope with this'.
> W: Well I knew that in time it would all work out, but at the time it was quite a lot to be hit with. Then in three or four weeks he was gone, travelling over here ... It was sort of uneasy, renting the house and selling the cars, not knowing if the work permit would come, wondering how we would get out of all of this if it didn't.
>
> (Wood/1)

The opening point for describing their unease in the new culture was language, and the lack of control over everyday encounters that is linked to inadequate mastery:

> H: The lack of ability to communicate is what makes me most uncomfortable.

WHAT IS STRESSFUL ABOUT MOVING ABROAD?

> W: Like being in a line where people cut in front of you, or come and get the cashier's attention. You could have handled the situation in your own language, but now you can't. It's very frustrating.
>
> H: There are two aspects. One is the frustration: people have no patience. The other is it sets up a barrier immediately, a wall. People recognise that you're not one of them.
>
> (Wood/1)

Such incidents were so uncomfortable that the subject came up again a year later:

> W: I waited half an hour to buy a toy for my son, because someone came who spoke French, and I couldn't. The salesperson demonstrated a toy car, then left to get batteries for it. I'd been standing there waiting for another lady to finish. Because I couldn't say to him: 'I'm first' I couldn't handle it, yet I didn't want to disappoint my child either. We had picked out a special toy together.
>
> (Wood/2)

If the feeling is one of not being in complete control of one's interactions, then a corollary may be an insecure feeling that one does not quite know the rules, or even that control lies with somebody else:

> W: Another thing really bothered me when I came. There was a sense of a loss of freedom. I was coming from a place where you felt protected; you knew the laws and rights and what was going on around you. Here I don't know what their laws are. I don't know what you can be put in prison for here. I don't know what I should and shouldn't say and do. I felt I didn't have the right to speak out against anything, or to do things, because it may be infringing on these people. That was something I never anticipated.
>
> H: It's the little things. We know for major crimes we're fairly safe, but things like where to put your garbage. And the traffic laws are different. I wanted to get some crutches for my son when he hurt his foot, but was told you have to have a prescription. You have to have a licence to fish. It's very regulated. It's not a free society. You can't go 25 kilometres in any direction without crossing a border, so you have to keep your papers on you at all times.
>
> W: You feel like somebody has got control over you.
>
> H: ... Anybody can just stop you on the street, and ask what you are doing, and for your papers.

WHAT IS STRESSFUL ABOUT MOVING ABROAD?

W: The first time I tried driving in Geneva they had a road block. I had to show my driver's licence. Fortunately we had someone with us who could speak French, and he translated. Then at the end the policeman let us know he spoke good English. This type of thing makes you feel even more uneasy.

M: They're watching you, and you don't even know they understand you?

Both: Exactly.

(Wood/1)

Such things are not just unpleasant. They caused Mrs Wood's first year, especially, to be not only stressful, but distressing:

W: I think we'll gain a lot, see things, learn about another culture. But you also give up a lot, that comfortable niche that makes you feel good. There's a loss. It's almost like a little death. You are falling apart, then you have to restructure.

(She starts to cry)

W: I find it hard to find my niche here. Everything is foreign. I feel a lonesomeness here I've never experienced before.

(Mr Wood explains, after looking to his wife for permission to do so, that an additional factor is that their last child has just started going to school, and that his wife is also having to adjust to having both children out of the house for the first time, an adaptation which is not easy for her.)

W: It's not like I'm not trying. I'll get in the car and spend the whole afternoon looking at things, but there's still being by yourself, and not knowing anybody. And there's still a foreignness, such a distance.

M: There's nobody here you know well.

W: When you tell people about coming, they say Geneva is wonderful. They never tell you about the problems, the adjustment. They just don't tell you you're going to have a bad time for the first few months.

H: (disagrees mildly) Somebody told us about the first few months being difficult, but you don't believe it. You think: 'I'm different, I can handle it'. We were told, but we didn't want to hear it. We didn't understand.

W: I didn't ever hear that. What rings in my ears is 'you're going to love it'.

(Wood/1)

WHAT IS STRESSFUL ABOUT MOVING ABROAD?

The Woods will appear many other times throughout the coming chapters, as they experience difficulties and critically important family effects of moving. First, however, the themes they have introduced are taken up.

Stress around the move itself

The people in the study often commented that the time before the move was very stressful. The decision to relocate may have been a difficult one, and, as the Woods demonstrated, timing of a move in relation to other family events may not be ideal. There was almost always a period of ambiguity before all the pieces fell into place, of signing contracts, requesting work permits, selling houses, and so on. Professionally, respondents were busy tying up loose ends at the old job, and making first steps in the new one, while simultaneously doing all the other things that needed attention because they were to be away:

> H: The most difficult period for us was the couple of weeks before we left. We were trying to do twice as many things as we had time to do. I was under a lot of pressure to finish things in the office, and didn't have time to help with the last-minute preparations. Our kids were uprooted from their home. Our furniture was shipped somewhere. We were living in a hotel. It was stressful for all of us.
> (Renton/1)

Reactions of family had to be anticipated:

> W: I was not only dreading telling the children, but also telling my mother ... I thought she was going to be unhappy, and make me feel unhappy and guilty.
> (Cady/1)

Even if it was to be for a short time, moving inevitably required making choices, deciding what to bring, what to store for an eventual return, what to eliminate. This could be good for the soul:

> H: It helped us throw away things that needed to be thrown away. It's sort of soul cleansing ... Who knows when we would ever have got rid of that old couch. It was the first thing we ever bought when we got married, but we couldn't leave it there for anybody else!
> (Y/1)

– or stressful:

WHAT IS STRESSFUL ABOUT MOVING ABROAD?

> H: In your normal day-to-day life, if you're established somewhere, you make very few decisions. You go to work, get home ... you may have to decide whether to put milk in your coffee or not, or where to shop for groceries ... but decisions that really affect your lives are few and far between. When you move you lose that frame of reference ... You have to rebuild it, to make decisions in a very short period of time that are going to affect your life for quite a number of years, like where you'll put the kids in school ...
>
> W: ... to buy or ship a car, buy or rent a house ... Almost every time we've moved he's left before me. Then he phones, and we have to make a whole series of decisions ... You think, what if I make the wrong decision? And there are doubts: 'did he really think that, or did he just say it because he knew I was upset?'
>
> (Newton/1)

The first few weeks after the move were also often described as unsettled: many families arrived in a state of fatigue, suffering from jet lag, disoriented. Most lived in temporary housing for the first two weeks, a time some described as one of inconvenience and suspension, of waiting to settle into a new life. In one-third of the families studied, the husband came ahead to start the new job. He usually lived in a hotel until the rest of the family arrived, a time described as lonely. When the wife and children stayed behind to allow the children to finish the school year, to sell the house, or while waiting for housing in Geneva, she had to deal alone with the packing and with the movers.

While most families received some sort of welcome and assistance when they arrived, usually from future colleagues, some had to cope on their own. One or two were treated with flagrant disregard, creating an initial impression that was difficult to overcome:

> H: I arrived to an empty office because everybody had gone to [another office in a distant city] for a month. Those first weeks really coloured our experience. There were a lot of practical problems ... For example we couldn't transfer money, and couldn't get a credit card, so we had no way of paying for anything for a couple of months. We had to pay a [large] deposit for the telephone, and later found out we shouldn't have had to.
>
> W: One of the children got sick when we had been here for only a week, and needed a doctor. We had heard the American Women's Club had a list of doctors, so [my husband] phoned. They told him to come down and register as a member first, *then* they would give the name of a doctor.
>
> (Friedson/1)

WHAT IS STRESSFUL ABOUT MOVING ABROAD?

Several people mentioned having been told they would get sick soon after they arrived, and there were, in fact, several incidents of illness during the first weeks, especially among children. Some were potentially serious. Several people mentioned symptoms that they or their physicians attributed to stress, and there were a number of minor accidents. These were far more stressful than they might have been had the family been more settled:

> H: One night about two or three months after we got here [our adolescent] fell while she was out with her friends. She had to go to the emergency room to get four stitches in her chin. It happened at midnight and we didn't have a phone yet, so her friends had to come and get us.
>
> W: I had been worried. I had wakened up and realised she wasn't back yet. The kids finally turned up at 2:00 to tell us what had happened. We had to go to the hospital to get her.
>
> (Gibbs/1)

Finally, and in spite of stereotypes to the contrary about the relative affluence of families such as those studied, financial worries were universally expressed at the first interview. The families were moving to one of the most expensive cities in the world. All had adequate salaries before they left – some would say more than adequate – and even higher salaries when they arrived. All had been told that in Geneva expenses were high for such basics as rent, food, and clothes (at the time the study was carried out, if one was not careful, a cup of coffee in Geneva could cost the equivalent of an entire meal in North America) and they all worried for the first few months. Several had depleted resources buying what acquaintances had told them they would need to bring, and, especially for those not liberally taken in charge by the employer, collateral expenses such as that of replacing household goods damaged or simply not worth moving, getting electrical appliances adapted to a different current, buying clothing, and paying deposits on rent and telephones, could be high.

> W: We knew the prices were high here, but the salary that [my husband] was to be getting seemed more than adequate. Now we've found there are a lot of hidden costs ...
>
> H: ... the price of insurance, the ability to finance housing ... meat ...
>
> W: ... milk. Things we use all the time, that now we realise are three times the price.
>
> H: Potato chips, snack things. There are some things we just don't buy anymore.
>
> (Foster/1)

Such things could properly be called hassles. Hassles predominated in the first few months after the move.

Hassles as a threat to feelings of adult competence

Hassles are easy to talk about, but difficult to take seriously, which is precisely what makes them stressful. During the interviews a few months after they moved, almost everybody had lists of annoyances, annoyances so trivial that people excused themselves before talking about them, so irritating that they very often did so at length, and so standard that in retrospect I found that after the first interviews I had usually transcribed them as 'etc.'. Some extracts:

> H: The stores are always closed, and when you get there it's too expensive anyway.
> W: You have to shop for groceries practically every day. I am fed up going to the stores, using my little bit of French . . . And we can't find any of the Swiss cheese we ate at home.
> H: The rooms are tiny. The bedrooms have only one electric outlet. Stupid windows: you hit your head on them, and if the wind blows they will bang closed and break . . .
> W: The biggest daily strife is driving. There are so many cars in such a small area, and people have absolutely no patience . . .
> H: To get a telephone we had to pay cash for security. They said: 'You're a foreigner so you'll probably skip out without paying the bill so we have to ask for a deposit'.
>
> (Allen/1)

Another example:

> H: The cat got hit by a car, and had to have lots of stitches. It's easy to find an English-speaking doctor, but not a veterinarian.
> W: The first month we were in a small apartment. The children missed all the North American food. There was quite a bit of complaining about why my cooking was so different, why they couldn't have their favourite foods . . . It's difficult to get used to waiting three times as long for a load of laundry to be done. The kitchen is so small there's no place to put the dishes . . .
>> One of the jokes you hear here is:
>> 'What are you doing?'

> 'I'm packing.'
> 'I've had it. I'm leaving.' (laughter)
> Everybody gets frustrated, it's the little things.
>
> (Cady/1)

Piled together, the repercussions of such hassles can be serious. After she made her joke about packing, for example, Mrs Cady laughed a bit too much, and was obviously upset by what she had just said. Protesting far too much, she phoned four days after the interview to say she wanted to correct a misimpression she was afraid she may have left: the remark about packing up and wanting to leave was just a joke: *not* everybody is saying this, just some people around her. They don't really mean it ... *she* didn't really mean it ...

In the above citations the person making the remarks commented that they sound petty, and study participants portrayed some embarrassment even while in the midst of diatribes about curtains, nails, laundry days, or lawn mowing. Two couples put into words the potential damage to self-image that make hassles so threatening. In both cases the wives had put aside careers so as to be able to make the move. The Rentons described a difficult period during the first year, with a child repeatedly ill, during which, to make matters worse, the husband had to be away from home frequently for his work:

> W: I was driving three hours a day to get the children back and forth to school. [Our younger child] was depressed. I was very frustrated, feeling that I was this highly disciplined person, used to working full time and more, and having kids and activities too. I thought I was coming to a place where *supposedly* I would have a lot of free time, and I felt I had not a second to myself. There was a total lack of accomplishment on a day to day basis.
> H: You no longer had any control over your life.
> W: I don't think depressed is the right word, but I was absolutely beside myself with frustration at not being able to accomplish what I felt I should be accomplishing. I'm not talking about reading *War and Peace*; I'm talking about it being nine in the evening and I still didn't have the laundry done, because I'd spent four hours in the car and had to take [our child] to the paediatrician and wait, then go to the pharmacy, then to the store, then to another store because the first one didn't have what I needed.
>
> (Renton/2)

WHAT IS STRESSFUL ABOUT MOVING ABROAD?

Although they only came for a year, what the Ys said was very similar:

> W: It wasn't as easy as I thought it would be, especially because of the language. I like to talk. When something doesn't work I say something funny, but I can't do that in French.
> H: ... You'd have to know how she was at home: 18-hour days: kids, work and so on. Here all of a sudden, boom ...
> W: ... ironing ...
> H: For her it's like the brakes being slammed on professionally, and she's still detoxifying, withdrawing from the stuff.
> W: Little problems, like having both Swiss and French money on hand, became big deals, partly because there wasn't anything else going on. If we'd had other problems these would have been nothing ... I thought I was losing my mind ... And it was hard on the kids to see me like that ... I felt just totally incompetent about doing the slightest little task, just the day-to-day things that should be easy but that weren't, like I couldn't get the dumb stove to work. I didn't have control over my day-to-day life. The hard thing was not feeling very confident, because I'm used to knowing what I'm doing.
>
> Part of it is I really thought I liked adventure, to try new things. I didn't know if I'd grown out of that, or had lost it ... I thought 'where's my sense of adventure? This person that likes to go out and try to think!' I was disappointed in myself.
>
> (Y/1)

It is undoubtedly not by happenstance that those who were best able to formulate these remarks were women who left highly invested professional lives in order to move. Hassles always imply threats to self image, but it is in *contrast* to an identity quite different that they become most evident. Mrs Y was not just reflecting on multiple roles, but saying something about what she felt she has become, when she contrasted being a professor with worrying about ironing the family's clothes.

Phenomena are similar when people talk about language.

Language

> W: I don't think any of us really understood the impact the language would have on us. The second night here the school across the street had a fête. We thought we would go to meet people in the neighbourhood. And they were speaking French! We knew this, but then it really hit.
>
> (Y/1)

WHAT IS STRESSFUL ABOUT MOVING ABROAD?

Language was of primary importance on the questionnaire, and also a major theme in the interviews. When they first arrived, all of the families studied said they felt they should learn to speak French, although actual commitment to language learning of course varied (one person got up at 5:30 every morning to study, and did so in the evenings after a full work day as well; others gave up after one or two lessons). Those less at ease in the local language had to depend on others to help them:

> W: I depend on friends who have lived here longer than me ... They can speak for me. They help me understand things that a small child would want to know! That's how I feel, very immature.
> (Davidson/3)

Such dependency was generally found to be uncomfortable, and also inconvenient:

> H: I don't like feeling dependent on people. It makes me feel menial. Also it means I spend a lot of time going places instead of phoning, for example to get the car fixed or for a hair cut, so I can be face-to-face when I talk with the person.
> (Vance/2)

One of the frustrations of language of which people most talked was that of feeling disadvantaged, even stupid:

> H: When we found out we were coming I had a crash course in French. By day three I felt like an ant, totally incompetent ... When I came I would find myself getting lost ... Somebody tried to help me, but I couldn't understand what he was showing me.
> (Rodgers/1)

Related was a feeling of being ill at ease, potentially vulnerable:

> H: That's an interesting theme, the strain of living in a society where you're not master of the main language. Even in [the last place we lived] I was in control of 85 per cent of the language, but not quite sure of the nuances. You always feel slightly insecure, not badly insecure, but you know you're not master of it ... which is why you end up socialising mainly with people who speak English.
>
> W: We socialise in French occasionally, but it's not relaxed. You can do it once a month for three hours, but if you want to have a good time, use slang and not have to explain yourself,

have people understand ... It doesn't bother me that I don't understand everything, but when I want to be in control of a situation, for example with a doctor or with the school, then I want to be able to speak English.

(Kennedy/2)

Those who mastered the language imperfectly were also vulnerable to being humiliated:

> H: Once just after we got here [my wife] and I ordered pastries from a store. The sales person didn't understand what I was saying. She mumbled something, and made a face. I didn't say anything, but I could have taken the whole case and thrown it right at her. Here's this little girl who is so ignorant she can't get a *decent* job: she's selling pastries. I probably earn thirty times more than she does, and she's got the guts to make a face because I don't speak her language.
>
> W: I had just seen exactly the same thing the week before – in New York. A saleswoman was treating some Japanese visitors rudely. They couldn't understand the money, and were giving her a lot of change. She was so rude, it was horrible. I felt terrible about the impression these people were getting of us because of this woman. When [the incident with the pastries] happened I felt: 'Now it's our turn.'

(Rodgers/1)

As discussed in the previous chapter, those who participated in the study felt that on the whole they had been in control of the decision to make the move: it had been their own responsibility. But in a difference somewhat equivalent to that between a major stress and irritating hassles, when they started living in a new culture people felt they had far less control over numerous less significant aspects of their daily lives. Examples given in the interviews concerned such things as maintaining one's fair place in a queue, as with Mrs Wood cited at the beginning of this chapter, or having unknown people come to do things for which one had not asked. At the Rodgers household, for example, the landlord had evidently arranged for somebody to come to do the garden work every week, work the family would have preferred to do themselves, and the gardener kept coming back in spite of their repeated requests in inadequate French that he stop:

> W: Every time I heard that broom sweeping I thought: 'Oh, no I don't want him to be here' ...

(Rodgers/1)

The feeling of helplessness, or of potential helplessness, could extend to roles as a parent:

> W: I used to take [the three-year-old] to a little playground while her brother was in school. It was usually just her and me because it was always raining. But one day the weather was nice, and the park was crowded. The children were on a little merry-go-round, and two Swiss kids started laughing at [the seven-year-old] because he couldn't speak French. That was uncomfortable. I felt sorry, but also scared about not being able to communicate with those kids. My children were into something that I would not have been able to explain. You know, if they accidentally bumped somebody I wouldn't be able to say: 'I'm sorry, it was just an accident'.
>
> (Rodgers/1)

Beyond the ability to communicate, and ultimately to influence one's environment, was a feeling that one may no longer be surrounded by the familiar. The usual signposts, the things that are taken for granted, and by which one comprehends the world, had shifted for several of those who participated in the study.

The comfortable known-ness of things, and what is taken for granted

Missing the comfortable known-ness of things started with that most basic of elements, food:

> W: (sigh) I like to cook, and none of my recipes work any more because I can't get the ingredients.
>
> (Foster/1)

Things that should have been familiar may suddenly have become strange:

> W: We had been in the house for perhaps six months when our seven year old's favourite programme came on the French television. I called him because I thought he would like it. He sat down to watch. First he got excited. But then he started crying, and said: 'I can't stand this. This is not how they should sound.' It was something that was close to home, and it was wrong. He got really upset.
>
> H: He was upset for hours afterwards.
>
> (Rodgers/1)

Missing the comfortable known-ness of things went on through the other senses, to physical orientation, or disorientation, in space:

> H: Our first summer here was bad. We brought too many things. The house was too full. We had to step over things. The bathrooms felt like prison cells they were so small.
> W: And the smells are different ... I was very disoriented. I couldn't manage to drive across Geneva.
>
> (Zelig/1)

It also covered cultural differences. The differences between North America and Switzerland are far from being as great as those with many other areas of the world, but several people nevertheless experienced culture shock, sometimes in a double sense:

> W: I was shocked by topless bathing suits. It really freaked me out to see ladies just standing there topless. In North America I was boycotting the local store for exhibiting pornography, and here I bring my children to the swimming pool where everybody is running around half naked, or more than half naked.
>
> (Zelig/1)

Although they may have been less susceptible to culture shock, those who had lived in other places also talked about losing orientation when they moved, and of not knowing how the system works:

> W: Adapting to a new culture has to be stressful: you don't know how the system works ... People think differently. You can't pick up the phone and call an ambulance. You don't know where you could take them if someone is sick. And that is stressful.
>
> (Madison/3)

Having already adjusted to vastly different societies did not necessarily make it easier to adjust to yet another. For some quite the contrary:

> H: Geneva is so much more sophisticated than the rest of the places we've lived. It's a very streamlined society here. It's a society where you don't go to a parking place without getting a ticket: you have to overcome that trepidation of 'what happens if I don't have the right coins when I want to leave this place?' It's a bit intimidating when you come out of a

system where there are not even traffic lights in the street (all laugh) – let alone hidden policemen, cameras, radar and parking places where you have to pay if you exceed the hour!

(Davidson/3)

Not knowing the rules, threats to identity

Several families described sensing that the ground rules for social interaction had somehow shifted. They felt ill-at-ease, not quite understanding either the geography of the new context or a set of unfamiliar rules:

> W: It was almost two months before I could get in the car without getting a knot in my stomach. I would drive down the street and worry about whether I was doing something wrong. One day I had a man really angry with me because I turned where I wasn't supposed to. He was writing down my licence plate number. I had no idea what I'd done wrong. I wondered what kind of city I'd moved to. The first month, just getting in the car and going to the store was a big deal.
>
> (Cady/1)

Some talked of feeling uncomfortable, criticised, as though the natives were frowning on them, that they were doing something wrong. These feelings were severe enough to lead some to think they might even be breaking the law without realising it, as did the Woods, discussed at the beginning of this chapter. All of those who perceived such hostility were living in a foreign culture for the first time, and may in fact have unthinkingly been making mistakes by inappropriately transposing old habits to the new culture. Few people like discussing embarrassing situations, so examples are rare, but one such incident apparently occurred when the Smithers made impromptu visits to sing Christmas songs in front of the houses of new acquaintances a few weeks after they arrived. Appropriate holiday behaviour where the family came from, this sort of visit in the more formal Geneva would have been at the very least surprising. The couple portrayed unease as they talked about the incident, and I did not probe. In another example, children were being 'a bit loud' while travelling in the first class compartment of a train:

> H: A woman nearby made nasty comments about us.
> W: We were bawled out for doing things we had no idea anybody would get mad about. We still didn't know what we had been doing.
>
> (Zelig/1)

Another example was described by the same family some six months later:

> W: I took a visiting friend for lunch to [an elegant restaurant]. We were a group of friends, and having a good time. We were talking, maybe a bit loudly because one is hard of hearing, but not *that* loud. We were swinging our hands and humming to the music that was playing, taking pictures of each other, taking turns going to the bathroom to take pictures of each other by a pretty flower pot.
>
> The waiter was horribly rude. He treated us as though we were being completely obnoxious. He was obviously talking about us, criticising us, following us to the bathroom. He gave us the impression we were doing something wrong. Is it the culture? Were we breaking the rules? Was he just hostile to North Americans?
>
> I would have liked to discuss it with the waiter, to find out what was wrong, but I couldn't. I couldn't even complain to the manager, as I might have done in North America. I felt like I was trespassing. I felt helpless. It ruined a fun occasion.
>
> (Zelig/telephone interview)

By the third interview the feeling of being criticised had disappeared in all of the families who talked about it, and had even been forgotten. As one commented:

> H: Over time you become yourself again. You learn there are certain things you do and don't do. Things become comical rather than stressful.
> W: You were stressed because you didn't know what was right, what was OK, and you just wanted it to be right and not to offend anybody.
>
> (Rodgers/2)

Mr Rodgers thought: 'You become yourself again', but others were less sure. Mrs Wood, cited in the introduction to this chapter, talked about loss, 'a little death', and about the need to restructure. It was when the equilibrium established in the new place was fragile that threats to identity were most acute, disorientation severe enough in at least in one case to be described as feeling like *Alice in Wonderland*. The following passage comes from an interview with Mrs Zelig, the woman who had talked of culture shock, and of feeling she and her family were being criticised in restaurants and in a train. This was the family's first move together. Some 16 months after their arrival Mr Zelig and one of the children found they were adapting quite easily, but Mrs Zelig and the other child were having a great deal of difficulty. We talked at length about her unease about the family's impending first visit back home:

> W: I really was kind of dreading going back home. You know, like in *Alice in Wonderland*. She went down the rabbit hole and was very disoriented, but finally she kind of got used to it. I was fearful I would lose the victories I had made. I just really wasn't ready, but we'd made the plans and had to go – all the relatives were expecting us. I wanted to go, but I had some ambivalence which surprised me.
>
> (Zelig/2)

In other words, the fear was of putting to test a certain tranquillity just barely attained in the new place. In this case the equilibrium held, and enough distance had even been attained to allow Mrs Zelig to see home in a new way:

> W: When we went home it was very easy. It was wonderful to speak English, to make small talk with a waitress at the airport. I had forgotten what it was like to make small talk with somebody, because I've become used to not saying anything unless I have to. In fact I had culture shock at home! I found it strange that in the grocery store somebody else was putting my groceries in a sack for me, and taking them out to the car.
> H: The sales person asked her if she wanted paper or plastic bags, and she didn't know what to answer. She just stood there!
> W: They must have wondered: 'Hasn't she ever been in a grocery store?' I just felt like I came from another planet or something!
>
> (Zelig/2)

A year later, after two and a half years in the new culture, the family was somewhat more comfortable, but annual shifting back and forth was nonetheless hindering attachment, or a certain gelling of the new identity.

> W: It's kind of strange here. The years seem to go so fast, maybe because the year is punctuated by all the school holidays, and also because we've been able to go home for the summers ... It's scary. You have this feeling of rootlessness anyway, and you're so disoriented. And to think you'll just be submerged in this culture and never get out of it. You think: 'I'll never

go back to anything familiar, it's all going to be ploughing through the unfamiliar until who knows when.'

(Zelig/4)

One final source of individual stress was loneliness.

Initial isolation and loneliness: 'Nobody would know if I left for three days'

Some of the families found very difficult an initial period of isolation immediately after they moved. New networks of relationships had not yet been formed, and it was even possible to doubt that they would ever do so:

> W: Our little boy was afraid he would not have any friends. We arrived during the summer vacation when most of the neighbours were away on vacation. We were walking in the street, and he kept asking: 'Where are the children? I won't have any friends!' He was panicked.
>
> (Nathanson/1)

Women, especially, described the first weeks as a time of disorientation and loneliness:

> W: That's a very uncomfortable, horrible time. The house is still a mess. The kids go off to school and your husband to work, and you're sitting there with nothing to do but sort out your house and find the grocery store and all that kind of thing. Even when you start meeting people you know names, but you haven't put them with faces. I have always hated that period.
>
> (Newton/1)

Mrs Rodgers, who was not particularly shy, but not yet very experienced in establishing a new social self, described the painful process of forcing herself to meet people. One of the main points of contact was with other mothers waiting for their children after school:

> W: The first person I tried to speak to happened to speak French. So the only comment I got back was: 'I'm sorry, but I don't speak English.' That intimidated and inhibited me. I watched until I saw one woman who showed up in jeans and seemed very relaxed, and I liked the way she was with her children. So I thought I would say hello. I felt like I was trying to ask

WHAT IS STRESSFUL ABOUT MOVING ABROAD?

> her for a date! I couldn't believe how I felt – nervous and uncomfortable. So I said hello and we talked a little bit ... Then the next occasion she made an effort to say hello and acknowledge me. I couldn't believe this ritual. It's years since I've made friends or set out to make a friend. I don't ever remember doing it, it's just something that just happened. This was a strange feeling.
>
> (Rodgers/1)

A little bit later in the same interview her husband reminded us that it is not only women who are affected by such feelings. He talked wistfully of walking down the street in a city as yet strange, wishing people would invite him into their homes. At a point at which new friends had not yet been made, and old friends were far away, he talked about how rarely the telephone rang, and about his irrational feelings of jealousy at the constantly ringing telephone during a visit to his sister's home in North America. Knowing that the phone was ringing for his brother-in-law's business didn't help:

> H: My sister had this stupid answering machine, and I kept saying: 'Why don't you answer the phone?'
> W: Our phone never did ring every five minutes.
> H: I know, but it used to be more, much more, than now ...
> W: That was before we moved to where we became a long-distance call.
>
> (Rodgers/1)

It was at the third interview, practically three years later, that Mr and Mrs Rodgers could formulate the full extent of the isolation they had felt:

> M: Was there a time when you were lonely?
> W: There was a time when – I wasn't lonely, because I can be alone without being lonely – but there was a time that I felt – alone. Like waiting for the kids at school. When I was at home I was fine. And then we had – I can't remember her name ...

(Her husband has to prompt her with the name of a person who, as a first friend, had been a very significant other, often referred to in the first interview two years before.)

> ... Yes – X – that I could call. So I had someone I could turn to, but she was very busy, and you feel you are going to impose.
> M: It was when you were with people that you felt alone?

> W: Yes. Because everyone around you is with each other. But there you are, not knowing anybody, just standing there all alone.
>
> (Rodgers/3)

For others, lack of attachment to other people amounted to feeling invisible:

> W: There is a stage you go through with every move – and it was even more acute with this move – where you feel invisible. You think if you disappeared off the face of the world nobody would notice. You could be gone for four or five days and nobody would notice ... That's the hardest, the loneliness part.
>
> (Vance/2)

Starting over again in relationships means repeatedly having to go over the most significant aspects of one's life history:

> W: One thing that is difficult in the beginning is that when you meet people who don't know you, you have to ... go through a number of things. You have to describe your family. If you get a call from your sister about a problem, and you want to talk to somebody about it, then you have to stop and tell them the whole story. If it was somebody who had known you, then you wouldn't have to go through all that – the understanding is immediate. That's something that's very comfortable, and satisfying, and fulfilling. That's something that you don't have with people you've just met. You're dealing with people you don't really know yet. What I do if I'm having a really tough day is call on my old friends that I've been through all that with, that know me. Eventually I'll establish that here, but it takes a while. And it's tough to do, to sort of reintroduce your whole personality to somebody.
>
> (Newton/1)

The more individual stresses raised by adapting to living in a new culture have been explored in some detail. A certain number of threads are left dangling in order to turn to the specific stresses, or pressures, such adaptation puts on families.

4

STRAINS ON FAMILIES

There are many sources of tension for couples and families in intercultural migration. The introduction to these particular strains comes from a group interview, which brought together three of the six couples in Geneva for sabbatical years.[5] The discussion took place one evening in the late spring. All three families had arrived during the previous summer, and were about to leave. They had not known each other before the interview, but had a great deal in common: each had two children, ranging in ages from six to 15 years; all were professors, scientists, or teachers. In all three families the wives were professionally active at home, but not in Geneva (although one had worked independently on an academic project): it was the husband's sabbatical which had brought the family to Geneva.

The discussion got off to a lively start when the group began contrasting the experiences of husbands and of wives during the initial weeks. Husbands were going out to an office each day, meeting colleagues and taking up the professional attachments which had brought them, whereas wives found themselves in the unaccustomed position of staying at home. Until they managed to set up a new structure for their time, wives and children were at decidedly loose ends, all the more vulnerable to the hassles referred to in the previous chapter:

> Mrs L: The first three months were very difficult. We had so much time after we got here . . .
> Mr J: (Protesting mildly) But it wasn't really horrible . . .
> Mrs J: That's because you were at work, the beginning was horrible!
> Mrs Y: That was a loooooong month. The kids and I were at home, and there were all these little things. Like the neighbours invited us to go to a swimming pool just across the border in

---

5 Focus groups had not been part of the original study design. The group interview was devised out of necessity when I had broken a leg and could not get to peoples' homes to do interviews. The families on sabbatical were about to leave, and three of them kindly agreed to come to discuss together.

France, and we didn't have the right currency to pay to get in. That's a minor problem, but it was *major* that day (murmurs of understanding and agreement). The children weren't in school, which would have given us a structure . . . You were off at work where you were appreciated, and I was having to work to compose a simple sandwich.

Mr J: Now *that's* a theme you'll want to talk about, the different experience for the two members of a couple! . . .

Mr Y: We've had arguments about things I thought we'd never have arguments about (laughs). I never thought the laundry would be an issue in our marriage. There are things we didn't realise . . . (he gets a bit embarrassed and confused, then corrects): we've argued about things, but I'm not going to say that any of those things have threatened our marriage.

Mrs J: They're just different from usual (laughs).

Mr Y: I don't think they've necessarily brought us closer together either, but . . . (laughs)

Mrs J: I'm still toying with this whole issue of whether or not moving makes families closer. For us living in an apartment means that (laughs) in fact physically we're closer.

Mr L: You use the same goddamn bathroom (laughter, everybody starts talking) . . .

Mrs J: Our kids share a room that is really tiny. There is just room for a bunk bed, and that's all. It's been a challenge to them. They spend a lot more time together. They get along reasonably well – they fight more than they did before because they're literally on top of one another, but I don't think it's been a negative thing for them entirely.

Mr Y: Our kids have become closer, only friends, allies.

M: . . . One other thing that I think can happen, and I'm using you here as informed observers, is that lots of little tensions become an issue.

Mrs Y: . . . which you've figured out how to take care of at home.

Mr Y: One thing on a more serious level in our case, is that my dear wife here, who's incredibly active in her career at home, has basically put it on ice here. And here I am, having a blast . . .

Mrs Y: . . . being adored and appreciated . . .

Mr Y: . . . and she's staying at home and ironing. So when I come home from work there's not a great deal of, let us say, conjugal feeling (laughs).

Mrs J: That's a typical problem.

Mr Y: If the roles had been switched I'm not sure I could have done it . . .

M: I've seen a couple of families who are having trouble. One of the things they say is that they went along in their habits at home. Their lives were all set up. Then when they came here all those habits were . . .

Mrs Y: . . . structural.

M: Yes. There may have been certain tensions between them that they hadn't realised, because of the way their life was set up . . . They were in a routine . . .

Mr J: You organise your environment to get around the conflicts, so they don't come up. Then when you get into a new environment, and you haven't structured your life that way, the conflicts come . . .

Mr Y: We talked about our kids getting closer. I can see the same things happening in a marriage as well. It's a lot more difficult to . . . I was going to say something ridiculous . . . to go bowling with the guys.

Mrs Y: (laughs) You have never gone bowling!

Mr Y: But you definitely find yourself, or at least you present yourself, as being more of an ally with your spouse. You never had to do that before if there were tensions, because you could escape into something else . . .

Mrs L: You have to talk more. There's so much more that you have to discuss. Just what you're going to do, how you're going to do it, where you're going. There's more communication.

(Everybody talks at once. Somebody jokes: 'She finally confessed to me she hates the music I play in the car!')

Discrepancies between husband's and wife's expectations and experiences, a potential for jealousy, and small hassles which may inflate to major irritations: as these couples point out, such irritations are all the more insidious since the family is away from its usual routines and structures, and family members may have only each other on whom to rely. The rest of this chapter elaborates on these themes, talking about the specific strains moving and adjusting to a new culture puts on couples, and on nuclear families. The chapter starts with the tensions raised within couples when there are two careers to be considered, and when only one can be pursued, then moves to strains immediately surrounding the move, which are especially severe when one spouse is seen to be responsible for displacing the entire family, and the other is 'not adjusting well'. Discussion of 'duty travel' then serves as a vehicle to discuss the somewhat more long-term tensions raised within families living abroad. A final segment goes to the family's external relations, discussing how they manage encounters with values that may be quite different from those with which they are familiar.

Two careers or one?

In any discussion of North American families moving, whether it is to another culture or even across town, it is impossible to avoid the issue of dual careers. The issue came up at the very beginning of the study, when couples were telling about their decision to move, and it kept coming up as interviews progressed. The ways women's child-bearing and professional careers affect each other is the object of a vast literature in itself, but the point here is that moving adds yet another variable in an already complex equation. It is difficult, at best, for a couple to maintain two serious careers when they change locations, and even more difficult when the relocation involves another continent.

Although it increasingly happens that it is the wife who gets the job and the husband who follows, it was the husbands who were coming to a new assignment among the cohort of North American families who moved to Geneva the year this study began. Many of the wives had worked before they moved, however, and in several families they had been actively engaged in serious careers. All were very well aware that working in Switzerland requires a permit, and that such permits were extremely difficult for foreigners to acquire: employers, official policy, and general hearsay all agreed that once the family moved, it would be practically impossible for the accompanying spouse to pursue a serious career, or maybe even to find a job at all.

The dual career families on sabbatical, reflecting on each other's observations, discussed the potential for tension between couples in such a situation. Among the five families retained that had to deal with them in the longer term, such tensions were less explicitly referred to, but certainly present. Mrs Bateson, for example, was a teacher dedicated to the point of occasionally getting up at four in the morning to prepare lessons for the next day. She had to put aside her career for the three years 'the company' had proposed the family live in Geneva, and had no guarantee of finding another teaching position when they returned. She commented:

> W: My first reaction [to the proposed move] was: 'You can go and I'll stay here and work, and see you at Christmas and during the summer.' That only lasted about a day, but it was my first reaction ...
>
> (Bateson/1)

She talked at length during the first interview about her frustration at giving up her career, and also covered the margins and back of the otherwise closed 'stressful aspects of living abroad' questionnaire with comments about lack of professional role, blows to her identity, and worry about what might happen to her career on return home. She referred several times, in retrospect, to having gone through a period of depression a few months after the family's arrival, related in part to her professional problem. The whole family agreed that it was not Mrs Bateson's destiny in life to be uniquely a housewife. As formulated by her very perceptive 15-year-old daughter:

> C: She doesn't make a good homemaker ... she's not the type. Some women are set out in their lives to be homemakers, that's what they're good at. My best friend's mother is just perfect at that. That's what she loves to do. But that's not my mother's type. She was grouchy when she had to do that ...
> W: ... depressed. I get very depressed if that's all I have going in my life, you're right.
>
> (Bateson/2)

In all of the formerly dual-career families in this study, dealing with the wife/mother's loss of professional role was seen to be a family matter. At the Friedson household for example, when I asked the couple about their hopes for the stay at the first interview, and in striking contrast to those who talked about travel, learning, and meeting a new culture, it was Mrs Friedson's professional frustration that emerged at the top of the list:

> M: What are your hopes for your stay?
> H: To see my wife find a job or find something to do. That would improve the state of the household ... the mood, not the money.
> W: ... Everybody had told us I couldn't expect to work, but I didn't *really* believe it. I was used to going places and finding a job immediately.
>
> (Friedson/1)

Two of the families in the same situation had, in fact, actually been counting on having the wife find a job when she arrived.

The Renton family

The career-driven Mrs Renton appeared in Chapter 2, when she talked of the complicated set of factors that had gone into the decision to put her demanding career aside in order to make an international move with her husband and seven- and four-year-old children. Deciding to leave her job so the family could move in fact became easier when her mentor mentioned the possibility of a position for her if she could get to the company's European headquarters some six hours away from Geneva from time to time. At the first interview, three months after the family arrived, she said she was for the moment simply enjoying having plenty of time to be with the children, and not yet thinking much about work:

> W: I'm more interested in making sure the children are happy. As much as I miss working, I really love being with my kids. They are great: well behaved, bright, very nice little people. I can say that, because it's not really because of me: they were practically raised in nursery school.
>
> (Renton/1)

There were a number of things not talked about at this interview, however. The four-year-old child was having great difficulty adjusting to the change of location, and, more pertinently here, Mrs Renton was more ambivalent than she had let on about no longer having a career. In addition, the vaguely promised possibility of a job in Europe was not working out. Her mentor had retired, and with him disappeared the possibility of a job for her.

> W: I miss my career ...
> H: You're dealing with two variables at the same time: adjusting to Geneva plus the disruption in the career situation ...
> W: I don't think there *is* any career any more ... I couldn't go back to the same job. I shouldn't fool myself about that. Not because the company has changed, but because of being out of touch for a year. You're just not aware of what is going on. And certainly after five years there's no way I could go back. The laws and regulations change.
>
> (Renton/2)

The Rentons had a very difficult first year or so. Mr Renton had to be away from home a great deal on work-related travel, and one of the children, in addition to having trouble adjusting to the change of location, was frequently ill. Nor was Mrs Renton using her new-found leisure in ways she found gratifying. Having left a hectic style of life juggling two serious careers in North America, the family found themselves living almost as frenetically in Geneva. They had chosen a house on one side of the city and a school on the other, thereby setting themselves a situation in which Mrs Renton had to spend three hours a day driving children back and forth.

The move also caused severe problems for a quite different dual career couple.

The Thomas family

The decision to move to Geneva had originally been much easier for the Thomases than for the Rentons: Mr and Mrs Thomas were both professionals in the same field, a profession in which one is expected to move every few years. When the time came there had been no doubt about the attractiveness of Geneva, both for professional and for sentimental reasons ('it just *felt* right'). As for the careers, the Thomases had been confident they would both be able to work after they moved. Things had worked out this way for friends of theirs in the same field, and, in addition, just before they left North America Mrs Thomas had been tentatively offered what sounded like an excellent position. As they explained when I first saw them:

H: It's a different process seeking a job in our profession than in industry. There are some shared positions when both are [professionals in our field] but it's hard to get one ... The norm is for one to take the job, and then hope something turns up for the other.
W: The week before we heard about the Geneva job offer we had turned down [another very appealing offer] hoping this would come up. If somebody had asked us five years ago where we would like to be now, we probably would have said doing something in Geneva.
M: So what does it mean for [her] career?
W: (She describes the position in an international organisation she would find ideal.) I could have tried to get that, then [my husband] could have come along. But the reality is that I'm more employable here. [The kinds of organisation in which we work] are bending over backwards to not hire white males, so the probability of his finding a job was slight. Mine was better.
(Thomas/1)

But by a few months after their arrival the situation was far less encouraging. The promised job 'didn't work out': complicated 'political winds' had shifted, and the person who had made the job offer over the telephone was no longer in a position to do so. Mrs Thomas had been interviewed for another, and was doing some freelance work but:

W: One is up against a lot of good people, and also there is a quota system. They need to balance male and female, geographical, other factors. I'm cautiously hopeful, but what is depressing is not knowing what will come, or *if* it will come. It's been hard for me.
(Thomas/1)

Over the course of the next very frustrating year Mrs Thomas was interviewed for two or three jobs, and just missed getting one of them. Finally she was offered one that 'sounded good on paper':

> W: What was happening was that the doors were closing one by one. Except for [one other] job, which was never sure, the job I'm in was the last real possibility. [After six months of this] I was pretty uptight, unhappy. I knew I was unhappy and depressed. I wasn't handling the time I did have very well, being totally uncreative, using a lot of avoidance, reading junk novels, sleeping a lot, eating a lot. I gained a lot of weight, and was just being generally horrible. It didn't help that I understood what was happening. I knew why I was feeling that way, but I had a lot of trouble just staying on top of things.
>
> (Thomas/2)

Discussion

The parallel with Mrs Renton is striking: both women were highly qualified professionals, very invested in their careers. They weighed numerous factors and chose to move, but thereby faced the possibility of giving up the important professional aspect of themselves, at least temporarily. Both were well aware that it would be extremely difficult to find employment after the move, but nonetheless had heard promises that they would in fact be able to do so. One cannot help wondering to what extent the two women had fallen victim to the temptation of simply hearing what they wanted to hear. In both cases the wife/mother's unhappiness with her professional situation was patent. In both families, in addition, one or more of the children was also experiencing difficulties adapting. Subsequent chapters return to how these families coped, and to how their situations evolved over the following year.

Partners not 'adjusting well'

Careers, of course, are only one reason for being reticent about moving abroad. In this study three of the women (Mrs Allen, Mrs Wood and Mrs Rodgers) admitted that they really would have preferred not to move in the first place. They had felt very comfortable and settled where they were, but thought, on the other hand, that concern for their own personal comfort should not hinder a move that would be good for their husbands' careers (see Chapter 3). A fourth woman, Mrs Newton, was frankly angry. For reasons that had everything to do with the world economic situation – in the form of severe problems affecting the employer – and nothing at all to do with her husband as an individual, the family had been obliged to move far too many times in far too short an interval. They had made four international moves in as many years. Even knowing full well that the family's situation was not his 'fault', it was on the husband, the nearest available target in an otherwise kaleidoscopic landscape, that the wife's anger and resentment could focus:

> W: I was furious. We had left [the place before last] a year earlier than we thought we were going to, and I was really extremely angry.
> M: Who were you angry with?
> W: The corporation, basically. If there had been anybody to strangle I would have done it ... So when it actually came to putting the house on the market, having the garage sale, the sort of steps one has to take, it hit me again. I just didn't want to do this. I didn't want to watch my house get packed up again. I thought: 'I could just die, I don't want to do this.'
> M: Who were you angry with this time?
> W: Life. I don't know. [My husband] thought I was angry at him. He misinterpreted it. I was expressing my anger towards him. I was shouting.
> M: The obvious target.
> W: He had left already, and I was dealing with the movers and was extremely distraught. He called me just an hour before the movers arrived, and told me there had been a change about the children's school. I said: 'Fine, I'm not going to do it. Just forget the whole thing. You stay there and I'll stay here. I don't care.' I was very angry, and it was coming out towards him, but I was just very angry at the disruption.
>
> (Newton/1)

Once a family has arrived in the new place, the loneliness and adaptation problems experienced by one of the spouses may also put considerable strain on a marriage. It was those who had gone through the process many times themselves, and watched numerous others go through it, who were best able to articulate these strains. Many of these people came from the business world, thus demonstrating that tensions around discrepancies between husband's and wife's expectations and experiences in the new culture are by no means unique to couples such as those cited in the beginning of this section, in which both are academics or professionals in international organisations. The family just cited, having experienced many of these strains, had given them a great deal of thought. Talking about other people, they returned to a theme introduced by the couples on sabbatical: one half of the couple is out 'being adored and appreciated', while the other is home – alone – learning to cope with less exalting aspects of everyday life:

> W: If you are isolated and he's the only adult you have to talk to it can be pretty tough. I remember when we moved to Brazil and I had the two babies he used to come home at lunch just to give me somebody to talk to. Even here, he will come home just to check on me, because he knows I have a tough time.
>
> M: (to him) That puts quite a strain on you, working and being the only one your wife can talk to.
>
> H: It puts a strain on the husband, but I think it's part of the responsibility. If the guy does not take that responsibility then he's pretty self-centred. Moving is much easier for the one who's working than for the one not working . . .
>
> W: I know a lot of the women feel their husbands let them down. They come, maybe it's a big promotion, and they're feeling very important. They travel, and have all these business lunches and whatever. Then he comes home, and if she doesn't have anybody else, if she doesn't have an outlet to complain basically, and deal with the frustrations of the plumber and the post office and the grocery store and everything else, then she will say it to him. He'll basically tell her to shut up: 'What about me, I have this job, I support you, what do you want from me?' I've heard about a lot of men who do that. You've probably heard more. [My husband] is a very considerate man, but I think he might be in the minority.
>
> Most of the women who move frequently are the ones who do pick themselves up and go out and make their lives. They decide that for whatever time they're going to be somewhere they might as well make their home as best they can. Whereas if somebody just decides to sit down and say: 'I don't like it here. I'm unhappy. I don't want to do this. I can't wait to get back home. I can't live without soap operas' or something, they are just going to dig a hole for themselves. Then if they complain, their husbands *should* tell them to shut up, or they should just go back home. But that's not always a viable option.
>
> (Newton/1)

Were there families such as this in the study, in which husbands were unable to cope with wives' unhappiness caused by the move? They would be hardly likely to admit it, and the unhappiest of the families in the cohort may not have participated in the study (see Chapter 6). But in the interviews, performed jointly with husband and wife, something very similar came out as unease and – participating in a study no doubt has its effect here – a tendency to analyse. In the following extract, as above, people talk not only about themselves, but about friends they have observed around them:

> W: There are a lot of things he doesn't want to listen to when he comes home tired after a long day. He wants to be a support to you, but the reality is he gets angry at me, and [my friend's] husband does too. It's like 'you are not making this move well, you are not adjusting well'. I kind of feel . . .
> H: (he interrupts) Mary could probably make $150 an hour for doing this . . . (we all laugh)
> W: The reality, and the brass tack fact of it, is that he feels guilty when I'm unhappy. He feels it's his fault. It's his business with the company that's made this situation which has made me unhappy. He sees a child crying, they're pulling at him from every angle at work, then he comes home and sees that I'm unhappy. He would never admit that, but seeing it from the angle of two different households makes me realise it.
>
> (Wood/1)

This was research, and not therapy, and we did not go further with the subject in any of the interviews. We will come back to discussions of severe tensions between husband and wife later in this chapter, however, and again in Chapter 9. But first we make a detour to a subject where it was socially more acceptable for couples to talk about family tensions raised since almost everybody experienced them, and 'everybody complains about it'. The underlying theme was that of separation, the overt subject that of 'duty travel'.

'Duty travel' and strains it may cover

Themes of separation of course run through practically every chapter dealing with migration. The strain of separations for some families at the beginning of a stay has already mentioned, when one member comes ahead to start a new job, and the others stay behind to finish school years and other business. Perhaps partly because it recalls the more substantial separations recently experienced, one of the recurrent topics of the first round of interviews was that of dealing with duty travel. Whether they were for 'the company', 'the government', or 'the organisation', most of the new jobs in Geneva required fairly extensive travel. Particularly in the early months after the relocation, several families found the repeated absences difficult. The Cadys are a typical example:

H: I have to travel about 40 per cent of the time for my job. I've been to North America three or four times in the past six months, but I mainly travel within Europe. I knew about it before I came. I had always travelled a bit for various jobs.
M: What does the travel mean to the rest of the family?
W: Travel is one of the hardest things to get used to. The children are used to their father being around more. He says he travels 40 per cent of the time, it seems to me 50 per cent. Somebody just joked on the phone: 'Oh, you're home this week!' He coaches the football team, but they've never been able to have any practices because he's never here.
M: (to him) Does the travel cause problems for you on the family level?
H: Well, you'd rather be home, but it doesn't really cause problems. You go three or four days during the week, come home on the weekend, and all you have time to do is what you didn't have time to do during the week.

His wife disagreed, pointing out that her husband rarely has any leisure, since he is either away or catching up between trips, and does not have enough time at home to keep up with what is going on with the family. A striking illustration came a few minutes later, when she mentioned that one of the children would not be passing to the next grade at school the next year. She had known for some time, but had not yet had a chance to tell her husband this relatively significant piece of family news:

W: That's the problem with travelling. You forget to tell things. It's not a major problem but something he should know.
(Cady/1)

The theme of his obligatory absences kept coming up. What started Mrs Cady talking after my introduction to the second interview, some ten months later, was the subject of travel. Objectively, her husband was away about two days, or one night, a week, with some additional day trips. She felt, though, that a week he had been away was a travel week, and most weeks were travel weeks. Evening meetings also took him away from home. She mentioned that this seemed to be the case for most of the families she knew in Geneva, however: it was not uncommon for a group of 'company wives' to find that their husbands were all out of town.

By a year and a half after the move she had become less frankly negative and more ambivalent about his travel. She was disappointed she had not become more used to it, but on the other hand, getting used to his travelling would mean getting used to her husband not being there, and this she felt she did not want to do.

The above portrays some of the problems involved with extensive work-related travel: little time at home simply to exchange information and discuss; lack of leisure for the person who is chronically trying to catch up with what has not been done at home and at the office during absences; husbands' and wives' differing definitions of both the amount of travel that is being done and the problems it causes for the family; the potential for family strains with repeated absences and homecomings. Implied is that the other spouse is left to cope with decisions that might better be shared, or sometimes to function practically as a single parent. It is difficult to evaluate the real weight of the problems caused by the absence of a spouse/parent, and the extent to which duty travel serves as a lightning rod for other tensions, however. At the simplest level, I learned to reformulate my original question:

M: Do you travel quite a bit for work?
H: I travel 20 per cent of the time ...
W: (at the same time) He travels 50 per cent of the time.
M: 20 per cent, 50 per cent???
W: My definition of travel is if he leaves at 6:30 in the morning and gets home at 10:30 at night he's been away. He thinks he hasn't travelled because he's home for the night. It's the same for one- or two-day trips. Most mothers feel the same way. If he's not here at any time during the day to help with the parenting, then I feel he's been gone.

(Renton/1)

When one parent was away, the other was of course left to cope:

W: He's usually here on weekends, but it's common that he's gone Monday to Friday ...
M: Does this change his relationship with the kids?
W: They don't think of him as a disciplinarian at all. He never scolds them for anything, because when he's around it's fun time.
M: Does that bother you to be the one who does all the disciplining?
W: No (silence). I mean I'm just keeping it going ... because I'm going to be around them more anyway. I always have been ... It's definitely not like a Dad that comes home at 5:00 in the evening every single day and has that dual discipline. That's

just the way it is. (Unusual for her, she is hesitating, sounding defensive. There is something here, but we let it drop.)

(Hill/3)

Repeated absences and homecomings could cause problems around rule setting and discipline with the children:

> W: It's hard for the children to have my husband gone. It's mother with children, then Dad comes home. The children feel they want to please him when he is here, to follow his rules. Then they let loose and do as they want when he's not ... The first year bedtime was a great bone of contention. I'm fairly strict about bedtime, my husband *laissez faire*. I nag, and he gets upset. I lost my authority over bedtime. I had to drop the issue.
>
> Often he would come home from a flight right at bedtime, with candy. I know it was because he was feeling guilty about being away. So it was like a party about twice a week every time Daddy came home. At 9:30 they would be eating candy. At 10:30 he would be boiling water to show them how to get a dent out of a ping-pong ball.
>
> (Zelig/5)

In each of the families in which a husband's frequent absences (or very long hours spent at work) were described as being a cause of severe problems (Cady, Renton, Rodgers, Smithers, Wood, Zelig) the children did require more attention during the time between school and bed about which the mothers complained: at an average of seven years old they were two years younger than the mean for all of the families in the study. Each of these families was on its first international move. But in each some other potential source of tension was underlying. One, for example, was Mrs Renton: she said she enjoyed being at home with the children since she was no longer working, but it is easy to imagine that her evenings at home with laundry and dishes must have contrasted in a particularly jarring way with her husband's trips around Europe's capitals as he mastered new professional challenges. The initial adaptation problems experienced by Mrs Cady and by the Wood family have just been discussed. As for the Rodgers family, whose graphic descriptions of their experiences the first year illustrated much of Chapter 3, the interview at which the following interchange occurred took place the middle of November:

> W: Do you know what [our son] said this morning? I was explaining that we were having this interview tonight and wouldn't be spending any time with him. He said: 'Well I guess it's not so bad, at least he'll be home for Christmas!'
>
> (Rodgers/2)

The comment elicited a tense laugh, first from one, then from the other, and it was obvious that there was considerable tension over the issue. They began to argue about whether or not he was actually spending less time with the children, but in fact it is quite possible that a certain amount of the children's distress could be attributed to the fact that *both* of their parents were now regularly leaving them in somebody else's care to – from the children's point of view – go off and do interesting things. The family had hired someone to help with the housework and child care, and Mrs Rodgers, gleefully affirming her new-found liberty, was leaping at any possible occasion to travel. She accompanied her husband on some of his business trips, or went on tours organised by the various women's groups to which she belonged.

What about the wives who said they were afraid of getting used to their husband's absences, as did Mrs Cady quoted above? The implication was that getting used to a husband's absences might somehow betray the way the wife, especially, would like the family to be. The point here is that complaints about something generally considered in the North American community to be somewhat stressful, or at least annoying (in this case duty travel), could also serve to convey deeper-rooted strains. Two families illustrate the subtle pulls and shifts set in motion by the move.

The Zelig family

Mrs Zelig was the woman met in the previous chapter whose disorientation after she moved was so severe as to make her feel like 'Alice in Wonderland' down the rabbit hole. The Zeligs had decided to move almost on an impulse, it sounded, although in fact things were far more complex:

> H: The transfer was sudden. At dinner one night a friend asked if we would like to come. I thought 'why not?'.
> M: Why specifically to Geneva?
> H: To have the children grow up close to mountains.

(He then describes his job in Geneva, which in fact marvellously fits his background, his complex life history, and his talents. It is clear that he delights in it at this point. I ask about the move for Mrs Zelig.)

> W: I was a bored, suburban housewife. We were both nearing 40. You start questioning: do we want life to go on like this, or do we want to have a last hurrah before we settle down? ... I wanted to see what grey cells were left after being a housewife.
> (Zelig/1)

In contrast to families who talked to everybody they could imagine before they actually decided to move, as well as reading books and attending courses, the Zeligs 'didn't have time'. Mr Zelig phoned a couple of people (who gave conflicting advice), but it was obvious that they had neither thought through the move nor prepared in a great deal of depth.

When I first saw them, Mrs Zelig, especially, was having a very difficult time. Her culture shock and feelings of unease and disorientation were discussed in the previous chapter. My summary of the first interview, to which she immediately and heartily agreed, was that she had more or less moved for a last fling before middle age, and now may have got into more than she had bargained for. In fact she felt she may end up getting stuck – making matters far worse was that the family had moved for a stay of unlimited duration:

W: The biggest thing is wondering if I'll ever get to live in North America again. It would be easier if we were coming for a limited period. I don't want to be Swiss.
H: This is the grief period, dark glasses.
W: I thought I would change cultures, come and have some fun, then go home. But [my husband] loves his job and the mountains, and [one of the children] says he doesn't like North America any more.

(Zelig/1)

Mr Zelig's comment about the dark glasses was characteristic. Throughout the interview, he consistently followed any of his wife's negative comments with a positive one, or attempted to minimise the importance of anything negative. During a long follow-up conversation on the telephone some six months later, the first thing Mrs Zelig said was that the interview had helped her talk with her husband. As with the Woods above, Mr Zelig had been defensive, feeling responsible, angry with her for having trouble, and not wanting to hear about her trouble precisely because he did feel responsible. With someone else present, he had to listen to what she had to say, and they had talked a bit after I left. An exchange in the next interview, following her summary of the good and bad points of the previous year, encapsulated their positions:

H: I don't like to dwell on the bad times.
W: Mary is *asking* about these. I'm not *dwelling* on them ...

(Zelig/2)

Mr Zelig's job called upon practically all of his previous life experiences and skills, and he described a number of anecdotes that made it obvious that he was in the enviable situation of considering his work as play. He also relished challenge and change.

H: I'm not looking for security. I would go crazy if I ever had to retire. I like to be where the action is. You don't get this by sitting in one place. If everything is comfortable you don't stretch enough.

(Zelig/2)

He most certainly did not, however, relish a more introspective approach: not dwelling on feelings summed up exactly the way Mr Zelig operated, and also one of the bases for tension between husband and wife. Mrs Zelig was having difficulty and wanted to discuss it; he refused to hear anything negative. In fact just hearing each other talk about the effects of moving during the interviews may have been too threatening: both readily agreed to talk to me separately, but would not let themselves be interviewed as a couple again. (The excuse they gave was reasonable however. Mr Zelig was travelling a great deal, and the family was unwilling to sacrifice a rare evening at home together for an interview.) Mrs Zelig commented to me (on the phone) that she and her husband never seem to have time to discuss, except on the phone, or on trips. Typically, in the interview with Mr Zelig alone, he claimed to have no idea what the move had meant for the family:

H: I have no idea. I don't discuss these things with them, because I don't want to stir things up ...
M: How is [your wife] doing?
H: Fine. She doesn't complain.

But he did have several comments to make about the children, and things the family was doing to help them maintain their equilibrium between two cultures. He also mentioned that he had just turned down an otherwise even more interesting new job because it would have meant moving the family to a place even more difficult for them to live in.

M: Do you have any feeling of being caught between work and family?
H: Completely. And I spend too much time with work.

(Zelig/3)

Mrs Zelig agreed, and talked about the problems this caused for the rest of the family:

> W: He's exhausted, so he doesn't feel like seeing people. He just wants to sit on the couch, or maybe go for a walk ... We're kind of isolated here. That's hard for me, because I'd like to do things, but he's too tired. I understand that, so I don't want to push him, but it's a problem.
> M: So the question is, how you cope with it?
> W: Well, I just take it day by day and hope it will change ... I have my own little world, my own little life with my friends, and it kind of shuts down when he comes home. I really don't even feel he's that curious.
> M: You'd like him to share that world with you.
> W: Yes. He did share that in North America. That's the hard part. He's just got so much on his plate it feels like there's very little room for anything besides just niceties, and not rocking the boat. There are days I'm on the edge of losing it.
>
> (Zelig/4)

The problem was not so much one of a wife's feeling of abandonment, of resentment at the time and energy her husband was pouring into his work, as it was a feeling that the family was slipping in different directions. The same feeling was quite severe in another family.

The Smithers family

The Smithers were the family who had jumped at the opportunity to move to Geneva since their goal had always been to live abroad (Chapter 2). As they discuss in the following segment, things were not working out at all as they had hoped, and the strain on the family was becoming severe. They had some difficulty when I asked them to describe their family, then in a dialogue reminiscent of the one above:

> W: It sometimes seems it's relationships through crisis. I don't know if it's because of having kids that argue with each other constantly, and a baby that whines and is difficult, or if that's a general description, but I find there's a lot of stress in the relationship. (To her husband) I don't know if you do ...
> H: Well the kids play outside most of the time. The only time they come in is when one is mad with the other, and they come in to complain or tell or cry.
> W: Sometimes I think the family relationship is frustrating, because we have so little time to devote to it because of other responsibilities. There are things we want to do with the kids, and don't get the time to. It's frustrating with [my husband] too, because we want to be together and there isn't time for it.

I don't know if you don't have your priorities right, or if it's just the way life is using up your time. Some of those choices you're making are out of your control.

(Smithers/2)

The 'way life is using up your time' had involved very long hours at the office for her husband since they moved, and to make matters worse, the long hours at work had not helped Mr Smithers' situation with his employer. He had just been eased out of his job, and was about to be transferred back to North America. The family was bitterly disappointed, and the final interview had a very depressive tone. We skated several times around a tension which did not seem new. They seemed to have already talked together many times about her feelings of resentment at the amount of time he spent working, and the fact that he did not see this as a problem for the family. In a word, she would have liked to spend more time with him, whereas he felt things were fine as they were. At one point, when she left the room to make coffee, he commented:

H: I tend to be less sensitive to the amount of time we spend together versus time apart, as you can tell . . . We do different things here, but it's not a significant change from the amount of time we spent together in North America.

But from her point of view:

W: I'm bothered that the two older children didn't notice [my husband's] absence very much when he was away for work . . . I wanted it to be important to the children that you were around, so that they'd notice it when you weren't.
H: It was important to them when they were younger. (They are now nine, six, and three).
W: It should be. [My husband] was gone for two weeks and asked the nine-year-old if he missed him. He just shrugged his shoulders and said 'I knew you'd be back'. It's good that he feels the stability and the confidence not to have to worry, but . . . (silence)
M: You want it both ways.
W: It's good that even a month's absence doesn't disturb them, but somehow we should need each other more than that . . . The three-year-old was missing him. He went back to crying when his father went to work, and would get upset if I didn't set a place at the dinner table for him. (To her husband) I guess I wanted the older kids to have you there so commonly for dinner that it would be unusual if you were not there, instead of getting to the point where they would just presume you were not coming home.

H: They're kind of go with the flow kids anyway. I'm not sure they have a routine established in any direction.
W: I guess I'd like that routine established.
H: They are not more aware of my presence than of my absence, or vice versa. Whoever is there to eat, is there to eat and that's it. They kind of approach it the same way I do: if we have dinner guests over the more the merrier, a few more, a few less . . .
M: (There is a great deal of tension in the air, and I try to lighten it) Maybe you'd better set a minimum level under which . . .
H: . . . yeah, all family members *must* be there.
W: No, it's not that way, it's never that rigid. But I wanted to go back to it being normal that we're all there to eat, and we're all spending time together a certain day of the week. I don't want the kids to look at me as the only available parent, the only available source of help.

(Smithers/3)

Discussion

The larger issue is the attention one half of the couple devotes to something outside the family, or tension between commitment to family and to work. This, of course, is far from being unique to families who change cultures, but in the cases just examined the move severed the attachments (to a wife's own work, to the community, to friends or to family) which had kept the accompanying spouse in equilibrium. As the Newtons pointed out at the beginning of this chapter, the resulting vulnerability puts a great deal of pressure and responsibility on the spouse whose job has uprooted the family, and not all were able to act as supportively as Mr Newton was said to have been doing. Tensions arise, tensions from which there is no place to escape when the family is new in a community, a situation common enough to have caused an uproar in the group discussion with Mr Y's remark about hypothetical bowling with the guys.

The final section of this chapter moves to a possible source of family tension stemming from its external relations, or the other people family members meet. How do families manage their encounter with values often quite different from those they have been used to?

Different values

Transferring to a culture different from their own means families encounter different values, differences that may force them to examine their previous ways of defining their terms with the world. It was not so much cultural differences, for which they had been prepared, that caused difficulties for the families studied, but significant value differences within their own community:

> W: What you get here is people bringing up their children differently. If we were living in North America all the neighbours would be bringing up their children in the same way. Here you're dealing with parents who may have different expectations of their kids. They let them stay up late, give them a lot of pocket money . . . I think it's really important for the children to realise that just because we're living in Switzerland with a slightly inflated salary that doesn't mean we have a lot of excess money . . . That is not our life style in North America, and we want to make sure our kids don't get that habit, because as soon as we go back they won't get this kind of money. This is an unreal life style, and we have to tell the kids not to get too used to it. It's not just the kids, the adults have that problem too.
>
> (Kennedy/1)

Although three of the families in the study had real financial problems after they moved, most of the others were comfortably affluent, although rarely ostentatiously so. Some mentioned living frugally in spite of generous benefit packages offered by 'the company', whereas others hinted at, or discussed frankly, having more disposable income while abroad. But Switzerland is a rich country, and in an expatriate community anywhere most members are notably further towards the wealthy side of a continuum than towards the opposite end. A few of its members would seem to be decidedly affluent, a novelty which can be very disconcerting, and with which families had to deal:

> W: One thing that happens in the international schools is that you are in a big expatriate group. Especially here, where you've got kids with chauffeurs, cooks and maids. You end up with kids who have an upper stratum life style, with a bit of money to play around with. If you take somebody from middle America, who usually makes [an average salary], and the kids get thrown into where they are invited to a chateau for birthday parties . . . (laugh) I mean it *is* a change in values. There is one kid at school who calls a taxi to take her home between classes. She flops money around like crazy. She's not the only one, but she's particularly splashy, and some of them have chauffeurs who sit around and wait for them. If your kids are friends with them, they drive you around and you go to their houses. You have 97 nationalities, different ideas, but you don't find poor kids. That's particular to International Schools.

H: You have a lot of normal kids too.

W: I didn't say they are all that way, but with the neighbourhood school concept in North America you go to school with people who pretty much live in the same type of houses and have the sort of milieu that you have.

M: How do you deal with these differences in your family?

H: They've always lived with these differences.

W: [The ten-year-old] has a friend who has a big house on the lake with two boats. She comes and says 'gee, her house is really nice!'. She enjoys it when she is out there, but it's just a comment. They have generally lived pretty well, and have been able to travel. I don't think they ever felt deprived. Plus there are a lot of kids here who are just everyday kids who don't have all that.

(Newton/3)

As implied, some of the affluence is only apparent. Some of what may seem like wealth does not actually belong to those who possess it:

H: It's interesting because so many of these accoutrements are job related as opposed to status related. One family has body guards and all sorts of domestic help, and I think they're genuinely wealthy. On the other hand some of the people with certain consulates have a driver and so on. Whether they are wealthy or not one never knows, because it goes with the job.

(Renton/3)

But it takes a certain amount of sophistication to perceive the difference between 'job related' and 'status related accoutrements', and the point here is that families who came from more homogeneous communities, especially, had to learn to negotiate the gap between how they live and how they, or their children, perceived other people might live. There seemed to be a fair amount of money circulating, and the risk was that young people would learn to demand more material *things* than they would have had they stayed at home. If the parents quoted above, who had lived in several expatriate communities, were relatively sanguine, several others in the study expressed concern about values children and adolescents might be learning under such conditions, and/or worried that their children might get used to a style of life that was unrealistic. On occasion parents noted actual changes:

W: Benjamin has had a lot of trouble. About the time we came here he seemed to change. Nothing is his fault. If he loses something: 'I'll get another one'. He likes material things. He's a bit of a snob. He wants the best skis, the best tennis racquet and so on. If he loses something, his attitude is: 'It wasn't my fault, just get another one'.

(Allen/3)

This family was, in fact, by all indications, living significantly more affluently after they moved to Geneva. We came back to the topic of values at the final interview a year later:

M: Children running into different value systems has been a problem for some people.
H: (joking) Our kids have lost all notion of the value of money. We have four irons in the basement, numerous vacuum cleaners.
C3: One of them talks. A voice says the bag is full!
W: [The seventeen year old] (who is not present) is especially bad about spending money.
H: He charges sports equipment, ski suits.
M: When we first talked you said that in North America you used to buy things without really thinking about it. Then when you got here everything was so expensive you stopped buying things. It sounds as though you are getting back to buying things again.

(He says yes, she protests, then observes:)

W: The kids do come in contact with people who have a lot of money. They always seem to know people who have this and that, and are allowed to go here and there. Our kids are not exactly on tight budgets, but it never seems to be enough.

(The discussion turns to Benjamin, whose materialism was mentioned the year before, and who is present during this interview, wearing a designer T-shirt. They start to argue about the things he has or has not bought with his parents' credit cards. He starts protesting about his low allowance, and a bit later he reasons, with impeccable adolescent logic:)

Benjamin: I want to go on vacation with my friends, but I don't have enough money. When I go on vacation with my parents we stay in nice hotels and go first class on the train. If they'd let me go with a backpack with my friends it would work out much cheaper for them. But me, *I* can't afford it.

(Allen/4)

Adolescents may have difficulties metabolising differences in values, but as the family quoted in the beginning of this section indicated: 'It's not just the kids, the adults have that problem too'. Another of the adolescents in the study, interviewed separately from her family, made a similar point. An extremely poised and observant 18-year-old, she had just spent a year at the International School. From this student's point of view, if some of her peers had problems it was not because they had too much money, but because of lack of parental supervision:

> M: Some parents have commented that there is too much money floating around among the students.
> C: Yes and no. There are some kids who are very rich, but the money doesn't show. They wear blue jeans just like the others. I only know they are rich because somebody tells me. But there was one who tried to use money to buy friends. Once when we were out in the evening and wanted to go somewhere else after the last bus he offered to pay for 12 of us to go in taxis.
>
> (She starts talking about kids who use drugs:) It's easy to get the money to pay for them. I've heard people say they can take a hundred francs from their parent's wallet and the parent won't notice. (She goes on to comment that in her case this sort of thing would not be possible since her parents always know approximately how much money she has, and where she is going.)
>
> (Graham/2)

One of the parents, making a point about people who experience large salary increases but who do not have the value structure to keep them on an even keel, was far more severe:

> W: Some people who have never lived anywhere else had a lot of debts when they came. Now they are rich and they go hog wild, and so do their kids. They say: 'we'll only be here two years, let the kids really enjoy it, we're not going to have it when we go back'. What they are doing is destroying the kids ... then they're *really* in trouble. It's a marvellous opportunity to live overseas, and if you have it, enjoy it. But you have to be sure of your self, of your own values. If you come with crummy values they are just going to get worse. If you are a shallow person coming here, if everything important to you has a price tag attached to it, then it's going to get worse here, because you've got more money to spend, bigger price

tags, and more price tags. I saw a lot of people in [other places abroad] do things they wouldn't do at home. (She gives examples.)

(Kent/3)

Such observations in the study were invariably about other people. Most of them came from those who had moved many times, who had worked out the issues for themselves some moves ago. Usually fine observers, most had given such matters a great deal of thought, and were more than happy to discuss them. As for those less experienced with moving, who were more likely to have difficulties handling different values, the two-year period of the study was insufficient for such observations to develop enough to be formulated. More significantly, families are hardly likely to admit to holding 'crummy values', or even to see that they might be going slightly overboard, as the Rodgers might in fact have been doing as discussed in the section on 'duty travel'.

A great number of themes have been raised over the past two chapters. The next chapter steps back a bit to review them, then addresses coping, or how the families responded to the stresses and the strains caused by moving to a new culture. Chapter 7 comes back to how families coped with the family strains discussed in the present chapter.

5
COPING

This chapter reviews some of the theoretical threads presented in the first chapter (sense of coherence and its components of meaningfulness, manageability and comprehensibility) as they relate to the stresses and hassles discussed in Chapter 3, and the strains for families discussed in Chapter 4. The theme of the chapter is coping, or how families manage the strains they encounter. Family sense of coherence is discussed, then coping is described through case histories. The chapter next discusses the quite different coping of four of the six families whose decision to move abroad was presented in Chapter 2 (the Gibbs and Jacksons, and the Grahams and Smithers). This chapter and the next two, which focus on social support (Chapter 6) and family 'co-ordination' (Chapter 7), serve as transitions between discussions of the stresses of moving abroad for families, and discussions of the effect of the move by two years later.

Event and meaning, comprehensibility and manageability

Chapter 2 was concerned with reasons to move. All of the families studied felt they had a choice in moving, and some had even worked actively to make it happen. Families were able to prepare for the move to a new culture, and some did so extensively. Some mentioned getting away from problems, but the sentiment that predominated for most was that they were coming towards a valuable experience. Most had formulated one or several goals. Fundamentally, then, most of the families studied were making a decision, sometimes a difficult decision, because there was something about which they cared. In Antonovsky's terms the underlying meaning was there: the problems and demands posed by what they were doing were seen as being worthy of commitment and engagement.

Behind the same event experienced by one rather homogeneous cohort of families, however, there proved to be several different sets of reasoning. These were presented according to the employment setting, namely 'the government', 'the organisation' and 'the company'. For the four families who moved because at least one of their members worked for 'the government', the meaning of this particular event – the move to Geneva – must be seen in relation to a series of similar events – other moves across cultures. A mobile style of life had been chosen long before, when the career was chosen, either by taste for travel, for the type of work involved in a government career, or – in one instance – because government work paid better than other options available. For these families the specific move to Geneva was a relatively low key matter in contrast to previous moves, many of which had involved significantly more adaptation (for example because the culture was very different or daily life more difficult). The specific city of Geneva was chosen, to the extent it *was* chosen, for a pleasant style of life. Hopes for the stay, a sojourn of two to five years before the family was to move on to other places, were relatively modest (examples were the Jackson and the Gibbs families).

Although most of the seven families who moved with 'the organisation' shared with the 'government' families the experience of already having lived in other countries, the event was qualitatively quite different. Most were coming to heady opportunities: this, they said, was the summit of their career. The hopes they expressed for their stays – and also the hopes their spouses expressed – were mainly job-related. Those who were to work for non-government organisations, especially, also spoke of idealism, of having a chance to do something about world problems. As for the specific place to which they were moving, the city of Geneva was simply where the organisation was based: these families were not moving to be in a specific place or towards a specific style of life. With one exception they moved for long-term stays, or perhaps permanently (examples were the Davidson and the Madison families).

The event was qualitatively quite different again for the 14 'company' families. All but one were experiencing their first or second move abroad. This was typically to be a two- to five-year sojourn, an interlude, after which the family expected to return to live in North America. The reasons they gave for making the move were usually mixed. This was an opportunity to advance careers, but also, they said, an opportunity for family members, especially the children, to experience new cultures, to broaden horizons, to see the world differently (examples were the Graham and the Smithers families).

The sense of coherence component of 'meaning' predominates in discussions of the decision to move abroad (Chapter 2), while the components of 'comprehensibility' and 'manageability' appear in Chapter 3, which deals with what is experienced as being stressful about the move. These components appear in the negative: it is the *absence* of comprehensibility and of manageability that poses problems. These are the hassles that strain the identity of someone used to coping easily with the mundane aspects of ordinary existence; not understanding the language being spoken around one; losing the comfortable known-ness of things; not knowing the rules and feeling criticised; all of these strain the individual's sense that the world is comprehensible, that it makes cognitive sense, that the information received is ordered, consistent, structured, and clear. The disorientation that was described comes from no longer comprehending the social, or even sometimes the physical, geographic, world around one. They also strain the sense of manageability, making people feel vulnerable, helpless, and as though they have lost some degree of control over everyday aspects of their environments, and especially of interactions, that should have been quite routine. A sentiment repeatedly described was that of feeling stupid, or like a child.

Antonovsky argued that the three elements of meaningfulness, comprehensibility and manageability are not dissociable: it is together that they comprise the sense of coherence. The next section brings them together and discusses how SOC was measured in families.

Family sense of coherence

The position taken for this study is that families, as they live together, develop shared constructs, or shared ways of seeing the world (Reiss, 1981; Oliveri and Reiss, 1984). As two individuals develop a relationship together, as they share daily life and friendships, they develop shared assumptions about the world in which they live. This becomes even more the case as they have children, as one of the major tasks of parenting will be to guide the latter in their development of their own such assumptions. There remains, however, the problem of how to measure such shared constructs. The basic construct used in this study was that of a family sense of coherence, but trying to discuss SOC directly with study participants did not work very well. The attitudes involved in either a strong or a weak SOC are largely unconscious: people are not very good at objectively evaluating how they see the world. A promising approach in an in-depth study such as this one would be to assess SOC indirectly, examining the ways in which families' responses during interviews reflected the separate SOC elements of meaningfulness, comprehensibility and manageability (for example by evaluating respectively whether or not there is something the family cares about and is committed to; whether they were perplexed about cultural differences and language as opposed to feeling challenged, curious, seeking explanations; and whether or not they did something about a problem that had been defined). For the purpose of analysis here, however, the more objective SOC questionnaire was used (Antonovsky, 1987, see Chapter 1 for a description). Family SOC scores were calculated on the basis of the couple's mean score, corrected for the gap in cases where there were differences between the scores of husband and wife (see Appendix, Table A.8).

The families scoring higher than average on family sense of coherence were the Allen, Cady, Davidson, Elm, Graham, Hill, Jackson and Wood families. Those scoring lower than the average, on the other hand, were the Gibbs, Kennedy, Madison, Newton, Ogbourne, Rodgers, Smithers, Exon and Zelig families. The prediction was that those scoring high and low on SOC would cope differently with the stress of learning to live in a different culture, and it is to this topic that the discussion now turns.

Coping with the stresses of moving to a new culture

Coping strategies are the behavioural and/or cognitive attempts to manage specific situational demands that are appraised as taxing or exceeding one's ability to adapt (Lazarus and Folkman, 1984). Coping is complex, and in a study such as this is best described in action. The next section describes how four of the families who talked in Chapter 2 about their decision to move abroad coped with the stresses and hassles caused by the decision. These are the high SOC Jacksons and the low SOC Gibbs, who moved because of 'government' employment, and the high SOC Grahams and the low SOC Smithers who moved because 'the company' proposed an overseas posting. The two other families who appeared in Chapter 2, the high SOC Davidsons and the low SOC Madisons, who moved so that one of them could work with 'the organisation', are discussed in Chapter 7.

The Jackson family

At first glance the move should have been less stressful for the Jacksons than for others. They had already lived in several European cities as well as in the developing world, and had deliberately chosen a less challenging post in Geneva in exchange for what they hoped would be a pleasant and easy style of life. On the 'stressful and positive aspects of moving' questionnaire they both listed many more positive than stressful aspects, and rated moving as being at most only moderately stressful. Yet they said at the last interview:

> M: Do you think adapting to a new culture is stressful?
> H: Of course it is. It's one of the more stressful things anyone can go through ... Once one knows where they are, then they are happy, but certainly not being in control of what's going on around you is stressful. It can lead to very paranoid feelings.
>
> (Jackson/3)

In fact the Jacksons had numerous complaints about hassles during the first interview. The main problem was that the housing they had found, which had seemed to be exactly what they wanted, turned out to be unsatisfactory. It did not take them long to realise they wanted to change apartments. Doing so, however, required great effort and delayed getting settled. The first interview, which was repeatedly postponed over several weeks until they found and settled in to their new housing, was marked by numerous complaints about the complex real estate system in Geneva, and about practical problems such as getting a telephone.

As for problems with language and culture, or with not understanding what is going on around one, and in spite of what Mr Jackson said about paranoid feelings, these were relatively minimal. Mrs Jackson already spoke fairly fluent French when the family arrived, and Mr Jackson took lessons, which he continued throughout the study period. The family had relatively little contact with the local Swiss population, but Mr and Mrs Jackson were subtle in their perceptions. For example, in contrast to some families who simply presumed that anyone they encountered in Geneva who was not North American must be Swiss, they realised that fully one-third of the Geneva population consisted of fellow foreigners:

> W: I find it hard in everyday dealings with people in Geneva. In Holland you deal with the Dutch, but here you just never know what nationality a person is. I don't know if they are Swiss, or French, or from Spain. I don't know what they are, and what is in their mind.
>
> (Jackson/3)

The point here is that, although it may be complex, the Jacksons perceived their social world as being comprehensible. They also saw it as being manageable, as can be discerned from their efforts to find more suitable housing or from their planning ahead for what they might do when Mr Jackson's father was severely ill (Chapter 6). They were able first to define problems, then to do something about them. For example preadolescent Beth had a very difficult year following the move, during which the new friends she invited home always seemed to have something else to do. Her parents provided her with a great deal of support, and also permitted her to maintain contact with her former North American friends through frequent telephone calls and visits. Mrs Jackson started to work full time during the family's second year in Geneva, but when Beth seemed to need to have her mother at home when she returned from school, Mrs Jackson discussed the problem with her boss and negotiated a change of work schedule. The situation improved almost immediately.

More fundamentally, the Jacksons ultimately felt they had a modicum of control over the path their lives took. They continuously and consciously weighed the advantages and the disadvantages of the choices they had made. For Mrs Jackson their mobile style of life meant giving up the idea of having a serious career. Mr Jackson had re-evaluated and relinquished his earlier high career ambitions in order to live in more agreeable places with his family, and had also decided that the priority for the next move would be Beth's education. As they put it:

> W: (to her husband) The interesting thing is the goals you had set for yourself you would have reached by now if you had taken hardship posts, jumped at promotions.
> H: ... I have choices. I have to work, financially, but I could do something different. To have a choice is a luxury, and makes you see life differently.
>
> (Jackson/2)

They defined and corrected errors, but did not waste time on regrets for what could not be helped. A striking example occurred during their second year in Geneva: they had determined that their most recent move back to North America had been a mistake, and when they decided to live abroad again the choice had been between Geneva and another city. They had chosen Geneva, but found that over the course of the subsequent year, world changes had suddenly and unexpectedly made the city they had *not* chosen an extremely interesting place to live. At the second interview they elaborated on both of these points:

> H: When we went back to North America last time it was after ten years abroad. We thought it was to be permanent. We thought we were going to settle down. It didn't work out that way. I don't quite know why. Was it the desire to travel again? Or to be in Europe again? Or leave the rush and hassle in North America?
> W: It was hard. Things had changed in ten years. We had expected to return to the nice little city where we had lived when we were just married. But we're getting older, and it's become an enormous city with traffic jams and everybody being in a rush. We realised that we did not have either the time or the money for all the things we'd looked forward to.
> H: We didn't have to leave, but I went around and asked what was available, and my first choice was [a city that had since then become one of the world's most interesting places to be for someone in Mr Jackson's profession].
> M: I was wondering what you thought about that now ...
> Both: It would have been great, oh my gosh!!!
> M: Do you have any regrets?

Both: No. It would have been interesting to be there, but there's nothing we could have done about it.

(Jackson/2)

Far from feeling 'it always happens to me', Mr and Mrs Jackson described the process of negotiating where the next move would take the family, then of formulating attitudes about the result:

> H: It might not be the perfect choice: we might want to go somewhere else, but this is the best we can do for this particular transfer ... You generate the type of a mental process that gets you in a good frame of mind about where you are going. Even if you're sent to a bad place you can generate the mental process: you say this is going to be an experience for us, or this is going to be good for my job, or whatever it takes to rationalise one's way into being happy about the move.
> W: Absolutely ... Our first post was to a place we basically just took, and tried to make the best of it ... If we have to be sent to a place, I'd go. I am not a person who complains and says this is horrible ...
> H: No matter where you go, there is going to be something.
> W: It just makes it worse if you complain. You simply have to make your life, and make the best of it.

(Jackson/3)

Mr and Mrs Jackson portrayed a feeling of mastery and control over their lives, control which ranged from dealing with the minor hassles to the feeling they would be able to influence such major factors as where they will work and live, and how they would like their child's education to be. Recognising mistakes, they could take steps to correct them, yet they accepted a certain number of disappointments as being inevitable: 'there's nothing we could have done about it'. When the situation could not be changed, then they worked on their attitude about it: 'you generate the type of a mental process that gets you in a good frame of mind about it'.

The next example is a family which had also moved several times, and with the same employer as the Jacksons, but which was low on SOC.

The Gibbs family

The Jacksons' active, take-charge attitude was in striking contrast with that of their colleagues, the Gibbs, whose leitmotif for their move was 'frustrating'. Although they had read the government's 'post reports' about living in Geneva, Mr and Mrs Gibbs found they had brought the wrong kind of clothes for the climate, couldn't find the things they needed to buy, and could not comprehend what people were saying to them:

W: I just get frustrated – there are a lot of things that make me frustrated ... I don't understand, or know what to look for ... the language gets me frustrated ... I tried some lessons but can't pick it up ... people talk French on the phone. For things like arranging appointments this is very frustrating.

(Gibbs/1)

The family was just getting settled when I first interviewed them four months after their arrival. Their possessions had been lost in transit, and they had been more or less camping in their new house with a few pieces of borrowed furniture. It was not the recent experience of this rather inconvenient period that seemed to be influencing the couple's outlook, however. They said they were not particularly bothered by the disruption: they had moved enough to know to bring things such as books and needlework to keep them occupied during the first months, and had used the time to explore the region and to learn how to use the public transport. But the word 'frustrating' kept coming up, even the next time I saw them two years later:

W: Switzerland is not our favourite place. I love the scenery, but can't learn French. It's frustrating to me. I can't buy things, can't read cooking instructions. I can look at words, but I just can't remember what they were.

(Gibbs/2)

Mr Gibbs worked in English and had not tried to learn French. Mrs Gibbs tried a few lessons but had given up after a couple of months. Handicapped by their lack of mastery of the language, they explored the region to some extent, but mainly on organised tours. One attempt to take a trip to the mountains on their own ended in ... frustration:

W: We didn't see much of Switzerland ... We wanted to see the glaciers ... We drove to the mountains. It was beautiful, but we didn't know what to do to get close to the glaciers. It was so frustrating driving that far and not getting right close to the mountain. We didn't know what to do, and they don't speak English, so we came home. We should have spent the night but didn't go prepared.

(Gibbs/2)

Not understanding the social world in which they were living, the Gibbs were hesitant to intervene, even with their own child. For example they preferred that their 17-year-old should not drink alcohol, but were perplexed about the community's norms:

> W: I don't want her to drink, it's not OK with me, but there's nothing I can do about it, really.
> M: Do you discuss this with her?
> W: We just tell her how we feel: she's going to have to make her own decisions. [The employer] makes rules about teenage drinking. I don't understand it: I guess they don't become alcoholics in [the government], or maybe they do and we just don't know it. That bothers me: it's as though they tell kids it's OK to go ahead and drink. Some kids even drink at home. I don't know what the rules are.
>
> (Gibbs/1)

Partly because of their lack of mastery of the language, when one of the family members received a substantial traffic fine which they considered unfair they were unable to formulate the complex explanations their defence would require. More profoundly, since the outside world was not understood, the Gibbs were subject to rumours and stereotypes they were unable to evaluate. For example:

> H: If you have an accident and call the police you have to pay for them to come. The son of one of the men I work with lost his passport, and the police charged money to fill out the papers. I don't know how it's set up: in North America the police are paid through taxes. I don't know how they do it here, but it seems to me it leaves it open [to corruption] to charge for these things.
>
> (Gibbs/1)

Swiss police, of course, receive salaries and do not directly charge their clients, and Mr Gibbs added in all fairness that it hadn't happened to them personally, that it was just something they had been told. The point, though, is that not understanding how things worked, the way was paved for the family to find itself in a hostile and insecure world.

The family also had much less feeling of being in control of its own destiny than did the Jacksons discussed above. As discussed in Chapter 2, once started in 'government' employment, the Gibbs just sort of went along. Extensive geographical mobility had seemingly caused family problems: Mr and Mrs Gibbs mentioned that an older child was having some difficulties in North America, and the younger, now in her last year of school, had 'had a bit of turmoil' in the past three or four years. She had been unhappy in a previous posting in a developing country, tried boarding school in North America, moved back with her family when that did not work, and finally seemed to be settling when a political crisis intervened and obliged the family to leave the country. Her parents thought she seemed relatively happier in the less tumultuous Geneva. The daughter herself did not directly participate in the interview, but throughout it made her presence and opinions known by means of noises from the next room. A strategic rattling of dishes led the interviewer to believe she was not entirely satisfied with life in Geneva. She left for university in North America the second year of the family's stay, then returned to live with her parents and work in Geneva when university 'didn't work out':

> W: She just was very unhappy, it just didn't turn out right . . . She hated dorm life. They gave her [an incompatible] room-mate . . .
> M: Was there any chance of changing room-mate?
> W: She didn't want to bother with the procedure to change.
> (Gibbs/2)

The Gibbs hinted at regrets and doubts about certain aspects of the mobile style of life they were living. They worried about the effects the family's mobility may have had on their children, but did not, in opposition to the Jacksons, talk about having actively influenced where they were to live. Even less did they talk of possibly changing jobs because of family factors. Like their daughter with her room-mate, it did not seem to have occurred to them to attempt to change things:

> W: Sometimes you can't help but make some mistakes about moving. If you'd stayed in North America maybe it wouldn't have worked out that way, like sending our daughter off to college, and she wasn't happy when she got there. Sometimes I'd like to be back in North America and have our own home. We've just travelled so many years. You just get settled and then have to move on . . .
> (Gibbs/2)

Sense of coherence elements of comprehensibility and of manageability are clearly weak. Life was neither very comprehensible nor manageable for the members of the Gibbs family: not understanding, or, more fundamentally, *not feeling they would be able to* understand, they were prey to the 'very paranoid feelings' to which Mr Jackson referred. Lack of understanding, of course, rendered life less manageable. In contrast to the active, take-charge stance of the Jacksons, the Gibbs simply let things happen to them: community norms could override parental wishes to determine their child's drinking behaviour, and it was not worth the effort to find a more compatible room-mate. More fundamentally, the employer decided where they were to live next. Mr and Mrs Gibbs portrayed a wistful regret about the negative consequences their extensive geographical mobility may have had on their family, but their unease remained non-formulated, and the underlying sentiment was that nothing could have been done about it.

The two families just discussed moved with 'the government'. The next families work for 'the company', but both the stresses and hassles encountered and the coping exercised are similar. The Grahams, who were high on SOC, had a number of things in common with the previous family, the Gibbs, including having already lived abroad at least once, having left older children in North America, and having moved with a child in her last year of school.

The Graham family

The Grahams were obviously subject to the same stresses and hassles as all the other families in coming to a new culture, yet seemed to subjectively experience none of them: positive aspects far outweighed negative in their responses on the questionnaires, and they talked far more about 'challenges' than about stresses and hassles involved in moving abroad. The interviews with the Grahams reflected their underlying paradigm of the world as comprehensible. They very obviously enjoyed figuring out how to live in the new culture, and asked for assistance if necessary. For example they used the visiting interviewer as a resource: when they had finished answering questions at the first interview they proceeded to extract everything I knew about local markets, then we translated the operating instructions for their stove. Experiencing the world as fundamentally comprehensible, they could then savour subtle differences in their new environment:

> W: If you come over here and try to live like you did in North America you're in for a big disappointment. You don't get the giant economy size jar of peanut butter and things like that. But if you're willing to live – I'm talking mostly about shopping – as a Swiss there's absolutely no problem ... you put up with smaller sizes and less closet space, things like that.
>
> H: I agree, but (to his wife) you're looking at the things that are, um, undesirable. You have to look at the things that they have here that we don't have in North America, and that are very desirable ... there are a lot of little positives, like (he gives a series of examples, such as containers that keep milk fresh, and a number of gadgets he has discovered) ... You have new experiences every day. Nothing gets stagnant as it does in North America where you get into habits, patterns.
>
> (Graham/1)

Mr and Mrs Graham's attitude to French is in interesting contrast with that of Mrs Gibbs, who had talked at length of how frustrating it was not to be able to communicate. The Grahams both spoke minimal French when they came, enough to manage basic 'supermarket' exchanges. Mrs Graham had intended to take lessons in Geneva, and watched some television in French with that in mind, but by two years later their good linguistic intentions had gone by the wayside. They managed the encounters they could not handle verbally with sign language and humour:

> W: I love going around seeing things, going through a castle, a chapel. But I'm not ready to buy the book at the door and learn all the details. I enjoy things – I love going to the top of [a nearby mountain] but I'm not going to sit in French lessons.
> M: What about [his] French?
> H: Very poor. I know a lot of vocabulary, perhaps more than [my wife], and have a better ear, but I can't converse ... If French was essential for being successful and doing my work I certainly would have made the effort a long time ago, but it's totally unimportant.
> W: I find that if you go into a store or approach a service man with a smile on your face and an honest look in your eye – even though you can't speak their language and they can't speak yours – if you really want to try and get your point across there is definitely a way to do it. If you go in with a chip on your shoulder saying: 'I'm an American and you have to speak English to me' they're going to reject you completely, but I never have a problem.
>
> (Graham/4)

The Grahams had become involved in other things of more priority to them, and were comfortable with their lack of mastery of the language. The point here is that they felt they had chosen their priorities: had they wanted to they *could have* mastered the language, or rendered that particular aspect of their environment more comprehensible.

The outside world was also manageable. Although the Grahams took due precautions (for example they asked for the researcher's references, and checked them, before they first agreed to participate in the study) once the precautions had been taken they more or less assumed most things would work out. While I was in their home for an interview on a Saturday afternoon, for example, their daughter's friends phoned to ask where she was: she hadn't appeared to meet them as arranged. Mr Graham assured the friends that she had left in time, must have been delayed somewhere, and would surely show up. He mentioned the incident to his wife, then calmly resumed the interview. Some parents might have become concerned, but neither Mr nor Mrs Graham appeared to give the matter any further thought. Later in the same interview they mentioned that a workman had come wanting to do something to the house. They didn't understand what he wanted to do, but, in contrast with many of the others who worried about strange people coming to their homes, Mr Graham commented: 'I knew who he was so I let him go about his business'.

Mr and Mrs Graham discussed stress at some length. Clearly they actively took charge of their own lives, and also of managing their own stress:

> H: I think one of your first allies is your own health. My health is important to me, and I know that it's important to my wife, too. Taking care of the health part will help you keep stress manageable.
>
> (Graham/4)

Managing stress also included deciding what can be controlled in life, and what not. Mr Graham spent a great deal of time in aeroplanes, and talked about a subject highly pertinent at the time of one of the interviews, worrying about terrorist attacks, and worrying in general:

> H: I can't let worrying about terrorism interfere with my life. I'm constantly in aeroplanes, and if I sat around worrying about terrorism I would never make my next trip, or I would give myself an ulcer. I just have to say to myself that I can't worry about it.
> M: You have the basic attitude that things will work out. The first time I was here [your daughter] had some friends call from downtown saying she hadn't shown up. You talked about it and decided she must have been delayed. Other people might have been worried.
> W: I'm very relaxed. I do worry about our children, but I do have the attitude that things will work out. And nothing could ever be so bad that it's insurmountable.
>
> (Graham/4)

Striking in the Graham family, as in the Jackson, was a feeling of weighed choices and anticipated and assumed consequences, of a modicum of control in the family's life course. Recall, for example, that Mr Graham said he would not have accepted the proposed job in Geneva without the wholehearted support of his family (Chapter 2). Their perception of stress differed: faced with similar requirement for adaptations, the Jacksons perceived a great deal of stress whereas the Grahams perceived very little. The Jacksons had more to cope with since their child had difficulties adapting during the first year whereas the Graham children had very few. The older Graham children left in North America successfully assumed vastly increased independence, and the child with them 'had a fantastic year', discovered far larger horizons than she would have done had she stayed at home, and she successfully began university in North America the next year. But in both families the attitude was that of going out to meet challenges, continuously evaluating, and feeling they would most likely be able to cope with whatever arose.

The final example of coping concerns the Smithers, the family who had moved, as discussed in Chapter 2, because they had always wanted to live abroad, perhaps practically at any cost, and who appeared again in Chapter 4, in a discussion of the strains involved for the family when Mr Smithers found that he had to work inordinately long hours.

The Smithers family

The Smithers had eagerly looked forward to adapting to a new culture, but instead ended up having to cope with a series of increasingly major disappointments. They had wanted to find a house with 'European character' and surrounded by Swiss neighbours so they might be able to integrate to some extent into Swiss society, but could only find a decidedly standard-model house surrounded by other international families. All other things being equal they would have liked to put the children in local schools, but after due reflection had chosen the English-language International School since they did not think their eldest child would be able to handle school in a new language. Already speaking Italian and loving everything to do with that language, they had hoped to come to appreciate French language and culture, but without much success: both took lessons but neither was able to learn the language nearly as well as they had hoped, and they never managed to overcome their avowed negative prejudices about French-speaking people.

A very busy family before they left North America, with numerous activities and a constant stream of people dropping by their home, they tried to reconstruct the open-door style by joining clubs and participating in activities, but made several wistful mentions of people who *did not* become friends, and of in fact being lonely in Geneva. Before they left North America they had invited plenty of people to come and visit, and many old friends did so, but the Smithers found that they had not quite appreciated that when people come as house guests they are continuously present for days and weeks rather than for hours. Mr and Mrs Smithers both spent a great deal of time and energy entertaining overseas visitors, preparing meals, and showing them places. But this, too, they described as being a source of stress.

The three children all had some trouble in Geneva: they fought a great deal, and were described as 'difficult'. During the second year of the study the eldest was found to have learning difficulties. The second, who had always been a very 'easy', 'good-natured' child, became 'negative', 'demanding', 'nasty with the baby', although Mrs Smithers commented: 'I don't think it's because of the move'. As for his younger brother, his parents were concerned that the three-year-old seemed to be developing behaviour problems, and were considering consulting a psychologist. Mrs Smithers was forthcoming in discussing the various problems the child was having, but 'forgot' until much later to mention that among them were great difficulties with orientation in space.

The Smithers had trouble coping with the accumulation of problems. By the second interview, although the words they were using were generally positive, both Mr and Mrs Smithers sounded depressed. As we talked about the reasons they moved, they even joked:

> M: You chose to work for a multinational company so you might be able to live abroad ...
> H: Right. It's a long-term goal that's being realised. Now we just have to come up with the next one.
> W: (laughing) We've used up the only long-term goal we had.
> (Smithers/2)

Mr Smithers never did get along with his boss in Geneva, and by the second year the latter had managed to shuffle Mr Smithers out, having him transferred to a company job back in North America. Mr Smithers felt he had no real control over the situation. He said he could have chosen to stay in Geneva against the wishes of his superior, but his position would then have been extremely uncomfortable, and seriously damaged his career. So with regret, but convinced it was the best decision, he had accepted an offer with the same company, but in a city different from the one they had left to move to Geneva. The last interview took place about a month after they had made the decision, and some six weeks before the family was to return. Mrs Smithers had commented on the telephone the week before:

> W: I was watching a TV programme last night about France and Belgium during the war. There were houses being bombed, and people dying in the streets, and I thought: 'and I'm worrying about moving from one house to another!'
> (Smithers/telephone interview)

When I last saw the Smithers they were continuing such relativisation, beginning to come to terms with the disappointment, and trying to find positive aspects in their situation:

W: I'm gradually thinking more about living in North America. I can sense the adjustment already: I'm thinking about what various things will be like, such as grocery shopping.
H: For work I've kind of clicked over. I have just been there for a couple of weeks, and I'm thinking about work there, the kinds of things we're doing here in Geneva that we'll be able to use there.
Both: You can get aggravated, or you can try to find good reasons for going home – and try to travel as much as possible in the time that's left!

(Smithers/3)

They listed a number of good things about going back, such as being close to family, and better help for the child with learning difficulties, but could not help adding that the move back was not so good for one of the other children, whose new-found fluency in French it would be extremely difficult to maintain.

Of the four families discussed as examples, it was the Smithers family that had the largest accumulation of problems with which to cope. Their move was driven by the lifelong wish to live abroad, yet the wish had an almost superficial quality. For example, the contrast with most of the other families in the study was striking when the Smithers had not been able to immediately formulate their wishes for their stay at the first interview, and their joke about 'using up our only goal in life' was perhaps more profoundly revealing than they thought. In retrospect, in addition, the decision was poorly integrated into other aspects of the family's life. They seemed to have made it without really taking into account what the change of job location would really mean for Mr Smithers' career and without objectively evaluating Mr Smithers' relationship with the boss with whom he would be working. They did not seem to have anticipated the adjustment that would be required in the family's relationships with the numerous people around them, or, and in particular, the different needs of their three children. Trouble with the 'meaning' of the event brought with it troubles with the sense of coherence element of 'manageability' as well. The couple felt that significant elements of their family's life were slipping out of their control, as Mr Smithers worked longer and longer hours, and as Mrs Smithers implied with her remark about the way life was 'using up your time' (Chapter 4).

At the same time the Smithers were perhaps gaining some control over their lives as they prepared to move back to North America. If they had probably not adequately thought through all aspects before they moved to Geneva, they were more thorough in exploring the implications of the move back. Rather than simply dreaming of the sort of house in which they would like to live when they returned, for instance, Mr Smithers had just used part of his recent business trip to the new place to determine exactly what sort of housing the family could realistically expect to afford. They were far more active this time in anticipating their children's needs, and also in envisaging which of their old friendships would be likely to have held up over the separation. Perhaps most importantly, although the decision to move back may have been made with difficulty and regret, Mr and Mrs Smithers felt it was their own decision, that they had had at least some control over what happened to them.

Discussion

Several provisos are in order at this point. First of all, it would be fair to recall that the families who participated in the study are basically healthy, well-functioning ones. As discussed in Chapter 2, they had either been screened by their employers or screened themselves before uprooting to a new culture, and families known to be having difficulties beforehand were strongly discouraged from making such a move. The less good coping described above is still relatively adequate: families muddle through. The Gibbs, for example, may not have found the glaciers, but they did get to the mountains. After they arrived they used the unsettled time during which their possessions had been mislaid to explore the region. And the problems experienced by their children – such as a first year of university 'not working out' – are decidedly far from the severe end of a continuum of problems that can potentially occur with maturing children. The Smithers couple was severely disappointed, yet the family was holding together as they prepared to return to North America. Indeed, when asked about the strains living abroad can put on couples Mrs Smithers had remarked: 'We knew in advance it wouldn't tear us apart'. And the children's behaviour problems had started to resolve themselves after a difficult first year or so, long before the question of return came up.

Second, the level of the goals set affects potential for stress, and thus the amount of coping that will be required. The four families given as examples in this chapter had in fact set rather modest goals for their stay. Setting more ambitious goals, such as seeking integration through having children attend local schools, entails more stress, stress which requires more coping. The next chapters return to this point. Third, although this study focuses on coping with a specific event, migration to a new culture, a complicating factor is that the stresses of adapting to a new culture often occurred in addition to other stresses and life events which had little or nothing to do with moving. Among the 28 families studied, for example, these included the loss of a pregnancy, serious illness in extended families, accidents, financial difficulties, and professional problems. There was thus an accumulation of stressors for some, creating a spiral of problems each of which made the others increasingly difficult to deal with.

A fourth problem in discussing coping is that it is a dynamic, moving target. It shifts and changes. It can be effective in one domain, less so in another. Family members may take turns coping well while others 'fall apart'. Families (or individuals) may be overwhelmed by a pile-up of problems, and not cope well for a time, then eventually 'kick in' and start dealing with them, reversing a downward spiral of functioning into an upward one, as the Smithers may well have been doing, for example. A fifth factor that makes it difficult for people to talk about how they coped in the beginning is that they very often forgot about their initial problems, especially when things later went well. Mr and Mrs Kennedy, for example, complained bitterly during the first interview about the treatment they had received just after they moved, yet by only ten months later had apparently completely forgotten the difficulties of the first days. Mr Kennedy, apparently forgetting that he had arrived for his first day at work only to find that someone had forgotten to tell him the day was a Swiss holiday and the office was closed, or that they had intensely disliked the way they were treated when they took the children to register for school, exclaimed: 'From the moment we arrived here everything has been a positive experience' (Kennedy/2). Furthermore, many families felt able to talk about problems only after the worst was past. The Rodgers, who talked in particularly fine detail about their humiliating, out-of-control experiences in Chapter 3, had in fact refused to participate in the study when they were contacted a first time. Mrs Rodgers explained that they had been in the throes of depression the first time they were approached, and felt unable to handle being interviewed, but that now that the worst was over they could talk about their problems, and even laugh about them.

A final factor that makes it difficult to discuss coping is that some forms of coping are easier to perceive and to describe than others: problem-focused active tackling of problems, for instance, is visible, as the individual or the family defines a problem and does something about it. It was visible in the preparations many of the families made for moving, by gathering together what they thought they might need, by talking to others who had undergone similar experiences, and by anticipating the problems and emotions they might encounter. It was visible when Mrs Jackson rearranged her work schedule so as to be home when her child arrived from school. Emotion-focused coping strategies are somewhat less obvious, but many are still quite possible to define from interviews. Analysing one's problems and defining those about which nothing can be done is an example, as when Mr Graham decided that since he had to spend a great deal of time flying he would not let himself worry about the eventuality of aeroplanes being hijacked by terrorists. Relativising was clear when the Smithers contrasted their disappointment about having to return prematurely to North America with the infinitely worse situation of people living under war conditions. It was also clear that they were reframing when they sought out what might be positive about the move back, or anticipated the things they would do when they got there. Other emotion-focused coping strategies are less obvious, however. Denial, for example, by definition cannot be talked about since the family simply does not *see* the problem. Mr and Mrs Smithers for instance did not see the move-related problems they were having, and did not admit even to themselves that they were unhappy about certain aspects of living abroad. Poor coping with moderate strains, similarly, is difficult to characterise since problems simply drag on when coping is not adequate (poor coping with acute stress is another matter, of course: denial of chest pain or a lump in one's breast, for example, can have catastrophic consequences).

These provisos in mind, it is nonetheless possible to see some of the ways in which sense of coherence affects coping. The most elementary is that the high SOC families were quite simply more able than the low SOC families to *see* the difficulties that would require coping. Those lower on SOC, the Gibbs and Smithers families, were less likely to admit to themselves when things were going just slightly wrong. They were not good at actively thinking through their difficulties, more likely to deny them, to let matters simply slide along. Less likely to define problems to themselves, they were thus quite obviously less in a position to do something about them. When the family high on SOC, the Jacksons, on the other hand, determined that they had made a mistake (in moving back to North America, or in their choice of an apartment) they most certainly talked of stress, but immediately took steps to correct the problems, inconvenient as such steps may have been.

Partly because they could allow themselves to recognise problems, but also, and much more importantly, because of an underlying sense that life is fundamentally comprehensible and manageable, the high SOC Graham and Jackson families were striking in actively taking charge, in talking about 'challenges', in making decisions that would affect what happens to them, in feeling they were at least partly in control of their lives. The opposite attitude of the lower SOC families, in contrast, is more difficult to put into words. It implies more passively following whatever currents life brings, experiencing disappointments, becoming frustrated. It involves not trying to work things out when one finds oneself assigned an incompatible room-mate at college. It involves assuming one will 'pick up' the local language without really giving the matter a great deal of thought, then feeling frustrated when one does not. It involves letting only partly understood community norms determine a child's alcohol consumption since to do otherwise would require increased sentiments both of comprehensibility ('I understand the implicit rules in this community') and of manageability ('I agree or disagree with them').

Finally, if SOC affects a family's definition of the problems that can be tackled or coped with, it also affects the definition of what is beyond the range of coping efforts. Some things may be beyond the range of coping efforts because individuals have determined that they do not have priority, as when the high SOC Mrs Graham decided she did not want to invest much effort in learning French. Others simply cannot be helped, and are thus not worth regret, as when world political changes later made very appealing the place the Jacksons had *not* moved to. Thus the high SOC families avoided the wistful regret that marked both of the low SOC families discussed in this chapter. Very far from finding that life was 'using up our only long-term goal', the high SOC families, who assumed that most things would eventually work out and that they would be able to cope with whatever came up, were able to take on new challenges, to expand limits in ever-widening circles.

The next two chapters discuss another major form of coping, seeking and obtaining social support.

6

GIVING AND RECEIVING SOCIAL SUPPORT

Previous chapters have given much attention to a major coping resource available to many of the families studied here: a sense of personal control or mastery. This chapter discusses a second major coping resource, social support, or 'the functions performed for the individual by significant others, such as family members, friends, and co-workers' (House and Kahn, 1985). The three major forms of social support – informational support, instrumental or practical support, and emotional support – are discussed in this chapter, as they are provided by the employer and by acquaintances and friends. At the end of the chapter social support in Geneva is discussed in relation to social support available in other posts abroad. Another major source of social support, that coming from within the family, is discussed at some length in Chapter 7. Throughout, the complex interplay between social support and coping is discussed, and the way in which social relations can help people cope with problems, but may also contribute to them.

The first segment of the chapter discusses one aspect of the still-very-pertinent links with members of extended families left behind. It starts with a very difficult issue, dealing with family emergencies and health problems over long distances. The chapter then goes on to talk about the help in the new place that may come from people outside the nuclear family.

Relationships with extended families

The people participating in the study remind us that those who move do not simply abandon relationships when they do so: respondents often talked at length of people they had left behind. Many described a feeling of living between two worlds, especially when they were dealing across oceans with children left behind, and with family crises such as the ill health or death of parents. Children newly attending university or in recently acquired jobs were especially present in parents' discussions, and many parents reported being surprised at just how difficult they found being far away from older children (Chapter 8).

Events occurring with parents and with other extended family members were also very pertinent for many. In a cohort of 28 young and middle-aged families and over a period of three years, a good many events occurred in the extended families: parents of several study participants became severely ill, and some lost fathers and grandparents. Other less normative events also took place: after many years of waiting, one mother, a political refugee, was finally allowed to leave her country to live near her children in North America. In another family a sibling gave birth to a severely retarded baby, and needed emotional support during the very difficult time she had coming to terms with the event.

Travelling back and forth to help, to visit, to support parents, to take care of practical details, and to share the burden with siblings, was obviously at times extremely difficult:

> W: My grandmother died . . . I knew my mother was having a hard time with it, and I had a hard time with being away through the illness . . . I felt I couldn't help my mother, and I couldn't be there with my grandmother. I felt rather helpless.
> (Bateson/2)

It is with the Vances that these things were discussed in most detail, and it is they who brought up the themes echoed by the other families. We had made, then postponed, several appointments for a second interview, one reason being that Mrs Vance had to go unexpectedly to North America. The story came out on the telephone as we were postponing yet another interview:

W: We had our first death in the family.

She went on to explain that her father had died the week before. He had been quite ill the previous year, but had recovered and seemed to be doing well when he died suddenly at home. Mrs Vance had gone back for the funeral, and described how the company had facilitated things for her, making all the travel arrangements, and delivering the plane tickets so that she was with her mother within 24 hours of receiving the news.

She had been worried about being in Europe with her father sick, and had been feeling far away sometimes, but now said she realised that the distance isn't really all that great. In fact she got home faster than she might have from some places within North America. In an odd way she found that reassuring, and said she will thus find it easier to cope next time: 'Life is the same sometimes no matter where you are. You cope anyway.'
(Vance/telephone interview/year 2)

We returned to the subject near the end of a long interview a month later, two months after her father's death. 'Life is the same no matter where you are' not only for coping but also for mourning:

> M: You've been through a major family event.
> W: Yes. It's the first time we've ever had to really deal directly with death.
> H: I was never one to visit family much ... but now I've started going to see them. If you're away for four or five months you see some deterioration, and it kind of hits you. You are far away and you can't be there at a moment's notice. That's frustrating ... But I don't think it would have been any different with her father's death if we had been any closer.
> W: No. It happened so suddenly I didn't have that feeling.
> H: You had to think about it for a day, travel with it for eight hours. Once you're there, once you've immersed yourself in it, it's a lot easier than anticipating what you're going to have to handle.
> W: Yes. I was surprised at my reaction when I came back here, though. I thought maybe it would be really easy when I came back. I could leave all that there and come back to a life where my father had never been. But it doesn't work that way (little laugh). It's still very tough. He had never been here, but I realised that all along I had been planning what I would show him. There were certain things that I had always thought: 'Oh, he'll love this when he comes', or 'boy, will he get a kick out of this' (tears). And I find those things still set that off, and then it hits. I think: 'Oh, you'll never be able to show him this, or he'll never see this' ...
>
> (Vance/2)

One of the things that made coping with severe illness in a member of the extended family difficult was the feeling that one was not necessarily being told the truth:

> H: Our families back there frustrate the hell out of us. They're extremely secretive. They don't want to *trouble* us. It just drives me absolutely insane. My grandmother had a heart attack and went to the hospital, and they didn't tell me.
>
> (Both talk at once, giving other examples, with a great deal of emotion not far from the surface.)
>
> (Vance/2)

Mr and Mrs Vance had only been told about her father's previous heart attack four days after it had happened, and about a sibling's major health problem in a letter written ten days after he had been hospitalised. Both said they had asked their family, in scathing letters, to be kept better informed so they would not have to worry in between.

Similar issues were pertinent in another family as well, as Mr Jackson's father had also had a very serious heart problem, but had recovered. Mr Jackson also discussed doubts raised by the practical aspects of such events:

> H: For a while it was touch and go as to what would happen. I wondered at what point I would make the decision to fly back. My father's physical condition? My mother's mental condition? The government's bureaucratic controls – the point at which they would pay for the flight?

He described the importance of keeping in touch through lengthy telephone calls during the crisis, with his father . . .

> H: It was reassuring to hear his voice gradually strengthen.

. . . and with other family members . . .

> H: I called my sister to find out what really was going on.

. . . and stressed that a difficult situation was made somewhat easier with the phone calls, simple and technically good, and in their case paid for by the employer:

> H: You have a lot of things on your mind for those phone calls, a lot of questions. It's frustrating: you hang up and realise you haven't asked all you wanted to.
>
> (Jackson/2)

The theme of maintaining relationships with extended families merits a far more extensive discussion than it can be given here, but this brief detour recalls at least two points that have already been mentioned in other contexts. The first is, once again, the potentially vitally important source of practical support that can be furnished by employers, mentioned above in the form of flight arrangements and telephone calls. The second is to recall that families 'straddle two worlds' when they live abroad. The next section continues the theme, discussing the non-negligible social support in the new place that came from old friends who were nevertheless far away.

Social support over long distances

Significant practical and emotional support right after a move came from old friends, from employers, and also from networks of people of the same nationality already living in the new place. In addition, important sources of social support for people just arriving were initiated from 'weak ties' (Granovetter, 1973), and from people geographically much more distant than the social support literature usually takes into account. Mrs Newton set the stage when she happened to remark at our first interview:

> W: I had a name of somebody I could call when I got here: a friend from Belgium who is now in Hong Kong had a friend she had met in Denmark who lives in Geneva now.
>
> (Newton/1)

Few of the people who participated in this study were notably shy: on the whole they were socially at ease, and knew many people. They kept at least minimal contact with old friends by sending an average of some 60 cards and letters at Christmas or the New Year. Out of necessity, or simply because they were at ease, they were also remarkably good at deploying very tenuous ties if required, or even asking unknown people for help. When Mr Rodgers, for example, developed a dramatic skin rash after surgery and could not reach his surgeon, he looked up a nurse who had been nice to him while he was in the hospital. She was able to get him the proper attention. Similarly, when one woman had an accident and needed both medical help for herself and somebody to look after her child while she was getting it, she went to a neighbour she had not yet met.

The telephone was extensively used by most of the families. In an emergency it brought assistance from people not necessarily in the same country, or even on the same continent. When an adolescent Newton child finally brought himself to tell his mother about an alarming health problem he was experiencing, for example, her immediate response was to phone a physician she had worked for in another European country. She got her former employer out of surgery, he gave advice, and on this basis the boy was operated on in Geneva within a matter of hours. Similarly, when Mr Madison needed legal advice he phoned a lawyer friend in Germany. And several people, such as Mrs Foster whose move-related marital crisis will be discussed in detail in Chapter 8, mentioned deriving considerable support during long telephone conversations with good friends in North America.

Such long-distance social support also operated with old friends. There were several mentions, especially at the beginning of the study, of the importance of contact with old friends for easing the transition. Adults eagerly went to the mail box each morning, and several adolescents were allowed unusual telephone privileges for the first few months in order to keep in contact with the 'best friends' they had left behind. Especially when there were difficulties making friends in the new place, frequent contact with an old friend or two, and/or the prospect of a summer visit, gave something to hang on to. Having old friends visit, learning the sights of Geneva as they showed the visitors around, made the first months far less lonely than they might otherwise have been, especially since the spouse who was working was often very busy with the new job or travelling.

When, at the second interview, respondents were asked to list the visitors they had had in the past year, the response was impressive: virtually everyone had had house guests at some point, most often in several different configurations. Family, friends, children's friends, acquaintances, and colleagues had visited, for a few days, or for a week, a month, or longer. Several people said that before they left, in the enthusiasm of the prospect of a sojourn in Europe, they had issued wide and general invitations for people to come and visit:

> H: We get all these students coming through on their rail passes. The first 90 nights in Geneva we had guests for 45.
> M: You're not a family that's closed to the outside world (all laugh).
> H: Sometimes we'd like that.
> W: We could use a little quiet time.
>
> (Thomas/1)

As for initial social support in the new place, it originated for many with that given directly by the employer, or from the spouses' groups that were linked with 'the company' especially.

Support coming from the new place

An obvious coping resource, available in varying degrees to all families in this study, was the informational, practical and also emotional support provided by many of the employers. The post reports and handbooks prepared for potential overseas employees by governments and by some multinational companies were important sources of informational support. Formal and informal practical assistance was provided in the form of annual home leaves, help with housing, and payment of school fees, as well as in instances such as that when 'the company' arranged to have Mrs Vance flown home within hours after her father's death. Several employers officially mandated someone to provide help when a family arrived. 'The company', especially, hired relocation consultants to help not only with finding housing and choosing schools, but also with a host of practical details to be attended to during the first weeks. Such consultants, as the only person a newcomer had as yet met, very often also provided less formal support, especially in an emergency. Mrs Rodgers, for example, phoned the woman who had shown the family houses when she was unable to understand the recorded message on a physician's answering machine: it was the real estate agent who listened and translated the message about how to reach the doctor. Similarly, husbands' secretaries were frequently mentioned as having been asked to help with the myriad of family transactions just after a move which required use of the local language (e.g. changing doctor's appointments, dealing with the telephone company, or locating veterinarians).

A potentially important source of initial social support was that provided by the spouse groups sometimes facilitated by the employer. Mrs Graham described the needs such groups may meet for their members:

> W: Companies have a very strong support system for women. If you have questions when you come, the first place you would go would be to one of the women you met at one of the coffees. A lot of the women who come have left careers, and are at loose ends. They get up in the morning, and don't have any work to go out to. A lot of us don't have our kids here, or our parents ... We don't discuss business – it's not that kind of a thing. It's more of a social thing, just gals getting together ... Most of my friends now are [company] wives ...
>
> (Graham/3)

Such groups could be significant sources of emotional support immediately after a family had moved, when relationships are very quickly made with people who are also in search of new friends. During the time of initial isolation, when husbands and children were busy with new jobs and schools, about half of the women who participated in the study became involved in numerous activities: coffees, handicraft groups, newcomers groups, spouses groups around the employer, volunteer work at the school. People attending such events, as Mrs Newton put it, 'understand exactly what you are going through'. Several of the women in the study made close friends from this period:

> W: The first month I saw X almost every day. She phoned every evening to ask how I was doing. It really makes a difference – it's like someone cares. There is someone who cares whether or not you're sitting there crying. The first month we were here it rained every day, and that apartment we were in while we were waiting to move into our house was horrible, dreary and dark. The kids were sick. [My husband] started travelling for his work ... I'd take my washing over to X's house, and we'd sit down and have a cup of tea, and she'd show me what she was doing. Or she'd take me out somewhere. We'd go grocery shopping.
>
> (Cady/1)

Initial support in adapting to life in a new culture thus came both from old friends – with whom relationships were maintained over long distances

– and from people met in the new place who were in similar situations – from 'first friends' and from company-sponsored spouse groups. Many of the former relationships could be quite significant, and many of the latter could later become so. The next section, however, brings up the opposite side of social support, discussing the potentially invasive nature of both old and new relationships, and what people did about them.

Gaining control over social relations

If seeing family and old friends was a source of pleasure, the other side of the coin was that such visits could interfere with getting into life in the new place:

C: We had visitors all the time. We'd have two or three days in between, then the next ones would come. And they stayed for three weeks at a time.

W: We had so many visitors that I did not have enough time for myself or just to do my daily thing. I enjoy visitors, but it was too much ... I couldn't get into my life here. I felt like my life was on hold.

(Bateson/2)

Having a great many visitors entailed costs. Such costs could be literal financial costs: admission to sights to be seen, special food prepared, meals in restaurants, or even telephone bills, such as that of more than a thousand dollars left by a teenager visiting the Madison family. Visits could also be costly in terms of energy:

W: My sister told me when she moved to England, be prepared for the guests, they will make you poor, and that's true.

(She lists several visitors they have had over the summer.)

W: It's fun. It's nice having people come, but if they expect you to do all the cooking and so forth, then it's hard work, and really expensive ... It sounds mercenary, but you think 'we came here to travel and have fun ourselves', and here we are spending all our energy entertaining.

(Elm/2)

Such demands could easily get out of hand. It was usually *à propos* other families that remarks were made about people who 'run themselves ragged' with exaggerated efforts to entertain out of town visitors, however:

W: Some people said they had people visiting during the whole summer. I had a friend who had 12 people here at one time.

> People expected her to accompany them to various places that she had already seen, and she didn't say no. She has been to [an especially picturesque village some two hours away] at least ten times. She was driving people to Amsterdam. She drove to Scandinavia.
>
> H: She's too nice to say no.
>
> (Graham/3)

Partly because 'everybody's already been here', and partly because families had learned to set limits on excessive demands, by the last round of interviews study participants no longer told stories, either about themselves or about others, of people feeling they were sacrificing themselves to flocks of visitors. Some of those who felt they had been too hospitable had formally and widely announced to all concerned after the first summer that 'the hotel is closed':

> W: We've informed everyone, even family, the hotel is closed for repairs until further notice (laugh). We'll invite people for a meal, but they'll have to find somewhere else to stay.
>
> H: Yeah, that's been a good change ... It was overwhelming us. It became too much to have all those extra people.
>
> W: And it affected our family life. We were with company from morning till night, so when do you sit with the children to help them with their piano lessons, or hear about school? And we took all our holidays to drive people back and forth to see places.
>
> (Thomas/3)

Hosts no longer routinely took all out of town visitors to the same lovely castle, but, if they did take people to see things, went to new places they themselves also wanted to see. They had less of a tendency to 'go all out' for their visitors:

> W: We just show them where the bus is and let them get on with it.
>
> (Kennedy/2)

Visitors were thus more enjoyed. Also, though, relationships had changed because ties and daily lives had been established in the new place. The discussion now returns to the early days after a move, to the second major source of support with the initial transition to the new place, that provided by 'first friends'.

First friends and newcomers groups

Some of the relationships with first friends proved to be quite transitory. Mrs Rodgers, for example, whose vivid description of approaching a new friend was cited in Chapter 3 ('it was almost like asking for a date') and who talked at length of this friend at the first interview as one of the people she could call upon for help, could not quite remember the woman's name when I asked about the relationship two years later. Support that may have been extremely important in the beginning, moreover, could later become cumbersome. At least four of the women in the study, including Mrs Cady cited above whose new friend had provided tea, sympathy, and laundry facilities, found that relationships which had been very helpful in the beginning later became burdens. Such massive help became invasive, and difficult to undo, later on when it was not as necessary any more, or when the new friends adapted differently. It was Mrs Wood who best put the phenomenon into words. She had been talking about her great difficulty adjusting, and about how a friend going through the same thing had helped:

> W: We learned our way around town together. We first met at the hotel when we were both waiting to move into our houses. We meet every Wednesday. We go to a new place, explore it, have lunch, give hints. She's been more support than anybody including [my husband].
>
> (Wood/1)

By two years later the good friends had gone their separate ways, however:

> W: We're not such good friends any more. She is one of the people who didn't make the transition well ... I feel very negative when we're together, because all I ever hear are insulting remarks about this culture, or complaints about not being able to find this or that. It's hard to listen to now, and it makes me feel very uneasy because I don't feel that way any more ...
>
> I was overwhelmed at the beginning with new experiences, all these new things to deal with. We met at a time when we needed each other. We were thrown together when we needed somebody, and were going through the same process at the same time. But I've changed more. She's still a friend, we still do things together, but it's not nearly the relationship we had when we first came here. We would talk daily at first. It was good to air my feelings with someone, but my process of adjusting might have been easier without her negative influence. She dragged me down.

(Her husband agrees that the relationship had hindered Mrs Wood's adjustment, and adds:)

> H: You can get the same thing moving anywhere. Misery loves company. Some people have a negative attitude about anything, and it is catching. I believe you should try to help people like that, but sometimes they just won't let you.
>
> (Wood/3)

The third source of support with the initial transition to the new place was that provided by the 'newcomers groups'. Here, too, it is clear that social support may come with a price attached:

> W: The company is very good at taking you in, showing you the stores, the school ... You don't have to go out of your way to make friends. I'm just sort of in a cocoon, a [company] cocoon.
> H: The bad part is that everybody knows everybody's business. There's a lot of gossip. But the good is helping new people, taking them around, stocking the apartment with food and flowers when they arrive, taking them to the grocery store ... It's really incredible support ...
> W: But after a year of it I'm beginning to feel almost stuck.
>
> (PP/1)

Attitudes towards company-related social groups quite often became ambivalent. Several people were critical of them from the time they moved. One criticism was that spouse groups, especially, were too uniform. First of all, they were made up only of women: at the time the study was carried out it was still very rare for a husband to be an accompanying spouse. Second, they were also usually monocultural, involving only people from 'home'. Several families specifically wanted to avoid such networks so as to meet people from other cultures, and were critical of those who insisted on sticking with their own:

> H: The people I always feel uncomfortable about are those who make no attempt to seek out people who are different, who need to stick with the expat community and the politics within it.
> W: People want to feel special, and they only associate with the people like them. That's very protective, like a shell.
>
> (Kennedy/3)

Finally, and perhaps most importantly, a major criticism of such company-related social groups was that they may be primarily frequented by people who, in sharing a common series of frustrations, may shift a delicate balance away from 'letting off steam' towards 'complaining' or 'whining'. In fact 'complainers' and what to do about them were a frequent object of discussion in the interviews. Although several people mentioned that sessions of complaining in moderate doses with trusted old friends could be very good for the soul, trusted old friends, of course, were what they did not necessarily have right after they moved to a new place. At times when they may have been feeling vulnerable, people were thus obliged to maintain a critical balance between revealing impressions to the extent necessary to construct a new friendship, letting off accumulated frustrations, and 'keeping a positive attitude'. Mrs Bateson, for example, who in moving to Geneva was coming to a foreign country for the first time, talked at the first interview about a 'wives meeting' she had gone to, at which several people had been very negative:

> W: I don't want to surround myself with a negative attitude. I don't want to fall into that myself. The people I want to spend my time with are the ones who maintain a positive attitude. Moving to a new country, culture, language is hard. It takes a lot of energy. Just to go to the grocery store at first was a huge thing, and I want to spend time with people who are staying positive about it.
>
> (Bateson/1)

She followed through at subsequent interviews, talking, as had Mrs Wood, not only about seeking out more positive people, but also about actively extracting herself from negative influences rather than letting herself be 'dragged down' in a social climate of people negative about their common experience:

> W: I had this job for a while, as co-chairman for newcomers to [the company] ... When I took it I never dreamed of the problems I would be listening to ... They complained about everything. They hated the schools, the town, the traffic, the parking. Too much negative conversation gets me down.
> M: You're no longer on that committee?
> W: No ... I don't mean to be too much of a Pollyanna, but it just didn't feel right.
>
> (Bateson/3)

In a cohort of people who had recently arrived in a new place, some inevitably felt lonely and isolated. Others, having gone through the same thing, and many of whom were free of the activities which might otherwise have kept them less available, were willing to reach out to help. But not endlessly, as the next section shows.

Limits to helping

Although they may be patient for a while, some talked of becoming impatient with, and actively avoiding other people who complain:

> W: I don't want to listen to a lot of the things foreigners complain about ... I have no time for complainers.
> M: What do you do if you run into them?
> W: I try to convince them, make them see differently.
> M: And if that doesn't work?
> H: They don't run into [my wife] a second time!
> W: (laugh) Only if I'm forced to be with them! I'm not that militant about it, but I just try to convince them.
>
> (Kennedy/2)

A rather striking example of the limits to families' willingness to help others in difficulty occurred during the study. Although the family discussed next was not interviewed as part of the study, for reasons that are explained, the husband asked that their experiences be shared:

> Although few people are as frank with a stranger on the telephone, one husband went into detail about the family's problems when I asked them to participate in the study. He hoped, he said, that the study would raise sensitivity to family issues among employers. This was the family's first move abroad, and they were having a great deal of difficulty adjusting. He talked at length about 'insane drivers', 'stupid rules', 'rude sales people', the fact that the language is 'almost impossible to learn'. None of the family could understand 'what motivates people here'. He observed that most other North Americans seemed to question very little, but that they themselves confronted everybody. He said the family was feeling betrayed, as though the 'nice little Europe' to which they had been thinking they would be coming, had turned out to be a very frustrating place, and that the things they were used to had been taken away from them.
>
> As to being transferred to Geneva, he felt that he had had some degree of choice, but that in fact his career in a multinational corporation would have stagnated had he refused the offer. For the moment he found that his career was interesting, but said that his wife felt penalised by living in Europe, that she had given up everything and received nothing. He said there was conflict developing within the couple: as for the children, they had been homesick, not an unusual reaction, but the conflict between their parents was beginning to affect them.

As for participating in the study, he would have been very willing. In fact he thought it could perhaps help his wife to talk about these things, but she had adamantly refused, and he did not feel he could 'push' her into it. Similarly, she had refused to go to a wives club that could have been of support to her. In fact she did not want to talk to anybody at all.

This family became well known in the cohort of families studied, and was referred to several times by other people interviewed. Many mentioned having tried to help, but the wife was simply too negative, and several people remarked that 'she would not be happy anywhere'. Others eventually started not wanting to see them, and the story, at least as far as it is known, ended sadly when the family returned prematurely to North America, the husband gravely ill.

The example is instructive in several ways. In hindsight, the employer can be faulted. A sensitive interviewer talking with husband and wife before they were transferred could perhaps have perceived a mindset or a fragility that would have advised against the transfer. Certainly, the family had been inadequately prepared for learning to live in a culture different from that to which they were accustomed. Their expectations were obviously inappropriate, and discussions with people who had already lived in Geneva, and/or a visit to the city before they moved, might have helped the family avoid the feeling of betrayal they experienced.

It is, however, what happened in Geneva that is of interest here. Members of this family had obviously made up their minds about the cultural differences they were experiencing very shortly after they arrived. The unhappiness of one member of the family was affecting the other members, and that of the entire family was affecting those who knew them, in concentric circles. As her husband pointed out, social support might have helped the wife, but only if she had been willing to go part of the way, to talk to people, and to reach out to the company wives club. As pointed out by several of the study participants quoted in this chapter, however, although there was a great deal of giving and of receiving of social support, there were limits to the community's willingness to help those among themselves having difficulties. When many of those who arrived at the same time were dealing with similar feelings, there was too much risk that 'a complainer', someone unwilling to make an effort, would 'drag the others down'. This brings us to the last theme to be discussed in the present chapter, mobilising social support – or failing to do so.

Mobilising social support

Not all families, of course, need other people to the same extent:

> M: Did you know anybody when you arrived?
> W: No, only one person I spoke to on the phone. She'd given her number to my husband and said to phone 'if your wife needs anything' ... The [company] wives have been very welcoming ... But I'm not really one for coffees and things. I have a lot of other things to do.
>
> (Hill/1)

A year later:

> W: The Women's Club ... was nice at the beginning. It was nice to have some sort of English speaking centre where you could go and not have to try and speak French, but I never became involved in many of their activities ... I don't know how you feel about these things, but any time you get a club together it takes hours to do anything. For example I went with the skiing group a couple of times, but the women would ski all day and have somebody pick up their kids from school, whereas I only wanted to ski half a day, then be home when the kids got out of school. I felt I was being a problem. And I didn't want to take ski lessons. I used to do a lot of skate boarding and surfing and it's pretty much the same thing, so I picked it up pretty quickly.
> M: You must have driven them nuts!
> W: (laugh) You got it! So I didn't go too often with them ... The next time I just found a ski lift and went by myself ... A lot of women around seem to make luncheon dates, and coffee dates, mosey around either going shopping or out to lunch. I've extracted myself out of that ... I feel badly refusing sometimes, but I don't need, for example, to go all the way across town for an exercise group. I do it here and get on with something else.
>
> (Hill/2)

We discussed the theme of family openness at some point during the second or the third interview, with a question formulated as follows:

> M: Some families always seem to have streams of people around. Others sort of try to protect their privacy, which side would you fall on?

There are some striking points in common among the families who defined themselves as protecting their intimacy. Far from being 'closed' to the outside world, 'banded together against a hostile environment' (Reiss, 1981) these families made contacts with people easily. Both husband and wife were sociable. Their work required a goodly amount of dealing with people, and it was partly in reaction to this that they tended to want to withdraw during their leisure times. Such withdrawal was distinctly voluntary, however. In a parallel with the difference between being alone and being lonely, these families, when they were alone, chose to be so. They were capable of defining their wishes, then being firm about them. They were polite, but not subject to social pressure that might push others to accept an invitation they really did not care about. Couples such as Mr and Mrs Jackson thought they had grown to this position with age or maturity, but there were also some young families among those who protected their privacy. All but one or two described their marriages as being particularly strong: they liked other people, but felt their family unit was strong enough not to actually need them, as will be discussed in the next chapter.

As might in fact be expected, the families who subjectively considered their families to be more 'open' seemed to have more trouble with moving abroad than those more comfortable with being alone. All but two of these families had difficulties making themselves a comfortable social space. Difficulties for families such as the Thomases, already discussed in this chapter, stemmed both from having set themselves ambitious goals of integration into Swiss society, and at the same time being too open to visitors from outside the family. One of the factors that hindered integration among some of these families was their very openness: playing host to the numerous people from the place whence they had moved kept them from constructing social networks in the new place.

There were exceptions, and it is interesting to speculate why two of the 'open' families (the Ogbournes and the Davidsons) may have had less difficulty with the transition to a new environment. Both families had already moved extensively around the world (thus perhaps having more realistic expectations of a transcultural move than the other 'open' families), and both were highly engaged in something outside their own family (music in one case, a set of specific religious beliefs, customs, and rituals in the other). The Davidsons and the Ogbournes had something else in common: for reasons difficult to define, both families simply seemed to draw assistance. As they reported with some wonder, good things just seemed to happen to them. The Ogbourne family, for instance, found an apartment that was both larger and less expensive than the one they had just when they needed it, when their second child was born. Finding housing in Geneva at that time was not easy, but Mrs Ogbourne just happened to be walking by as a vacancy notice was being put up. The person renting the apartment took a liking to the young family, and let them have it in preference to several other candidates. The Davidsons, also, consistently attracted not only minor, but major, assistance. One example (among the many of which the Davidsons told with gusto) also concerned housing: when the family bought a house during their second year in Geneva the real estate agent, a friend of the sellers, withdrew to save his commission and help reduce the price for them. The people selling the house then helped the Davidsons with arrangements such as settling administrative formalities and registering the children at school:

> W: When he sold his house he acquired a family. He just adopted us.
>
> (Davidson/2)

Other families told similar tales of rather mysteriously mobilising social support. For instance the adolescent girls in the Graham and the Bateson families had their paths facilitated for them by girls from Geneva whom they had met only briefly before they moved. Their new acquaintances had enthusiastically told others of their arrival, thus preparing the way for the newcomers to fall quickly into circles of friends when they arrived. Some of those in the study, such as Mrs Hill, reported that their Swiss neighbours were kind and helpful, and two of the families on sabbatical found that local residents went out of their way to do helpful things for them, such as telephoning to make sure the recipients had understood a letter in French that had just arrived from the local gymnastics team.

Some of the families, on the contrary, and for reasons that also remain ultimately mysterious, simply failed to mobilise social support. To use the researcher as an example, I am still at something of a loss to explain why I freely gave post-interview information or translations to most families, but failed to volunteer a most ordinary piece of information to Mrs Foster when I might very easily have done so. More generally, it is difficult to understand why people such as Mr Foster just seemed to attract hostile comments and criticism (see Chapter 9), or why the Friedsons continued to be lonely well into their second year after the move although they had made efforts to meet people.

Part of the explanation undoubtedly lies in a paradox: individuals or families who did not really *need* other people were those who generally met many anyway. Part of the explanation is certainly that some individuals or families seemed so desperately in need of help that they frightened others. Part of the explanation is also that the receiving of social support may have a subjective element: the same gesture might be taken for granted – or not even perceived – by one person, whereas it is seen to be extraordinarily helpful by another. Another part of the explanation is certainly that those who reported receiving social support also liberally gave it, and because they were more oriented towards giving help, did not expect it for themselves.

In sum, all of those who moved needed both social support and to make new friends. Some attached themselves to the first people or groups that came along. Others waited, weeded out and chose. What is underlying, implicit, for many of the families in the study is the feeling of being able to exercise control over their social environment. Several actually did exercise such control, by correcting the balance and limiting hospitality that had been overextended to old friends and acquaintances, by rejecting certain relationships, or by avoiding certain groups. Some, who had formed relationships that proved unsatisfying and unhealthy during a time of need and vulnerability, were able to extract themselves from these later on.

The meaningfulness, comprehensibility and manageability components of the sense of coherence thus appear once again, in the depth of commitment to something other than oneself that certainly affects how people relate to each other, in the ability to define negative as well as positive elements of social relationships, in the ability to conceive of changing something that is less than satisfactory, and to then attempt to do so. This chapter has been concerned with social support coming from outside the immediate family. The next turns to social support from within the family, or that which comes from families functioning together.

First, however, the chapter makes a small detour to discuss a factor from outside a particular family, but which very much affects the social support it will mobilise.

Social support in Geneva and in 'hardship posts'

Study participants who had previously lived in developing countries remarked upon one further paradox concerning social support in a place such as Geneva. They pointed out that support is more readily available in situations known to be difficult. The comparison eventually came up with virtually all of those who had lived in other areas of the world. Several of those who had been living in physically more difficult places both relished the minute practical details that facilitate everyday living in a developed country and found them somewhat intimidating, as Mr Davidson pointed out when he talked of suddenly having to deal with how to pay for a parking spot and other sophisticated forms of traffic regulation (Chapter 3).

Some families were well aware of the disparity between living in certain other regions of the world and living in a place such as Geneva, a disparity which can be a source of ambivalence. One of those whose career trajectory normally requires living in developing countries had given the matter a great deal of thought:

> H: We have never had so much choice of magnificent places to see ... the attention to detail, quality of life for everybody.

> I know what it's like to be a poor student living downtown in the smog without enough money to get out into a field. Here *anybody* can just get on a bus and go out to the country for a walk. People who have been brought up here take it for granted.

But:

> ... You lose sight of 80 per cent of the world living in Geneva, the starvation, refugees, pollution, housing, the population explosion. Some days I walk down this lovely street and want to jump for joy, but I tell myself I mustn't forget.
>
> M: How do you deal with that disparity?
> H: I can cope with it. It's like I'm on sabbatical while I'm here. I just make sure I don't forget what it's like for the other 80 per cent. But in the end you and I belong to the developed world. [My wife] and I get thrown into Third World countries, but we are outsiders. We're not part of that world, no matter what effort you make to assimilate.
> W: We can always leave.
> H: And in fact we do leave.
> W: ... I'm certainly prepared to go to another Third World country, there's no doubt about that, but you can't help comparing ... The biggest problem we face now is knowing that in three years we will have to leave this place. We know we will never live this well again.
>
> (Kennedy/2)

If practical details of Geneva are very well organised, making everyday life more comfortable than in many other countries, this relative ease has another side. In countries known for being difficult for such practical matters a great deal of help is available: expatriate families would have a great deal more assistance than they received in Geneva, where they are expected to manage on their own:

> H: This is a much more difficult post than some place like [Nairobi] where you are picked up at the airport and taken to a furnished house that's all leased for you. General services will even come and change light bulbs for you!
> M: Is Geneva known to be an easy or a hard post?
> H: People say after six months to a year you can relax and enjoy it, but for example it took two months to get a telephone.
> W: That takes five days in North America. This is thought to be like North America: you should be able to do everything yourself ... The general services staff here is very small, probably

because it's so expensive – salaries for drivers in Geneva are about the same as professionals' salaries in North America.

H: Also, our work here is not so urgent that we can't miss an odd meeting or two. If you're calculating, it doesn't really matter how much of our time is used for errands. If you're not there when you're needed in [Nairobi] and something falls flat it can be a disaster. Here it hardly matters.

(Quincy/1)

But it is socially that many interviewees said a place like Geneva is most difficult. First of all, many of those in the international community are living in a place where they do not feel they belong. To many expatriates this is not 'home':

W: It's a strange environment . . . People go on 'home' leave every year or two. How to make it home here, when home is somewhere else?

(Thomas/1)

One of the families on sabbatical had particularly fine observations on this theme:

H: A lot of people here are extended transients. They may be here 20 years but are still transients. Like the secretaries at work: they are here 20, 25 years, their whole careers, but it never dawned on them not to go back to England. It's surprising to me that people wouldn't be living where they *want* to be living. It's strange. Almost everybody I talk to is not necessarily here because they want to be here, they'd rather be somewhere else.
W: They do their shopping when they go on home leave. They have to go back, get nourishment, then they feel comfortable for another year.
H: They're not assimilated . . . It's an odd place in that respect. In North America after six months you're North American, fully into the system.

(AA/1)

Second, social customs are far more structured and formal in a city such as Geneva: several people said they missed the kind of visits such as those common in Africa, for example, where people simply drop in. Perhaps more important is that in many developing countries the expatriates are culturally, socially and also physically distinct from the local population, immediately identifiable as foreigners. In such situations the foreigners, including those who may have preferred to integrate, tend to band together:

> H: In Geneva we have formed fewer friendships than in any other place we have lived. The system is different. In [the last post] you were all thrown together. You developed close ties to people you worked with.
> W: Here we never see colleagues outside of work. The closest person lives only a few minutes away, but I have never been to his house, and he to mine only once.
> H: Expatriate communities are always closer in developing countries ... Here in Europe there is a lot more that you can do on your own. If you can get spare time you want to try that new little restaurant, or take a weekend trip, or maybe a Sunday drive to see some church. So you don't have the same feeling of solidarity in the expatriate community ... You don't develop the same level of need to spend time with people who are more like you.
>
> (Quincy/3)

The Jacksons took the theme further, observing that some people tend to be attracted to expatriate communities in developing countries:

> H: In our experience the smaller the society, the closer it is. In Africa there's practically no contact with the locals, so you over-talk about experiences with the other expatriates. People talk about the weirdest things – like their crazy aunt – that they wouldn't talk about in Paris or Vienna or somewhere else where you don't get very involved in somebody else's experiences or family problems. There's nothing else to do but watch the sun come up, and there's a lot more conversation about ourselves, our unhappiness, or happiness.
> M: Are you saying people get more intimate?
> H: Yes, not physically, but in relationships, yes. There's nothing else to do.
> M: Would you say it's harder to come to a place like Geneva where you don't have that?
> Both: Definitely, yes.
> W: I know people who just *love* hardship posts. They seek them out. They like to be important, have servants and all that.
>
> (Jackson/2)

In conclusion, the families who had lived in developing countries, or in culturally very different countries, contended that socially, and at least at the beginning of a stay, living in Geneva was more difficult than in what are known as 'hardship posts'. The paradox is that in a culturally relatively similar situation adjustment is thought to pose no special problems, and new residents are not thought to need special help with complicated formalities at the beginning. There are no outside forces to make the expatriate community band together. Except for the very limited company networks there is no homogeneous community into which a newcomer will be immediately welcomed, and many external distractions of things to see and do. In such a situation the newly arriving family must make its own way.

7
SOCIAL SUPPORT FROM WITHIN THE FAMILY

Social support coming from outside the family was discussed in the previous chapter. A major source of support discussed in this chapter is that which comes from within the family itself. Family unity, or sense of itself in relation to the external world, affects how families cope with the strains discussed in Chapter 4. Three of these – separation and loneliness, partners not adjusting well, and encountering different values – are discussed in this chapter. Case histories of the 'organisation' families introduced in Chapter 2 discuss how a strongly bonded family (the Davidsons) helped its members deal with highly stressful situations precipitated by the move, and how a lack of a sense that 'we are all in this together' increased another family's stress (the Madisons). First, however, some basic concepts of family togetherness.

Families operating together

The concept of family togetherness used in this book is that which D. Reiss termed family 'co-ordination', and defined as 'the family's belief that they, in fact, occupy the same experiential world, a world which operates in the same way for all of them' (Reiss, 1981, p. 74). Families high on this characteristic share common principles and patterns of the universe. They work as a group. Co-operative exploration of the environment is facilitated for these families, in contrast with families who tend to approach the world in a less related fashion. Reiss and his colleagues assessed 'co-ordination' by observing the way families worked together at a common task in a laboratory setting: while sorting cards into logical sequences, families high on this dimension continuously shared information and observations with other family members as they arrived at common solutions. In 'low co-ordination families', in contrast, family members each worked separately, coming independently to solutions to their common task.

It was not possible to recreate laboratory conditions in this study to evaluate family 'co-ordination' rigorously and mathematically in the way it was done by Reiss and his team. A family's attitude about itself in relation to the outside world may be sensed, however, from what members say in an interview; from references to a shared sphere, where it is assumed that all family members are influenced by the same things, that what affects one affects all. The data contained several indicators of such an attitude, such as whether or not the family had made an effort to move to the new city together, and also whether they carried out leisure activities together. I asked if families deliberately organised schedules so as to have particular times of the day together, such as breakfasts or dinner time, or other regular events such as the family meetings some mentioned. Verbal and written answers about what the family did were backed up by observations made during the five to eight hours we spent together over a span of two years: of the way children were sent to bed during evening interviews, of what family members had been doing when I arrived for an interview, of just which members it was assumed were to be included when 'the family' was to be interviewed, of reflections made about the activities and absences of family members. A particularly revealing indicator concerning families such as those studied here was just which members it was assumed would travel together on family voyages: some couples frequently left their children with a babysitter and took trips together, whereas others – with children of the same ages – went to great lengths not only to include the children on trips, but to include a range of sights, experiences and foods that would interest both generations. Such observations were backed up by more quantitative indicators from two of the questionnaires used in the study. Table A.9 in the Appendix lists the families considered as operating together in 'the same experiential world' and those that tended to approach the world as less related individuals. These families coped differently with how they went about dealing with loneliness and reconstructing social networks, with separation, and with the strains that occurred when family members were having a difficult time adapting. These strains, introduced in Chapter 4, are the object of the next sections.

High family 'co-ordination', meeting people and family separations

'Openness' was discussed briefly in the previous chapter, as the propensity some families have to open their homes to other people, to actively encourage others to stop by. It was noted that, on the whole, those of the opposite tendency, those who rather tried to protect their intimacy, and who were thus comfortable with being alone, had less trouble adapting to moving to a new culture. This section takes up a related but slightly different theme. 'Openness' and 'co-ordination' refer to somewhat different aspects of family functioning as the former taps the way in which a family relates to the outside world, and the latter the way members are together within the family itself. But the latter clearly affects the former: most of the couples high on 'co-ordination' said that although they felt they were naturally outgoing and sociable, at the same time they felt no urgent need to be surrounded by other people:

> W: [When we first arrived] we were happy to be by ourselves. The preparations were hectic, so when we finally got here it was nice to have a few days to ourselves. It was lovely to just sit and relax, just the four of us, to play cards, be able to go for a walk and not have anybody bother us, or bother [my husband] about work, not have the telephone ring.
>
> (We talk about how they are meeting people since they moved, and they comment:)
>
> W: I take the initiative to phone people. I don't wait for people to phone me. I'm meeting people easily ...
> H: In my work I meet new people every day ... Meeting people is not a problem. It's rather the reverse: keeping them at bay!
> W: I could pick up the phone and arrange a party right now after three months in Geneva. I've met some people I feel very comfortable with, but the good friends won't happen for two or three years ... It takes time. But we also like to be by ourselves. We don't sit around asking ourselves 'do we have any friends?'. Because our relationship is enough for us. If your marriage is not strong I would think it's kind of dicey to go abroad, because all of a sudden you are very dependent on each other's company. Your marriage has to be tough. If you don't really like each other, you're in trouble.
>
> (Kennedy/1)

The Jacksons, took the point a bit further. They actually had trouble understanding how individuals who moved with their families could be lonely:

> M: Something that people find extremely difficult at the beginning is the period during which, if they went away for a few days nobody would notice.
> W: I can understand that if you are single, but not as a family. How could you be lonely? I could never be lonely, even if it's just the two of us.
> H: I would say it's very tough for a single person, but for a family?
>
> (Jackson/3)

Far from seeking social support in community groups such as the wives groups described in the last chapter, both of these couples were critical of people who become very busy attending such activities, and avoided doing so themselves. In fact they made conscious efforts to protect family intimacy:

> W: I never liked women's gatherings, people who have to *do* something, *go* somewhere. There's a lot of that.
> M: How do you explain that you don't need that?
> W: I just don't like chattering.
>
> (Mr Jackson and I both encourage her to come up with a more elaborated explanation.)
>
> W: I don't know. People always ask me to join things, but I just don't want to.
> H: Well I'd hope that we're fairly content with each other and we're not driven out to other activities just to get away from each other . . . We could have a lot of contacts through [work], but don't . . . We don't go out that much . . .
> W: If we want the community we can have it. It's our choice not to. We're very home-oriented.
> H: For example, a friend said to me last week, 'I wanted to invite you over last Saturday, but I knew you had something planned'! We were not going out that day, actually, but whatever we're doing it's planned. Even if we're just sitting at home, it's planned: we've decided what we're going to do with that day. We may have decided to do nothing, but that's a decision we've made.
>
> (Jackson/2)

For families 'living in the same experiential world' it was simply taken for granted that the difficulties of one family member would require action on the part of the others. When the Jackson child had problems, for example (Chapter 5), these were seen to be a family matter: it seemed natural for the mother to rearrange her work schedule to meet her daughter's needs. Similarly, Mr Jackson had said that his child's well-being will determine the place to which he will be willing to move for his next job: if the place is not acceptable he would consider finding another employer. The above examples notwithstanding, it is not the child's needs and wishes that take precedence in the family, nor that of either of the parents. Rather, the needs of each of the members of the family, parents and child, are balanced with those of the others: the whole is taken into account, and in fact takes precedence over the parts.

SOCIAL SUPPORT FROM WITHIN THE FAMILY

Loneliness and meeting people was one of the problems discussed in previous chapters. Another, separation, was also greatly influenced by family 'co-ordination'. In Chapter 4 the socially acceptable theme of duty travel was discussed as a vehicle for a more central but more difficult theme, that of separations. Of interest here are the families who said duty travel was *not* a problem: all were relatively high on family 'co-ordination'. The Batesons illustrate how such families coped:

> M: How is it for the rest of the family when he travels?
> C: We also travel as a family. He travelled a lot in North America too ... It's not that bad.
> W: We usually watch movies and have fun foods he doesn't like. We go out to restaurants he doesn't like. It's just a fun time for us to be together in a different way, really. If he was gone all the time and was a stranger it would be another thing, but that's not the feeling. It's a break in the routine, kind of fun.
> H: Because I really don't do it all that often.
> C: Mom and I will maybe go on a day trip ... Not that it's better at home without him! (All laugh. Her father makes a joke about her being in trouble when I leave.)
>
> (Bateson/2)

Several things are noteworthy about the interchange. The first is the definition of travel: the family was convinced that he 'doesn't really travel all that much', although, objectively, Mr Bateson travelled about the same amount as the husbands in the families for whom their 'extensive travel' was a problem. Second, the family focused on the pleasurable aspects of a change of routine rather than on the separation itself. Mr Bateson enjoyed some aspects of his travelling, sometimes taking extra time to see places he had not seen before. He was frank about his enjoyment, and, rather than complaining about his absence, the other family members were glad for him. As somebody else put the same idea:

> W: This week he's off the coast of Spain at a business meeting with his tennis racket (laugh). Well he deserves it.
>
> (Elm/2)

Third, they all relativised the travel. This was not new: he also travelled a lot for work in North America, and they were also able to travel together for pleasure as a family. Fourth, the family treated with humour what can't be helped: they joked about enjoying the time when one of them is absent. Finally, family members enjoyed being together, but were not bound to one another. In contrast to the women discussed in Chapter 4 who were afraid of getting used to their husbands' absences, they were free to enjoy the difference when one member of the family was absent: 'We just enjoy being together in a different way'. Each family member to some extent goes in his or her own independent direction, and also enjoys the coming together again. In other words, living in the same world means family members can give one another freedom.

We turn now to the other family strain discussed in Chapter 4, the tensions raised when one member of the family is having difficulty adapting. This time it is low family 'co-ordination' that provides the framework for discussion.

Low family 'co-ordination' and family members in difficulty

Several people in the study commented that with a husband learning a new job, and children getting used to new schools, it fell mainly on the wives and mothers to orchestrate emotional well-being for the rest of the family.[6]

> W: I think it's one of the hardest things a wife and mother has to pull together, to handle the physical and emotional work of moving and guiding a family through it, plus her own emotional upheaval. Doing it successfully is a big job. Your husband is busy getting oriented to a new job, there's pressure on him. So it is up to the wife and mother to pick up all the loose ends.
>
> (Vance/1)

There was considerable difference, however, in just how much a woman's difficulties in this respect were shared and discussed with the outside world as well as within families and between spouses. It was in low 'co-ordination' families, especially, that several women felt that to best help their families with the adjustment they should keep their own difficulties to themselves. In other words they felt they should maintain a strong facade. The best example occurred in the Allen family:

> The Allen family had an extremely difficult first year, with many stressful events in addition to the move to Geneva: an unplanned pregnancy; a premature birth at the time of which, to make matters worse, Mr Allen was on another continent and could not be reached; a baby with a number of worrisome health problems;

---

6 See, also, a substantial literature directed towards people 'moving abroad', for example Piet-Pelon and Hornby, 1985; Albright et al., 1986; Kohls, 1979; McCollum, 1990; Seidenberg, 1973.

two or three accidents which immobilised one family member or another; adolescents who gave their parents cause for concern in their personal development and at school. They were in the midst of these things when I first interviewed the family, but talked about none of them, choosing to focus instead on the numerous small complaints and hassles on which they were quoted in Chapter 3. It was only a year or two later, once the worst was well past, that they were able to talk about the most stressful times, and about the extent to which the wife had felt responsible for the emotional management in the family:

M: You had a really stressful first year.
W: It was a lot, and one thing after another. And trying not to let anybody notice exactly how you felt (tears). I couldn't have said anything to [my husband] or to the kids about how I really felt that first year because I thought, if I start to say just how unhappy I felt I just would have lost it. So I kept it all to myself. It was easier . . . We were all having a hard time. For the kids, especially, you had to be strong.
M: You kept up a front for the kids.
W: Yes, and [my husband] too. He had his own worries at work.

It was only at this point, almost two years later, and after I had opened the door by raising the subject of stress, that the Allens revealed the most stressful of the events of the first year. One of their adolescent children had witnessed a suicide. The child had been present by sheer happenstance, and the victim was a stranger, but the event, described in vivid detail, had been traumatic. It had also been difficult to know just how to help the child, who had been unwilling to discuss it. We talked about the event itself, then discussed the family's unwillingness to refer to it at the time:

W: I probably didn't mention it. I think when we spoke the first time we discussed the insignificant things like going grocery shopping.
M: You talked about the cars, about how you weren't happy with the house, that sort of thing.
W: But not on a real personal level. I was very cautious as to exactly how I worded everything. If anybody asked me I'd say: 'Yes, well, we're adjusting'.

(Allen/3)

Mrs Allen chose to try to keep family waters smooth by keeping her troubles to herself. In other families, such as the Zeligs and the Smithers discussed in Chapter 4, tensions were more open, although here too the husbands tended to side-step problems by slipping into a joke. But the point here is that low 'co-ordination' in families means that one member will be more liable to be left to cope on his or her own, refraining from formulating a request that could result in assistance, trying not to 'rock the boat'.

Imbalances of authority, encountering different values

Family strains, of course, are not limited to those between husbands and wives. Relations between parents and children, also, may shift in subtle ways when the family is living in a foreign country, in the absence of the external structure normally available in the home culture. Several contributing factors have already appeared throughout the chapters, such as dual careers, preoccupation with stresses and hassles that make it difficult to assist other members of the family, or vague feelings of parental guilt. Another theme that appeared was that of the imbalances of authority and of power relations within a family. Such imbalances may occur when children learn the local language faster and more adequately than their parents. Although most of the parents who participated in this study talked proudly of their children's progress in French, and several told anecdotes about their children understanding the language better than they did, or being able to interpret for them, in families who went beyond English-speaking subculture in Geneva such differences in fluency could give children more power than they might otherwise have had, and potentially undermine parental authority. The problem occurs when parents become dependent on their children for translations. Those in the study most affected by such dependence were the high 'co-ordination' Davidson family, who freely recognised the potential problem, and could also laugh about it:

> W: It's a reversal of roles, and you have to be careful. There has to be a balance. The children have to maintain the same respect for you whether you are fluent in that language or not. At the same time we also have to appreciate the effort they've gone to to learn all the French they have.
> M: That's a potential problem for some families.
> H: It's not unresolved with us. For example if we're talking to an auto mechanic I will take [our 13-year-old] with me if there's something I can't explain. I will ask him to translate and he will say: 'Why do you want to say that?' Rather than just do it he begins to critique it. It's a little bit of an embarrassment. It's awkward sometimes because they realise the roles are reversed.

> W: It is not all that easy for them. It's hard for them to shift gears. They are talking about things they don't understand.
> H: A normal child doesn't deal with a plumber or a mechanic. It's not expected of them in a normal home.
> W: ... Teenagers sometimes have a lot of disregard and disrespect for the parents. And if parents look dumb that doesn't help.
>
> (Davidson/3)

Or as they had said a year before:

> H: We've never had anybody ridicule us at all about our French.
> W: Other than our own children (laugh).
>
> (Davidson/2)

One of the potential strains for families discussed in Chapter 3 was that of encountering values quite different from those to which they had been used. Here, too, there is risk of introducing differences that potentially add to a family's feelings of perplexity and alienation, as well as possibly creating imbalances between generations. One of the examples in Chapter 3 was that of the Zelig family, who had been shocked at seeing women going topless at the swimming pool. More than two years later the family was only slightly more at ease with the different norm, and coped by making a detour around it:

> W: I still don't like it but have to live with it ... We don't positively *avoid* the beach, but we try to see the things we really want to see while we are here, and the beach is not one of them.
>
> (Zelig/5)

Since the precipitating factor is the same, the contrast with another family is striking. With the same cause of unease, and many other similarities (children practically the same age, never having lived overseas before, working for 'the company') the higher co-ordination Wood family used the difference as an occasion to discuss their own values:

> M: What about different values, like kids having more money, or ideas about drinking?
> W: We've run into the money thing, yes. Others have more, but others have less too. This has sometimes made me uncomfortable, and my children uncomfortable, but it has given us an opportunity to sit down and talk about money, and to reassess our own values too. I think values are something you

teach in your home. We talk about differences, things I don't think are right.

H: My wife doesn't drink, but I do, so that's one difference the children are exposed to ... What we're exposed to here, that they're not exposed to at home, is a visual thing – on the beaches here the ladies are not dressed as we would think they should be (little laugh, and a joke).

W: But that's the real world. It's the world they live in. I think it's better for the children to have the exposure. How can you have values unless they are in contrast with something different? A value is something you feel strongly about because it's good for you.

(Wood/3)

The two citations illustrate opposite ways of dealing with one particular difference the families have encountered. Neither approved of the different way of dressing, but one family side-stepped the issue, whereas the other used it as an occasion to re-examine, and possibly to reinforce, their own ideas and values. Several of the families participating in the study volunteered that, far from causing problems, they thought it was good for children to run into other values. They agreed that the encounter with people who think differently had provided a chance for their own family to reflect upon, and perhaps strengthen, their ideas about right and wrong. Successfully handled, the result can be that adolescents, especially, in encountering different values in a different culture, may have forged a set of their own attitudes and values stronger than they might otherwise have been. The point here is that high 'co-ordination', or 'living in the same experiential world', will clearly facilitate such working through for families.

Two case studies make up the remainder of the chapter, discussing two families who were dealing with significant stress. The first was low on 'co-ordination', the second high.

The Madison family: low 'co-ordination' and significant stress

The Madison family was one of the two 'organisation' families sketched in Chapter 2. When I first contacted them by telephone asking for an interview, Mrs Madison agreed readily, even eagerly, but said her husband was very busy supervising refugee settlement in a war that had just broken out half way around the world. At the moment he normally arrived home from work between 9:00 in the evening and midnight. As she had predicted, we were able to make an appointment when things calmed down a month later. At the first interview we talked about the extensive travel he had been doing for his work, and how he had been working especially hard since the most recent troubles, including during the recent holiday period:

M: What did you do at Christmas?
H: Dealt with refugees. A colleague's daughter and our daughter held 'the organisation' together for the crisis on Christmas Eve when no one could reach us because the switchboard was closed ... [My wife] is happy since at least she saw me for a couple of hours on Christmas Day (he laughs).

But this is the nature of the work I do ... I'm away three months out of the year on the average. But even when I'm in Geneva I'm not necessarily at home: when there's a crisis going on I may get home at two in the morning then go off again by seven.

(Madison/1)

The work obviously made great personal demands, and Mr Madison mentioned that the family had no vacation during the summer because of work pressures. At the same time he spoke with enormous pleasure of his children's involvement in it, when he talked about his daughter's contribution on Christmas Eve, or when he proudly mentioned seeing his children's pictures in a magazine article describing some of the activities of 'the organisation'. The pre-adolescent children as yet had little to say about the way the family functioned or about their contributions to their father's work, but during the second interview it became clear that Mrs Madison did not quite share her husband's commitment. In a discussion that became quite tense we explored the strains that such unshared commitment can put on families:

W: [My husband] is a workaholic.
M: How does that affect the family?
W: I don't mind the hours unless they interfere with my life (he laughs).

(She talks of an incident three weeks before, when she had returned from a trip in the middle of the evening to find that her husband was still at the office. The pre-adolescent children had been alone since they came home from school, and had not had dinner. He protests, and they argue about whether or not the plans he had made for the children's dinner were realistic. She goes on to another example. Tension mounts as they argue about who in the family is or is not available to go on vacations at various intervals during the year, and refer to an incident they agree not to discuss at the moment ...)

SOCIAL SUPPORT FROM WITHIN THE FAMILY

H: I'm a normal individual that does a job, that's all. She says I'm a workaholic.
M: Well, you do work long hours.
H: So did my father.
W: He rarely saw his dad in the evenings, or weekends, or even on vacations ... They didn't do a lot of things together, but he grew up to be a very responsible mature person, to have a responsible job, and he doesn't see why his children can't grow up to be the same way.

(She looks to her husband, who nods his permission, and goes on to describe severe problems in the extended family, some of which they both attribute to parental absence. Then they try to put things in perspective:)

H: [My wife] complains, but she knew about my work style before we got married. She worked with [an organisation that operates under similar conditions]. There's no easy solution to the problems. Oil rig people work six months on and six months off. Military wives have similar problems.
W: (agrees) I'd rather have [my husband] as a workaholic than as another kind of person. That's an evil that I feel I can live with ... His mother used to tell him if you're sitting there doing nothing you're wasting. ...
H: ... your life.
W: ... you must be doing something. [My husband] cannot go to the beach and sit and relax. He has to be doing something, so if he goes to the beach he either takes work with him, or he takes the newspaper and starts marking things, which is working.
H: [My wife] worked for 'the organisation' for five years, so she's seen the good side and the bad side. There are times when she's had enough, and she lets me know. She acts as a brake: she gets me away from it so I can get myself back together again.
(Madison/2)

The work was objectively demanding, and in contexts dealing with crises there was also a certain amount of pressure, both objective and social, to work long and hard. Even within this context, however, Mr Madison was notorious: he was referred to by one or two others in the study as being at the far end of a hypothetical continuum of workaholic ways. This was undoubtedly partly his own fault: part of his attention throughout one of the interviews was devoted to a routine job that somebody in his position should have delegated. Also, as he made clear in the passage cited above, he obviously learned to be this way in his family of origin.

The family had other problems, however. They had arrived with debts, and one salary with 'the organisation' was not enough to keep them out of financial difficulty. After a year or so Mrs Madison obtained a full-time 'secretarial support' job with 'the government'. This was not the best of jobs. The good thing was that it was easy to arrange time off to be with the children or visitors, but Mrs Madison said she was thoroughly bored until one of her co-workers went on sick leave, leaving her, with two jobs to be done, enough work to keep her occupied. For various technical reasons Mrs Madison received a salary less than half of that of the person sitting next to her doing the same thing. She was paid far less than she would have to pay someone to help with the house cleaning, and the interview in which we discussed family division of housework became tense indeed. Another problem that was brewing by the third interview was that the problematical family members left in North America were now talking of moving to Geneva – in order to be able to live closer to the Madison family.

The Madison family was low on 'co-ordination': they were rarely together for meals, and travelled separately (partly because work occupied so much of the time of one member of the family). In the interviews it was only Mrs Madison who talked about children's schoolwork and other activities, whereas Mr Madison talked about the children mainly in reference to his pride in their participation in his work. In a word, Mr Madison was deeply committed to his work for 'the organisation', but the commitment was mainly *his* commitment: the rest of the family followed along as well as they could. The strains on the family are obvious, and the Madisons let us see some of the cracks. The risk, of course, is that of growing apart over the long term. At the moment Mrs Madison was complaining, and the couple were quarrelling: there is no reason to suppose that the sort of tense argument they had while I was there was a unique event. On the other hand they were in some sort of equilibrium, with Mr Madison acknowledging that his wife's protests at least prevented him from disappearing entirely into his work.

What does this have to do with moving? Spending long hours working, or commitment to a profession, is, after all, hardly unique to people who migrate to a new culture. Nor are unsatisfying and underpaid jobs for women. The point here is that when a transcultural move intervenes, an additional source of stress is added to an already difficult situation: tension may be more severe since family members are away from their usual supports. In addition, moving around the world, or at least extensive travel, is built into the work in which people such as Mr Madison are engrossed. If moving comes with the job, then the sorts of family strains they discuss also come with the job. The second case study shows how high 'co-ordination' can help a family cope with these strains and others.

The Davidson family: high 'co-ordination' and significant stress

The Davidsons' reasons for moving were discussed briefly in Chapter 2: Mr and Mrs Davidson had come to Geneva with three of their six children, and after several moves to developing countries, so that Mr Davidson could take a position in 'the organisation'. This, he said, was to be 'the summit of his career'. The family's plan was to stay until Mr Davidson retired in ten years or so, then to settle in the place to which they felt strongly attached in North America. As for Mrs Davidson, although she had training in a technical field, and proudly told me she had maintained her licence, she had been thoroughly occupied helping the growing family throughout their numerous moves across cultures. She was contentedly home-oriented, and in fact the Davidson household so invariably smelled of baking when I visited that the odour of carrot cake seemed to float around the tapes months later as I was transcribing the interviews with the Davidson family.

Their religion was very important to the Davidsons: family members prayed together at meal times and observed several religious rules that made them somewhat different from their colleagues and neighbours. They attended church regularly, and had usually quickly become leaders in the church they attended throughout their moves. Their religious affiliation was also an extremely important and effective source of social support: church-related networks mobilised rapidly to provide all sorts of informational, practical and emotional supports to members in need. During the three years I followed them, for example, it was with the help of network members that the Davidsons found not only one, but two quite exceptional houses, then successively moved their possessions into them. Similarly, the interviews were full of passing mentions of giving or receiving assistance to or from church members, but also from a host of others such as neighbours, police, sales people and simple passers-by. Such support included giving and receiving food, providing shelter, help with the children's homework and with translating, listening to troubles and providing counsel. Although none of the family spoke French, they had decided – together – to take the more difficult path of having the children attend local schools rather than the International Schools attended by most of the other children in the study. They had expected the children's first year at school to be difficult and stressful, and also that they would probably lose an academic year in the process.[7] However they also expected the end results to be worth the extra complication, and

---

[7] Policies in North American schools may make it extremely uncommon for a child to repeat a year of schooling. Such is not the case in Geneva, where even a bright child may for one reason or another repeat an academic year. Such 'loss' of a year does not necessarily carry stigma or damage future academic prospects.

considered stress to be a normal part of moving, with which a united family could help. At the time of the first interview five months after they moved to Geneva:

> H: The children are not well accepted by their peers yet. They come home with stories of being bullied or picked on or called names because they don't speak the language. We try to explain that it's this way in any society when a foreign kid comes. They will prove themselves this year.
> W: We all have so many adjustments to make, and of course it's a supercomplication, but it's not unusual. We know that this too will pass.
> H: As a family we have our own built-in support systems. A single parent would have more of a challenge. We adults have stress too: a different work environment, and we can't communicate with the neighbours very well. But we can all get in the car and go for a drive or something.
> (Davidson/1)

Several members of the family were still under stress a year later. School difficulties had caused stomach-aches and other stress-related problems for the child described as a perfectionist and competitive, and the two other children had been kept back one or two academic years before they finally found that they could function adequately. Changing houses for a second time had caused some temporary financial difficulties (about which the family did not complain, however. They said the situation would soon resolve itself, and that in the meantime they were coping by reducing expenses, for example by giving home-made Christmas gifts). Furthermore, Mrs Davidson said she was having some minor health problems. But it was Mr Davidson's professional situation that was perhaps the most stressful. The job described as the summit of his career was not working out as expected. At the second interview, after describing his pleasure at being able to work at a world level, and at being in a position to perhaps put his ideas into effect, he also mentioned budget cuts, restructuring, and doing more bureaucratic work and less substance than he would like. He had thought this was temporary, but his position of lesser responsibility than he had anticipated had become permanent by the next year. He had been affected by a restructuring programme, and was struggling with what was in effect a demotion.

To cope with the stress he felt, Mr Davidson jogged every day, and his commitment to family and community life helped him maintain perspective. He also attempted to maintain perspective by reframing, interpreting his hierarchical loss of professional status as a chance to master a somewhat different set of tasks and defining it as a purely administrative event, carried out independently of individual merit or performance. It is, however, Mrs Davidson's support that was striking in the following exchanges, as she listened to what her husband had to tell me, then gently asked a probing question, or made a suggestion, to help him bring out aspects that were difficult for him:

M: (to him) Tell me how the work is going.
H: Well, since you were here last my office has undergone some organisational restructuring. This has been a bit traumatic in the last year because my role has changed. I'm no longer chief of a unit ... It's not just our family that has been subject to this reorientation and role of the father. Everybody in the division, about 80 people, has gone through a period of uncertainty, career identity crisis and role reversals.
W: But didn't you say it's run straight through the organisation?
H: Yes, division after division ... I have been moved from being an administrator over a unit to being just an ordinary professional ... I've always liked doing what I'm doing now, it's been a secondary interest of mine, but it's becoming the main thing. It's challenging, and I've accepted this as being an opportunity to learn some new talents, new strategies, new approaches. I have a chief who is very bright, very hard-working, probably the most dynamic person in our whole division in terms of ability to get work done. It's a challenge to work with him ...
W: You did mention, though, that your chief is the kind who has to have the last word on everything, which makes it difficult.
H: Yes. He and I have had several very frank discussions. We sit down and express our feelings and views. Months back I made it very clear to him that I admired his work ethic, that I would adapt and learn as much as I could from him, but that I'm not going to become a workaholic like he is. I think he accepted that pretty well. I said it in a very open, non-hostile way and he and I have a very good rapport now.

(She mentions again that others have found it very frustrating working with this particular boss, giving an example.)

H: This is not too unique though ... I've had a discussion with someone who worked with him for five years, and they got awfully frustrated with him. But I think I've seen beyond that. I think I've accepted him as someone with whom I can work, from whom I can learn, rather than seeing him as someone who is imposed upon me. I've tried to turn it around as a more positive opportunity to grow.

W: But you have to come to acceptance of that feeling.

H: Yes, you have to. You go through a lot of frustration ... I think I've felt more stressed in the last year than I've felt in a long time, because it's been unknown, hidden things, lack of definition for what your activities are, maybe feeling a lack of acceptance. I couldn't identify uncertainties. But my body knew I was under stress.

(Davidson/3)

The point to the above extract is the way in which Mrs Davidson gently brings her husband to see the opposite side of the story he is telling. He determinedly wishes to see the positive, and it is his wife who helps him formulate and express the negative feelings that, as he says himself, are there anyway, and are better ventilated. In other words her role is not just that of logistical helpmate, but emotional also. Clearly, the two are sharing the same emotional world, as they do with the rest of the family also. The Davidson family, in sum, was strikingly united in their commitment to their religious ideals and to each other, and their commitment, as well as their 'co-ordination', their sharing of the same 'emotional space', clearly helped individual family members deal not only with the potential disequilibrium in the family caused by their children's more rapid adaptation, but even with relatively severe psychological stress.

Discussion

The importance of 'co-ordination' for helping a family adapt after a move to a new culture is clear. High 'co-ordination' families are very much more than the sum of their parts: the world of husband and of wife, as well as those of the children, comprise 'our world', as opposed to the separate worlds of members of lower 'co-ordination' families. Families who 'live in the same experiential world', who 'come from the same place', who operate together rather than as a collection of individuals, are clearly at an advantage when they are removed from their usual social supports, as they are when they have just moved to a new culture. Loneliness, one of the major strains discussed in Chapter 2, is a strain such families have difficulty comprehending. Members are less likely to rush off into the first group or friendship offered, thus less likely to later find themselves entangled in unsatisfying relationships that had been based mainly on mutual need for company. They are also, paradoxically, less afraid of the absences of other family members, absences that were another major source of distress after a move: spouses who are 'living in the same experiential world' can, at least to a degree, share an experience that only one of them may have. To caricature just a bit, they both enjoy the tennis, although only one of them is 'off the coast of Spain at a business meeting with his tennis racket'. More substantially, as in the example of the high 'co-ordination' Davidson family discussed at length in this chapter, one spouse can help the other formulate, recognise, bring out the difficulties he or she is experiencing, and the entire family may thus be able to maintain relative serenity in the face of fairly severe stress. In the example discussed family members were even able to choose a more difficult route – having the children attend local schools – in pursuit of a goal they valued – a degree of integration in the new place.

Low 'co-ordination' families, on the other hand, rather than living in 'their world' portray a feeling that between husband and wife theirs is 'his world' and 'her world'. The two worlds may not have a great deal to do with each other. In the example discussed in this chapter one aspect of the world of one of the family members, Mr Madison's work, was very highly invested, and required a very high degree of commitment, commitment that was not necessarily shared by the rest of the family. Each member coped (or in the case of Mrs Madison's poorly paid and non-gratifying job, floundered) relatively independently. In case of problems in adapting to the new culture, members of low 'co-ordination' families feel they need to keep their difficulties to themselves: they cope alone, and try to keep a brave face for the rest of the family.

The next three chapters discuss outcome, or the effects the move had on the families that were studied. Chapter 8 serves as a transition, focusing on the effect of the move for the children. Chapter 9 describes events occurring over two years for each of the families, and discusses two case histories at some length. Chapter 10 then discusses the effect of the move for the families as units.

8
EFFECTS ON CHILDREN

As they did in the discussion of strains on families in Chapter 4, it is the three couples who came together for a group interview who introduce the effects moving can have on their children:

> Mrs J: They discovered lots of different languages. There are people from 17 or 18 different countries in each class at the school.
>
> Mrs Y: They were able to really experience not being able to speak the language . . . We *knew* people spoke French here, but it was different actually experiencing it. The younger child, who is usually not shy about trying things, really clammed up. It was a long time before he was willing to try *anything*. Now he's not afraid to try, and he's realised that many of the kids in his class speak several different languages fluently . . .
>
> Mrs J: We had the same experience. Our younger child . . . was just totally taken aback by this *wall* of language he felt he couldn't penetrate . . .
>
> Mrs Y: And they are learning about different countries . . .
>
> Mr Y: I think that when they grow up, having lived in another country will have corrected a political bias you get living in [a major North American city]. You get other views of world politics.
>
> Mrs J: They now have friends from countries they'd never even *heard* of, and that makes a big difference in their world view . . . They are interested in their classmates' countries. There are difficult kids, and there are bullies, just like at any other school, but in general there's a sense of supporting one another and accepting the kids for whoever they are, with their differences. Whereas the kids in the schools we've been familiar with in North America really emphasise conformity. They want everybody to be alike. Here it doesn't matter if a kid doesn't wear the same kinds of clothes the others do. Nobody really cares . . .

Mr Y: A couple of other things will affect them when they grow up: in our travels here we've probably exposed them to a lot more cultural and artistic things than we would have at home. (murmurs of agreement)

Mr J: ... simply the fact that travel is interesting. To most people where we live travel outside the *state* is unpleasant and dangerous.

Mr Y: ... how to find a place to stay, even late at night ...

Mrs J: ... you can travel and have a good time even if none of you speak the language ...

Mrs Y: ... realising when you are in another country that, in contrast, you know more French than you think. Taking kids to art museums and so forth because if you want to go they have to come, and they end up enjoying it. Learning mythology. Developing a taste for ruins because they are something you can climb, and they have interesting insects and lizards. I grew up thinking that certain things were boring, because I didn't do them very often ... They don't have that mind set.

Mr Y: In such things as eating they've been a lot more adventuresome than they would have.

Mr L: You mean they didn't notice the McDonald's every three blocks in Paris? (laughs)

Mr Y: It doesn't interest them any more. And there are some things that are just totally bizarre – we were sitting in a restaurant in Paris at lunch and all of a sudden the 11-year-old said 'You know, I think it's about time I tried snails!'

Mrs Y: I told him: 'Get serious, order a steak!'

Mr Y: And, you know, he did try snails, and he's had them since. I don't know why. Maybe it's the water (laughs). They're trying more things than I think they would have in North America.

When they arrived, the 28 families brought 55 children, then added two more. The children ranged in age from the two who were born during the study to 18 years old. In addition, 14 older children remained in North America, at university, or working. This section makes a slight detour, to discuss the effects of moving on children. Although the whole focus of the study is to see the family as a whole, and not to separate worker, spouse, or child from his or her context, at the same time some effects specific to children are simply due to their age and development. Shifting the focus, turning the object on its side so to speak, helps shed some light, to prepare for a discussion of the effects on the family as a whole. The discussion starts with school-aged children, before turning to their younger and older siblings.

School-aged children

Although most parents said that the well-being of their children was a major factor influencing the decision to move, this, of course, was the parents' definition of the children's well-being. The children, had I asked them, might have formulated opinions quite differently:

> H: Choosing where we are going to move next is beyond our child's age. At 12 years old she has very facile desires ... We would try to make her feel part of it, but she is not going to be very adaptable to listening to reasoning that has nothing to do with her.
> M: It's your decision, taking into account what you think is best for her.
> H: Yes. We try to talk to her about it, but what she would like is to move to southern California and have a swimming pool and have movie stars say: 'Hello Beth.' (We all laugh.) But we're not going to do that (laugh).
>
> (Jackson/3)

Moving for the children was tinged with regret at leaving the old place and apprehension as to what living in this new place might bring. The poignancy of leaving and arriving had usually dissipated by the time I interviewed the families, but occasionally was portrayed. Mrs Foster, for example, told of finding nine-year-old Sam sitting on the floor of his empty bedroom, crying, shortly before the family left North America, the packers gone, the house empty. Six months later Sam complained to me that he can never get to sleep at night in the new house. He had arrived in the winter from a warm climate, and talked of how cold and boring the first winter in Geneva had been for him. The weather was always bad, there were hardly any other children outside to play with, and in any case they were not friendly, and moreover 'most of them speak French, and I don't want to learn French'.

School-aged children are very much affected by two decisions made by their parents: the time of the school year at which the family moves, and the type of school chosen. There were several indications that arriving during the school year, when a child would have to break into already existing friendship groups, posed more problems than did arriving during the summer vacation, after which classes are usually formed in new configurations: all but one of the families who arrived after the school year had started complained of school-related problems of one sort or another, whereas only half of those who arrived during the summer break reported problems. The other side of the coin was that children who arrived over the summer vacation faced the prospect of an unknown school. One family (the Thomases) defused such anxiety by arranging to arrive in time so that the children could attend the new school for a few days before the holidays instead of dreading the unknown for several weeks.

There were many new things to get used to in the new schools: classrooms were different, and there were cultural differences from the schools the children had previously attended. Some teachers had a style and a language that needed getting used to: the 'waste basket' suddenly became a 'rubbish bin', and at least one child was shocked when he encountered the somewhat brutally frank: 'Come here, Paul, I want to see why you screwed up so badly', rather than the kindly and far less direct North American: 'Do you have any questions, can I help you?' In a phenomenon of newness obviously all the more striking in the local schools, the focus was suddenly shifted on matters that ranged all the way from what one wears and has for lunch to how world events are perceived, and the influence of one's country in these events.

A major decision families had to make when they arrived was whether to put the children in the local school or in one of several private schools available. The most popular choice among the latter was the 'International School', which specialises in educating children of families such as those studied, in either French or English. Some parents chose the International School simply because somebody had recommended it, but others had reasoned that their children would adapt better since the school caters specifically to the needs of foreign children. Most of those families whose career assignments involved moving through several countries felt there would be more continuity for their children if they attended a series of similar International Schools wherever they lived. Others thought their children would need to be educated in English since it would be in that language that they would pursue higher education in North America.

A number of the families in the study chose to put their children in local schools, in a language that was foreign to all but one of them. Almost all did so deliberately, so that their children would learn French, and also so that they might be able to integrate into the local community. Most of those who chose this route had done so with full knowledge that this was the more difficult course. By the end of the study, among the relatively small number of families studied here, most of the children who had started out in local schools had for a number of different reasons been transferred to the International School that was thought to be more oriented towards their needs. It should be noted, however, that all of the children whose parents insisted they learn French (including in the International School) had done so by two or three years after they moved. Some became bilingual.

School-aged children had experiences with new friends similar to those of their parents: finding a good friend the first days after the move could make a very significant difference for a child's immediate adaptation.

EFFECTS ON CHILDREN

As Mrs Kennedy put it: 'all it takes is one friend each'. As with adults, 'first friends' could be both very important and double-edged (see Chapter 6), however. For example, the transition was greatly facilitated for one nine-year-old when she was befriended by an English-speaking classmate, but the relationship with her former helper later became difficult when the new girl outstripped her friend, and the other children started teasing the helper about how much better her *protégée* was now doing.

Some of the children in the families studied were described as being inherently sociable, able to simply go up to people and make friends regardless of language. They did adequately at school, but as children who 'would just rather be playing', tended not to be remarkable students. Such children quickly and easily made new friends, and their adaptation was described as having been remarkably easy. On the other hand, moving was especially difficult for the children described as shy, private, quiet. One seven-year-old, 'a quiet child who likes structure and stable situations' kept drawing pictures of the family's North American house. The five school-aged children in the main sample of the study who were of mixed race were reported to have found themselves more at ease in an international setting than in the more homogeneous North American ones, but other children who were different for one reason or another could have trouble. Their capacities and limitations had been recognised in their former settings, but they had to make themselves known all over again in the new place:

> W: Our 11-year-old is very big and looks much older. He's been having a hard time. At home his friends and the others at school know he's big but clumsy, and has trouble with gym and so forth. They just accept that ... But here he keeps being treated as though he should be older and able to do better.
>
> H: The first time we went to the school we went into the library. The librarian told him he couldn't take out a book, because this was the library for the lower school. She didn't even ask him how old he was. He told her he *was* in the lower school. He's had to live through these things again that had already been dealt with in North America.
>
> (Y/1)

As might be expected, children who had acquired a reputation for being bright in their former schools had to start over again and prove their brightness. Several parents talked of the fact that their children could no longer count on receiving good grades on the basis of their reputations as good students. Similarly, the transition seems to have been much more difficult for children who had been leaders before they left, who had to

EFFECTS ON CHILDREN

carve out a new social space after they moved. Benjamin Allen is the best example:

> The second child, Benjamin was described by his parents as having always been as close as possible to a perfect child. Twelve years old when the family moved, he had been in a special school programme for gifted young people. He had never been very 'social', not because he was shy, but simply because he didn't need to seek others out: he was content to play at his friends' houses. Indeed, reading between the lines of his parents' descriptions, he seems to have been a natural leader, casually comfortable with himself and looked up to by other children.
>
> Coming from an environment in which he had been known, secure and protected (and driven around by his parents) he had a very difficult time at first. He had trouble with freedom, such as that given by public transport, and according to his mother 'changed personality' from being 'very secure and comfortable with himself', to being 'insecure, needing to be popular, trying to be someone that he's not'. He was bored and unhappy at school, transferring to French, then to boarding school in an attempt to give him both some challenge and some structure. Adolescence intervened, and his continuing struggle with freedom got him into trouble with both school and parents on issues involving trust and responsibility.
>
> By the end of the study Benjamin had changed schools for a third time, and was back at home. He had done something serious enough to make his parents punish him rather severely, forbidding him to leave the house in the evenings for several weeks. He remained present for most of the last interview with the family: he was resentful and somewhat sullen in several of the things he said, but also commented that he'd given his parents every reason not to trust him. As for his parents, they were firm in their restriction, yet at the same time allowed him to not discuss the details of whatever it was that had got him into trouble.
>
> In Benjamin's case the family's move would seem to he heading towards having very long-term consequences: breaking away from the family for this child, now an adolescent, involved distancing himself from their North American culture in ways that could well become permanent. His parents assumed he would be going to university in North America in three years or so, but Benjamin was proclaiming that he wanted to stay in Geneva, and to become a Swiss citizen. Already, and in contrast with the other members of the family, especially with his brother just one year younger, he talked and dressed very much like a European, had abandoned

baseball in favour of tennis and skiing, and wanted to travel around and stay in youth hostels rather than accompany his parents on 'home leave' . . .

One benefit few had anticipated at the outset was more freedom in space than most had experienced in North America – and thus increased independence. Safe and reliable public transport was available in Geneva, meaning that, starting somewhere between the ages of seven and nine, a child could move around the city alone or with friends, without having to be driven around by parents as in most North American settings. The change required some negotiation and getting used to for some of the families, but was ultimately liberating, giving children a freedom and independence they might not otherwise have had.

Overall, parents found that the benefits of living abroad for their children were those they had hoped for when they moved: a broader outlook, increased knowledge of the world and of its peoples, learning a language, acquiring experience and skills in meeting new people. Mr and Mrs Renton, for example, talked proudly of how their child, around the age of nine, went off with his lunch bag for a whole day of judo in French in a group in which he knew no one. They remarked that this sort of adventure was bound to help him in the future. Such skills may well be learned over many moves and startings-over in new schools: it is perhaps not by happenstance that some of the children who had moved the most were among those described as having the skills of meeting new people easily.

Younger children

Two babies were born to the families during the study. The Ogbourne pregnancy was planned, and the birth and infancy went smoothly and easily. The baby in the Allen family, on the other hand, conceived during the move, came as a surprise. The family was experiencing a number of other difficulties, and Mrs Allen was having her own problems adapting, but trying to keep up a brave front for the rest of the family (Chapter 7). The baby was born prematurely, and had a very difficult first year. Whether or not his difficulties may have been caused by the family situation of stress, it is certainly plausible that they were influenced thereby. In any case many of the family's other problems were resolved during their second year in Geneva, at which time the baby's health problems also cleared up.

As for somewhat older children, before they moved parents in almost all of the families had given a great deal of thought to how their children might react (Chapter 2). School-aged children and adolescents would be interrupting habits and leaving circles of friends, and their parents had expected to devote extra time and attention to them just after the move.

EFFECTS ON CHILDREN

What was unexpected, however, was that it was among the nine pre-school children in the study (aged 1½ to 4 years) that perhaps the most difficulties were encountered.

Quite apart from any other events and processes that may have been occurring in their families, strikingly similar disorientation was described among several of the small children. The children were too young to understand the explanations adults may have given about time and space around the move, and they had experienced a number of changes of habitat. Families typically moved from their house to a hotel and/or to grandparents while the packing was being done in North America, then to an apartment while waiting for their possessions to arrive in Geneva. Many had also used the waiting time to go on vacation, thus adding at least two more temporary changes of abode – to a vacation hotel or apartment, then back to the temporary housing – before finally taking possession of the place they would eventually be inhabiting. Somewhere in the midst of all these various housing changes the children kept asking when they were going 'home', calling the new home a nice hotel, asking to go back to where the family had just been staying. Three of the children were very disoriented. The three-year-old Ogbourne child, for example, became upset if either of her parents merely left the room, and became extremely anxious when she saw an apartment recently left empty by the neighbours with whom the family had become friendly. The four-and-a-half-year-old Smithers child became, in his mother's words, very 'negative', 'demanding', and 'nasty' with his younger sibling (Chapter 5). As for the four-year-old Renton child, she was often found lying awake in the middle of the night, or would pick up a blanket and wander off to find somewhere different in the house to sleep. Described by her parents as a heretofore 'happy, talkative, outgoing child', she withdrew, was sad, practically stopped talking for a year, and also experienced many minor illnesses.

Their parents had not been expecting trouble with any of these children. On the contrary, they had been exceptionally 'easy, good natured' children, and it is possible, although paradoxical, that it was precisely because the children had always been 'easy' that nobody had anticipated trouble, and that the parents had not anticipated the children's very natural lack of maturity in conceptualising space and time. Although the Rentons and the Smithers had been quite worried about their child, and had considered seeking psychiatric help, in all three families the problems eventually cleared up without outside intervention. Both families who made visits back to North America during the first summer remarked that the visit had helped, demonstrating to the child – exactly as when a younger child plays peek-a-boo – that loved ones were still there.

It is noteworthy that in the instances in which the children's difficulties took longer to resolve other family members were also having difficulties (Mrs Renton with putting aside her career [Chapters 2, 4 and 5] and the

Smithers family with Mr Smithers' increasingly demanding and unsatisfactory job situation [Chapter 4]). Parents' temporary adaptation problems had repercussions in other families as well, such as the Rodgers. The family was living in a hotel during the difficult first few weeks. Mrs Rodgers, who had never left North America or even thought about travelling, was wondering about the wisdom of the decision to move (Chapter 3). Mr Rodgers was away on frequent business trips, leaving his wife, during a period in which it seemed to rain constantly, to fight with public transport every morning to take the older child to school, and to find a way to spend the rest of the day with the three-year-old. It is not surprising to hear that the latter did not always behave properly in restaurants, and had one or two incidents of 'crying hysterically' on early morning bus rides to her brother's school. In sum, it is quite possible that it is the younger children who, since they are more completely dependent, most reflect even the temporary difficulties other family members may be having.

Adolescents and older children

Adolescence is supposed to be a poor time for moving children, and in this sample of people generally well versed in both developmental psychology and in the literature on 'moving abroad with families', virtually nobody had done so without giving the matter a good deal of consideration. It was among the adolescents in the study that some of the most surprising adaptations took place.

Fourteen-year-old Karen Bateson is one of them. Moving a child for the very first time just as she entered the all-important 'high school' in a small North American city would seem to have been a risky endeavour, but Karen not only coped beautifully, she thought after some two-and-a-half years that the move had had an entirely positive effect. She said the move had forced her out of the groove she would otherwise have stayed in, making her examine herself and her values, and learn to do and to think for herself:

> Karen: Since I've been here ... I've come to terms with myself in a more mature way. I don't do things any more just because I'm not supposed to. Before, I didn't work in school, ate a lot etc., because I wasn't supposed to. I used to think it would hurt my parents if I got bad grades ... Now I've realised bad grades don't hurt them, they hurt me. I don't have to prove anything except to myself now ... When we moved here I didn't have values. I have my values now.
> M: How much of this comes with moving, though, and how much is just because of your age?
> Karen: I probably wouldn't have had the same if I had stayed

in our home town ... I would have kept moving along in the same groove. I would have had no time to assess myself. And my friends here are more for real. My friends in America were superficial ... they just talked about their hair or their boyfriends or their cars. Here they really care about you. So my values are different because of that, and also because of the emphasis on the academic at school.

(Bateson/3)

The benefits were similar for the 18-year-old Graham child. In retrospect, she said the year had changed her considerably: she felt she had become much more independent in her thinking, having discovered other cultures and 'broken away from small town snobbisms'.

In only one of the ten families with adolescents was moving seen by all concerned to be clearly and unambiguously bad for the child (see also Chapter 5):

Seventeen-year-old Nancy Gibbs had 'been in some turmoil' for the past couple of years. When she didn't like the developing country to which her parents had been posted in their work for 'the government', she returned to North America. When that didn't work, she moved back with her parents, and was just starting to settle and to enjoy school when the family had to leave for political reasons. Nancy was the only adolescent in the families studied that I did not actually meet, but if she did not participate in the interview, she was obviously following the discussion from the next room. She made it clear that she had not wanted to move to Geneva (see Chapter 5).

She started college in North America the second year after her family moved to Geneva. When that 'did not work out' she came back to Geneva to work for a year. When I last saw the family she was soon to start school in North America again, this time near other family members who could keep an eye on her.

According to her mother, extensive moving around has perturbed Nancy: she feels she has no roots, always hated having to move away from her friends, and is jealous of her cousin who has always lived in the same place. Mrs Gibbs sighed, but without elaborating: 'you can't help but make some mistakes about moving. If you'd stayed in North America maybe it wouldn't have worked out that way'.

At least three of the family moves with adolescents involved rather substantial risks. One family we have met several times throughout various chapters, the Vances:

Eighteen-year-old Stephen came to Geneva with his family on the understanding that if he still wanted to after one school term he could go back to finish secondary school in North America. In his last year, leaving friends, football team, several clubs, and a girlfriend was hard. Although his parents did not talk about it at first, his more complicated story came out over the next two interviews.

Stephen had always been of concern to his parents. At one point a psychologist had described him as 'marginally emotionally unstable', although the various professionals consulted over the years did not seem to find his state as difficult as the family and intimate family friends did. Coming to Geneva was a risk:

W: We had been warned by the psychologist that a move like this can either solve something, or help in the solution, or it can kick it right back because of the stress. And he's not someone to handle stress well.

(Vance/3)

In fact the gamble seemed to have worked out beautifully: Stephen decided to stay longer than the original minimum of one semester, then eventually even for an extra year. One effect of moving was getting away from a friendship group that even Stephen himself hinted was problematical. Not entirely by happenstance, the house the Vances had chosen in Geneva was located within walking distance of adolescent gathering places, and Stephen's suburban friends often stayed there after the last bus had left on weekend evenings. His parents thus saw quite a bit of them, and although they might not always share their taste in clothing and other body adornments, found that basically Stephen had made 'a nice group of friends'.

During the last year of the study Stephen started university in North America. His phone calls had been varied, talking both about successes and homesickness, but he had successfully handled his first major holiday alone. He was about to come home for the first vacation, and the rest of the family was eagerly awaiting his arrival.

This raises a more general point about children who are 'different'. Newcomers have to re-establish their identities, a process that might be more difficult for those who are unusual in some way, such as the boy already mentioned who everybody at home had come to accept as simply being bigger than others of his age, or the gifted children who can no longer slide through school on the basis of their reputations. The point raised by Stephen's story is the opposite:

W: Stephen learned a lot about himself. He learned that he could fit. For someone who had always felt he had to work really hard to conform, it was good to come into a community where there was no conformity. There is no standard because so much is different. He could grow a little bit more confident about himself in this kind of an atmosphere.
M: You can be yourself because there's no standard model.
Both: Yes.
H: That's interesting about the kids here ... There's no clear-cut grouping. When our eldest child was at home she had a clear-cut group of girl friends. They all belonged to the drill team ... Stephen's buddies were always the athletes and all that routine, they could almost be computerised.
W: Like they had been cut out with cookie cutters.
H: Over here it's a big minestrone of things.

(Vance/3)

Finally, although the focus of the study was to be on families with school-aged children, almost one-third of the families studied had in fact left a total of 14 older children working or studying in North America. Leaving children in North America for their first year of university proved to be difficult to an extent that surprised all those who had done it:

W: It was terribly tough to have 5,000 miles between us. I felt very isolated from our daughter, and she felt isolated from us, even though she had no longer been living with us. All of a sudden she had no home to make visits to from college.

(Vance/2)

The normative course of events for a North American child is to leave the family 'nest' around the age of 18 years for university, coming home for holidays and school vacations. Most typically these holiday visits take place fairly frequently at first, then less and less often. Moving abroad interrupts the sequence: it is the family who moves away from the child, rather than the child who leaves the family. The effect was underestimated. Visits are facilitated when multinationals pay for two or three overseas trips a year, but even here the subjective distance was felt to be far greater than families had anticipated. Two of those in their first year at university (one in the main study as well as one in the single-parent 'B' family) in fact interrupted their studies to come to live with parents in Geneva, at least temporarily.

The nineteen-year old in the Vance family, for example, found coping with university on her own very difficult. She had problems, academic, emotional and social, and decided to come and live with the family in Geneva for a year to get herself back together, and to learn French. As the study ended she was studying near Geneva. Her parents said calmly that they would not be surprised if she settled permanently in Europe, and they themselves, although they had never lived abroad before the present move, were now hoping to find another overseas posting when this one was finished.

It is, of course, far too early to have any clear picture of what the eventual outcomes might be either for the children or for their families, but some long-term processes have clearly been set in motion. The next section summarises, then the book turns to the effects of the move by two to three years after the event.

Discussion

There are obviously numerous factors at play that will influence a child's reaction to a move abroad. Maturity will affect how much he or she will be able to understand of what is happening when the outside world suddenly changes. Outside factors which have little or nothing to do with the child in question will be influencing the family (difficulties at work are an obvious example, economic factors another). One child will be influenced by the successes and difficulties other family members may be having (for example when unfavourable comparisons are made with a more talented family member, or on the contrary when a sibling having trouble occupies most parental attention). Even luck may be important (for example, whether or not other children in the neighbourhood or in the same class are compatible).

Children have been somewhat separated from their families in this section, but the family characteristics that have formed the backbone of the discussions thus far come up once again. Family sense of coherence and 'co-ordination', especially, may or may not necessarily affect whether a child has difficulties in the first place, but they will most certainly affect what is done about them. It is family 'co-ordination' that emerges most clearly. A family that 'lives in the same experiential world' will be more likely to have taken a difficult decision together in the first place, helping older children, at least, feel less as though something has been imposed upon them, and more as though they are equal participants in a process. This was strikingly the case, for example, in the Davidsons' joint family decision that the children attend local schools, and also in the decision for the Graham family to separate so that some members could move to Geneva (Chapter 2). It is quite possible, also, that such families will make more of an attempt to balance the needs of all family members when

EFFECTS ON CHILDREN

arranging the modalities of a decision that is taken. The example here is that of arriving in Geneva during the course of the school year, as opposed to during the summer break: proportionally more of the families lower on 'co-ordination' arranged to arrive in the new city at a time which is more difficult for the child, during the school year. Fewer of the families high on 'co-ordination' did so. The tendency may be for families who 'live in the same experiential world' to do what they can to ensure that conditions of a move are as favourable as possible for each of the members of the family group.

Families higher on 'co-ordination', moreover, are more likely to intervene when problems do appear for one of the members of the family. The traditional, generally well-functioning families such as those who participated in the study (Chapter 2) are hardly likely to abandon children to flounder on their own in case of problems, but there was a qualitative difference in the way more and less cohesive families reacted when a child was having difficulties. For example, when a child in the lower 'co-ordination' Zelig family had trouble when he started in the neighbourhood school his parents were certainly concerned, but there was little mention of the whole family gathering around to help him: he was simply withdrawn from the school. Similarly, it is quite possible that a spiral of interaction was affecting the Allen baby's health during his first year, a time at which Mrs Allen was attempting to cope alone with her own difficulties, as well as with those of some of the other children. The feeling is of attempting to cope as individuals or as dyads (mother and child) rather than as a larger unit. The feeling was quite different, on the other hand, when the 'high co-ordination' Jacksons all attempted to work together when Beth had trouble making friends, or when the Davidsons talked of sharing the children's more stressful adventures attending school in a language they did not yet speak. In each of the latter instances the feeling was that of a group working together from a common shared emotional space.

9
THE EFFECT OF THE MOVE: TWO CASE STUDIES

Two case histories are presented in this chapter. The Foster family appears in detail for the first time, as the chapter analyses the complex and interrelated factors that caused the move to have disastrous consequences for at least one family. The second case history is that of the Wood family, who have already appeared in several chapters, and for whom the move may well have precipitated an equally important, but this time positive, set of changes.

The Foster family[8]

Mr Foster moved first, his wife and children following some four months later. They were living in a large house in a neighbourhood of look-alike new houses inhabited mainly by foreigners. The whole family had already been in Geneva for half a year when I first interviewed the Fosters, but their living space still had the echo of a place recently moved into – there were naked light bulbs hanging from the ceilings, and little furniture. Some of the children were having dinner with the au pair when I arrived, and a large-screen video was playing American cartoons to keep them occupied as they ate.

The most important reason to move to Geneva was clearly Mr Foster's excellent job opportunity. In North America he had been the author of an idea that had literally revolutionised the telecommunications industry, and he had been offered a position which would give him the opportunity to put the idea to work on an international level. He was very flattered, and enthusiastic.

The Fosters moved with their five children, the eldest of whom was now ten years old. The youngest, now age three, was somewhat bluntly described as having been 'one too many'. Mrs Foster complained that there was never enough time to spend with each child, that she did nothing

---

8 As already discussed, names of the families and of their children are pseudonyms, and details have been changed to protect the anonymity of those who participated in the study.

THE EFFECT OF THE MOVE: TWO CASE STUDIES

but take care of children's physical needs. She had worked in the same industry as her husband until the children started coming, and although the prospect of resuming her career was very important to her, in the meantime she was very involved in her husband's work, discussing details, advising, and even writing reports for him. She had been waiting impatiently until all the children were in nursery school to have some time to herself again, maybe to finish university, but moving to Switzerland meant postponing her own plans for at least two years. She said she had wanted to make the move since it was such a good opportunity for her husband, but from the first minutes of the first interview it was clear from tones of voice that there was tension around this point.

Against this difficult, but relatively rational, series of reasons for moving was a background of more menacing themes. As secondary in their reasons for moving they talked about drugs, kidnapping, and general insecurity in North America (see Chapter 2), and also wanted to get away from the extended family and the neighbours. One of Mr Foster's sisters had been living with them for several months while going through a messy divorce, and their house, with a swimming pool and lots of babies to play with, served as the neighbourhood youth gathering place. Mrs Foster said she felt she spent every weekend cooking for masses of guests and never had any time to enjoy the party herself. In sum, having had too many children, and been too hospitable to family members in trouble and to neighbours, Mr and Mrs Foster, rather than attempting to put a bit of order into their relationships, were trying to slip away, to escape. They were also one of only two families who spontaneously mentioned that as part of the preparation before they left they had their wills written (the others were the Madisons).

When they arrived they found much the same world as the one they had left. The problems crystallised around their immediate neighbours, whom the Fosters simply assumed must be Swiss. There were disputes, for example about weeding the hedge between the houses. The main problem, however, was that, for reasons they failed to understand, the neighbours, whose children were about the same ages and one of whom went to the same school, had forbidden their children to play with the Foster children:

> W: ... The parents apparently told the children not to play with our children. I don't know why. I just assumed they don't want their children associating with ill-mannered American kids. That's the only explanation I can think of.
>
> (Foster/1)

Mr Foster protested that it was not worth getting upset about the family's relationships with their new neighbours, but Mrs Foster, obviously bothered, came back to the subject several times during the first interview.

THE EFFECT OF THE MOVE: TWO CASE STUDIES

The attitude was more generalised than just concerning tensions between neighbours: the Fosters found that people in Geneva were rude, cold, aloof. Mr and Mrs Foster both carefully refrained from saying that the locals should speak English, in fact Mrs Foster talked about how people such as they should learn French, and she later invested a great deal of energy in doing so. But at the same time they maintained that the locals should do more to recognise the needs of English-speaking residents, to cater more to the North Americans. It was nine-year-old Sam who wistfully told me at the first interview that there was nobody to play with in Geneva, because they all speak French, and ought to learn English.

It is far from uncommon for those in the community studied to talk about the Swiss 'police state', especially just after they have arrived and registered with immigration officials, got the car and the dog in order, and discovered that it is not permitted to mow the lawn on Sundays. Respondents such as the Kennedys considered such rules as the price to be paid for a certain quality of life, but the Fosters complained lengthily about the price of traffic tickets, one of the 'hidden expenses' the company had failed to tell them about. They both reported being scolded, for example for not taking care of grass cuttings properly, or for putting up an unauthorised notice on the neighbourhood bulletin board:

> H: No one tells you these things. You have the best intentions, but you're always wrong. We certainly don't mean to do wrong or offend people, it's just a point of information that we don't have – if they'd just tell people.
>
> (Foster/1)

People did eventually explain to the Fosters: after their grass cuttings sat uncollected in plastic bags for several weeks the president of the neighbours association came over and explained why, and where they should be put for composting. The landlord, also, eventually drove Mr Foster to a recycling station to demonstrate how to sort the garbage. But Mr Foster complained about 'their little minds', and in ways that are ultimately mysterious, in several instances the family attracted petty or unhelpful behaviour in the most ordinary of interactions, including from the researcher. For example, and for reasons I am totally unable to explain, I listened to Mrs Foster complain bitterly and at length about not being able to find a typical North American food, and failed to tell her after the interview was over, as I often did with other study participants, what most people do to make a simple substitute. Another example of strangely negative behaviour on the part of others occurred when someone went to the extraordinary length of tracing their licence plates and writing a letter to complain when Mr Foster parked his car in the wrong place for a few minutes on the other side of the city.

THE EFFECT OF THE MOVE: TWO CASE STUDIES

Follow-up

Things were clearly not going well with the Foster family when I saw them for the second interview a little over a year after they arrived. They started the interview by talking about severe financial problems. Mr Foster felt his employer had not been forthcoming with him about financial aspects of living in Geneva, to the point of having lied about certain things in order to get him to come. He went on to complain about the neighbourhood problems discussed above. Things were not uniformly bad: they had given a very successful party in the neighbourhood around a North American holiday (so successful in fact that the neighbours asked for another one the next year) and had, to their satisfaction, started to go to church, and to meet some people.

It was around a discussion of the problems that some of the children were having that the couple's troubles began to emerge:

> W: The fact is that after more than 15 years of marriage we're having marital difficulties.
>
> (Foster/2)

I saw Mr or Mrs Foster, separately, four more times over the next year as the family deteriorated. They had hesitated a bit about accepting the second interview since they were already in crisis and not sure they wanted to talk about it, but:

> W: We gave it some thought and decided sometimes you have to go out on a limb. Our story could help somebody else. You can't close yourself off.
>
> (Foster/5)

The story came out gradually over the interviews, partly as both Mr and Mrs Foster themselves came to recognise the difficulties in their relationship. Although neither had been aware of it at the time, Mr and Mrs Foster agreed that the couple had been in trouble before they moved. After the last pregnancy, coming immediately after the previous child was born, and definitely not planned, Mrs Foster had started to become depressed. She had been hanging on to the prospect of finally being able to have some time to herself when all the children would be in school. The youngest had been enrolled in a particularly good nursery school in North America, but no such facility was available in Geneva, and moving meant postponing this moment for a full two years (the youngest child was now three years old: on several occasions during the interviews Mrs Foster cited the exact date at which he was to have started school had they stayed in North America).

THE EFFECT OF THE MOVE: TWO CASE STUDIES

As the young family rapidly grew, Mr Foster, involved in a difficult stage of his career, was often away from home, and his wife started resentfully feeling that she had given up a great deal for the family, and now was receiving inadequate support from her husband. She also depended on him for most adult contact, waiting for him to come home from work to talk to her: she loved having him discuss his work and problems, enjoyed being consulted and also enjoyed the feeling of 'helping him'. Always, it was Mr Foster's job that took priority in the family, as Mrs Foster said it had for her own father when she was growing up. Mr Foster thought his doing well professionally would be good for his family, but did not seem to have thought much beyond his comment to me that he had to work hard to earn enough to pay for the children's education.

Mr Foster arrived in Geneva full of ideas about the fantastic professional challenge awaiting him, moving his ideas from a North American level to a European level, but the 'honeymoon' period did not last long. Although he did not talk about it at the first interview, he was extremely frustrated after six months or so. He had undoubtedly been naive in trying to transpose North American ideas and methods directly, and at that point, as his comments about the neighbours and about the Swiss in general indicated, had little cultural sensitivity in any case. Working with an international bureaucracy with little formal power, he was beginning to wonder if, professionally, the move had not been a mistake.

The still-unpacked, unsettled state of the house when I first interviewed the Foster family six months after their arrival in Geneva had been indicative. In retrospect, Mrs Foster said she was very depressed, and withdrawn, during the first year. She experienced weight loss, insomnia, 'nervousness', and went through several incidents of what she described as severe depression, and crises of one sort and another. In one critical incident, for example:

> W: It was 6:30 in the evening. I was trying to get dinner ready. My husband was late coming home from work. The kids were screaming. One of them spilled some juice all down the cupboards and over the floor. Cleaning it up I almost lost it sitting there on the kitchen floor. I got completely hysterical. I was down on my knees, so tired of cleaning up other people's messes. My husband finally phoned. One of the children answered, and told him: 'There's something wrong with Mommy'.
>
> (Foster/2)

It was about at that point that the Fosters began to seek help: they engaged an au pair to help with the children. The adolescent they found was of great help at first, but may well have been affected by the general unhappiness of the family. In any case the interval during which she was

THE EFFECT OF THE MOVE: TWO CASE STUDIES

of help did not last long: Mrs Foster said that after a little while she 'just wanted to party with her friends'. She was not replaced when she left. More alarmingly, Mr Foster later said that at that point he had been thinking about legally obliging his wife to seek psychiatric care, a measure made unnecessary when Mrs Foster eventually sought psychiatric help on her own initiative.

Frustrations and barely formulated doubts on one side, depression and resentment on the other: Mr Foster started spending less and less time at home, and more and more time with someone who understood his problems. The affair actually began not long after the Fosters moved to Geneva, but went on for over a year before matters came to a head and Mrs Foster 'discovered' it. All of the children began to experience difficulties. Most alarming were those of the oldest. Sam, a sensitive child, took his role of oldest brother with a great deal of seriousness and responsibility. It is undoubtedly indicative that, although I had said nothing of the sort, prior to the first interview with me his parents had told him that as the oldest child I would want to talk with him about moving. He had seriously thought out what he wanted to say, talking about how he can never sleep at night in the new house, about how lonely and bored he had been the first winter, about how all the other children in the neighbourhood only speak French. He was described by both of his parents as seriously lacking confidence. Mediocre at school and sports, he was 'the sort of child who always gets passed over by teachers', as described by his mother, who cried as she talked of his problems at school. He had always had trouble at school, and difficulty making friends. The only exception was for a brief period in a new school he attended for a few months just before coming to Geneva, where his mother said he was considered special by the other children because he was about to move abroad to Switzerland. He could not make friends in Geneva, and several times ran away from school. It was when, after a particularly bad day, Sam started talking about suicide that parents and teachers finally realised he needed help. And it was while talking with school officials about her son's problems that Mrs Foster also got a referral for psychiatric help for herself.

As for the next children, the second, who always had friends, was described as 'rough and tough, and active'. He was referred to a psychologist during the family's second year in Geneva after performing some potentially very dangerous acts of vandalism. The third was described by the school psychologist about the same time as being 'tuned out', 'day dreaming', and in need of professional help (according to his mother). The fourth was found to need special help with reading difficulties. The only child who was not in school played in the periphery during one of the interviews, and could not help overhearing as his mother poured out intimate details of her marital difficulties to me, and presumably to other people on other occasions as well.

The Fosters separated after about a year, Mr Foster gradually moving to another area of the house, then to his own apartment. He did make an attempt to save the situation, seeing a couple of psychiatrists, although without much conviction, talking childhood traumas, relationships and so forth when I interviewed him alone, but as though he were speaking an unfamiliar foreign language. He said he had also talked to Mrs Foster's friends, to try to understand what had happened. As for Mrs Foster, she switched from psychologist to lawyers as she undertook divorce. The process itself was extremely messy, with acts of hostility and of imprudence, melodramatic flights to North America, 'helpful' interventions by extended family, and the use of the children to convey messages between husband and wife. Mrs Foster finally found the energy to finish unpacking and make the house look settled the day after Mr Foster moved out, and also started trying to establish some order and structure in the family's life: having meals together without the video and television, insisting the children put their toys and clothes away, setting up routines around bedtime, and so forth.

The ambivalence and lack of clarity of the situation was reflected during the last two interviews I had with Mrs Foster. Three weeks before she and the children were to move back to North America the house was nicely decorated for Christmas, yet the basement was full of boxes and collections of toys being packed to be sold the next day. The family had continued to go to church together. Mrs Foster said this was because her husband did not want anybody to know about their separation, but it was she who had not yet managed to inform the younger children that in less than a month they were to move permanently back to North America. I saw her for a last time a few weeks later. She had taken the children back to North America, where they had just had their first day of school, and was back in Geneva for a few days to supervise the movers and take care of some last-minute details. She was extremely distraught, having just discovered that due to a technical error they would have to keep the Geneva house, now empty, for an extra six months. The owner of the house was aware of how difficult it would be for the family to now maintain three separate dwellings. He was perfectly within his legal rights to insist that the Fosters stick to the terms of their contract, but it would have been a simple matter for him to find new tenants had he wanted to help them. Decidedly, the Foster family did not bring out the best in other people.

The role of moving in the family's disintegration

It is impossible to know if the rupture would have happened had the Foster family stayed in North America. They might well have simply gone on in the life they had set up for themselves, Mr Foster rising in his career, neighbourhood children gravitating around the swimming pool, Mrs Foster taking up university and recommencing a life of her own once the children were in school. It could have been the family's move to Geneva that precipitated the spiralling down of the relationship: the doubt and frustration around Mr Foster's job, which after all had brought the family to Geneva at some substantial sacrifice, was compounded by the social isolation typical of the beginning of a stay in a new place. Mr and Mrs Foster had only each other on whom to rely during a difficult time and their lack of ability to help each other highlighted and worsened the cracks that may already have been present in their relationship. Mrs Foster sometimes said the events had blasted her out of a depression she hadn't realised she had been in, and that she was looking forward to her 'new life' which was to start with going back to school. But on other occasions she referred to the move as having 'destroyed our lives'.

As for Mr Foster, his comments on the matter must be understood in the context of his distaste for dwelling on the negative. (At one point he told me on the telephone that his wife and one of the children were in North America at the moment, but that 'things are going great'. On her return three weeks later Mrs Foster informed me, also on the phone, that Mr Foster was about to move out of the house, and that the couple were getting a divorce. Both later related separate versions of dramatically hostile acts that had made Mr Foster return prematurely from a family vacation in North America with most of the children – a few days before he told me everything was fine . . .) What he said when I interviewed him alone a bit less than three months before his wife and children left was that he thought the marriage was not necessarily over. Certainly adapting to a new culture caused specific strains in the family, however. These are now discussed in detail.

Work

The stresses of Mr Foster's work have been mentioned. He eventually learned to deal with Europeans, and undoubtedly became more realistic about the way things work and what he could accomplish. When I interviewed him in his office almost two years after the move his pleasure at certain aspects of his work was obvious. Apparently, having survived the professional test in Geneva, he was being considered for an important position back in North America, which he said he was contemplating in order to live nearer the family. Professionally Mr Foster was certainly successful: the idea he was responsible for promoting took effect after a few years, and has modified an aspect of daily life in Europe.

But, as indicated above, Mr Foster's move to Geneva came at the expense of his wife's plans. There was no talk of negotiation prior to the move, and little indication even of serious discussion: his career simply came first.

In a word, Mrs Foster felt she had been sacrificed for her husband's career. At best she pursued career interests vicariously, trying to 'help' her husband by consulting with him in the evenings about the problems he may have been having at work, at a time of the day when he may well not have been particularly eager to continue thinking about such things. Just before she moved back to North America she read me a long letter that she had written him about the divorce, in which jealousy and feelings of martyrdom seeped through every paragraph.

Not having enough company support

In contrast to the others who worked for 'the company', as well as to many who worked for international organisations, the subdivision for which Mr Foster worked did practically nothing to assist newly arriving employees. The Fosters were far from having all of the expatriate advantages accorded to many of the families in the study, and from the very beginning they felt a persistent and very irritating resentment about not having been treated fairly. The lack of company support created severe financial difficulties for the Fosters. Seen from North America before he signed his contract, the salary had seemed high. Having visited Geneva on several occasions before they moved, Mr Foster knew that the cost of living was high, but had failed to take into account what he termed 'hidden expenses' of moving, such as having motor vehicles converted to Swiss standards, or paying deposits on rentals for the house, telephone and car. When they actually started setting up house they discovered that many of the foods and items of daily life they had taken for granted in North America were imported in Switzerland, and cost much more than they had calculated. Unthinkingly trying to reconstruct a North American way of life when they arrived, the Fosters made several unwise decisions in the beginning, signing contracts into which they were then locked. Almost half of Mr Foster's salary was spent in rent, and a good deal more went to maintain the two cars that were necessary to drive to work and to the three different schools the children attended.

As a result, the Fosters were not able to afford many of the things they had formerly taken for granted, and that others in the North American community in Geneva had easily, such as extensive use of the telephone to keep in contact with people 'at home', travelling, going out for meals. They had to budget to send the children to camp, or to ski, and buying furniture was difficult. This is the sort of thing that 'the company' smoothed out for employees, clearly and honestly informing, advising, covering installation expenses, even helping out with the rent. While their economic misery was most definitely relative, the point for the Foster family is that they were constantly in a position of feeling that their situation was very inferior to that of most of the people they saw around them.

THE EFFECT OF THE MOVE: TWO CASE STUDIES

Lifestyle and social isolation

It did not help that the decisions they had made in the beginning were not what they had wanted. Mrs Foster, especially, had wanted to change lifestyles when they moved, to live in an apartment and even travel around Europe by train with the children. The couple had tried, but, undoubtedly realistically in Geneva's housing market at the time they moved, had not been able to find a suitable apartment.

Their relations with their immediate neighbours had been hostile from the very first, and the Fosters had assumed that they were bordered by Swiss who simply did not like North Americans. It became clear in later interviews, however, not only that the Fosters' immediate neighbours had trouble with most of the other neighbours as well, but that in addition they were not Swiss, and in fact culturally and linguistically were even more distant from the Swiss than the Fosters. What is important is that the Fosters had jumped to conclusions about a generalised 'other'. They simply presumed that since the neighbours spoke a different language, and since they were living in Switzerland, they must obviously be Swiss. It did not occur to either Mr or Mrs Foster that 'other' might have more finely defined characteristics, or in this instance that the family next door might also be foreign. Furthermore, the Fosters somehow felt they, as foreigners or North Americans, were uniquely responsible for any interpersonal problems there might be. In other words, if there are tensions 'it must be our fault, and because we are North American'. Not being defined beyond a vague, generalised 'other', the neighbours could not be seen to have their own problems – family, social, of adaptation, or other – which might, in fact, have explained their apparent hostility. In sum, their undifferentiated generalised definition of 'other' made it impossible for the Fosters to perceive subtle differences and tensions which could have explained interpersonal problems. These not perceived, the only explanation that remained was that there was something wrong with 'us', as individuals, as a family, or as a nationality.

A final factor was the family's social isolation in Geneva. They were removed from the usual social supports and structuring that had framed their lives in North America. The Fosters were a little ambivalent about the social life they had left in North America: on one hand they spoke with pleasure about the many people around the house, especially neighbourhood children. Mrs Foster had one good friend from the place they had previously been living, a source of comfort in lengthy telephone conversations as trouble developed after the move. And extended family were very present in their lives: Mr Foster's sister had been living with the family before they left, and Mrs Foster's family provided substantial support, both emotional and very practical, as she and the children moved back to North America. On the other hand one of the reasons they had left was to get away from such ties. They also mentioned that over the years they had rarely entertained Mr Foster's business colleagues, the excuse being that their very child-oriented house was not up to standards for such entertaining.

In any case, they remained somewhat isolated in Geneva, partly by choice to change from the way they had been living in North America, partly because taking care of numerous children did not leave a great deal of free time. The Foster family did get out to such child-focused social activities as school events and sports, and had also left their mark on the neighbourhood with the party they had given the first year, also child-focused. But neither as individuals nor as a couple, although they made many acquaintances, did the adult Fosters make any close friends during their two years in Geneva. Certainly partly because their marriage was deteriorating, but undoubtedly also in a spiral process, they did not seem to manage to invite people to their house, and dinner invitations to others' homes gradually declined when they were not reciprocated. The reason they gave for not inviting people was that they had no dining room table . . .

The next family to be discussed started out in a way similar to the Fosters, without enthusiasm, feeling depressed and overwhelmed with problems. However they later went on to do more than simply settle in. The consequences of the transition would seem to have been extremely positive for the Wood family. They are presented in somewhat less detail since they have already appeared several times throughout various chapters.

The Wood family

If adaptation went far differently for the Woods, this was certainly not what I would have predicted at our first meeting. The interview, which took place four months after they arrived, was one of the more difficult ones of the first series. A 'company' family, the Woods had agreed easily to participating in the study, but when I actually arrived at their house to talk with them Mr Wood was reticent. He had a great deal of concern about confidentiality, and tested me by asking if I had interviewed others from 'the company'. I told him I had, but in response to his next question refused to give names, to which he replied: 'OK, you passed'. He also objected to my taping the interview, only reluctantly agreeing to give it a try. He soon forgot about the tape recorder, and later relaxed to the point of lying down on the couch and joking about how much I might charge for an interview.

Although the family had moved once or twice within North America the trip to look for a house in Geneva was the first time they had ever been off the continent. The offer of the job abroad was not a complete surprise, though: good friends had just been transferred, and Mr and Mrs Wood had already discussed what they would do if ever they received a similar offer. Although 'the company' gave them plenty of time to make their decision, and even though Mrs Wood was just out of the hospital after an operation (Chapter 2), they took only a few days to accept.

Mr Wood, a young middle-level manager in 'the company', was vague about what the move would mean for his career, other than: 'it puts more arrows in your quiver'. Mrs Wood had been a secretary before she was married, but had stayed home to take care of the children. The year they moved to Geneva was the first both children were to be in school all day. Mrs Wood said she had seen the move as an opportunity to see a new place, meet new people, learn a new language, and meet new challenges:

> W: I was ready for it. We had moved in North America and I enjoyed it after the first six months or so. We talked with the children about it. They were positive, excited.
>
> (Wood/1)

As for their hopes for the stay, in addition to the career aspects for Mr Wood, they talked about meeting new people, understanding other cultures, countries, governments, religions. Also, and perhaps most important, was what the experience might mean for the children:

> H: Certainly it will have negative points to it, but it will be something they can build on, and be more well-rounded people.
>
> W: This was our very first opportunity to come overseas in any way. I found from the very first trip to choose houses and so forth, there was something that changed, a perspective on people and lives that was different. It's such a growing experience to leave your culture and what you're comfortable with and to go into something that's so foreign and so different to you. All your life you'd heard about Europe, but all of a sudden it's really real ... It's changed my perspective on a lot of things: it's a growing experience. It hurts sometimes (little laugh).
>
> (Wood/1)

As for ideas about the Swiss and about what people say about living in Geneva, they talked about various things they had heard, but both reported that as far as they were concerned: 'the jury is still out'. They talked about exploring the area, and made many tentative observations about the culture. Both found it frustrating not to be able to speak the language. Like the Fosters, they had several anecdotes about doing the wrong thing or being controlled: parking in somebody else's space, needing a prescription for something one can simply buy in North America, having papers checked the first time Mrs Wood dared to drive. Mrs Wood, especially, felt less free than in North America, more regulated, and worried about breaking rules because she didn't know what the laws were (Chapter 3).

What bothered them especially, though, was that they found people more reserved: people don't smile at strangers as they do where the Woods came from. Also, the locals are not as courteous. Mrs Wood went into detail about her feelings of humiliation and incompetence in front of her child as she was repeatedly passed over by a sales person while waiting to pay for a toy, the sort of incident she would have been able to handle easily in North America (Chapter 3).

Working his way into his new job, Mr Wood had to travel what both he and his wife felt was quite a bit, in any case more than before the move. His absence was a problem for the rest of the family: they were used to spending time together in the evenings, and Mrs Wood was having trouble finding things to do to keep the children entertained on her own in a strange place. The children, who were experiencing adjustment difficulties of their own, may well have been unusually dependent at first (for example, they would not go to bed while I was there, and kept asking for their parents to come and read to them). The elder child, ten years old, in addition, was having difficulties at school. As described by Mrs Wood, the teacher was at best very strict, with a pedagogical style different from that they had been used to. At worst the teacher was a tyrant who humiliated his pupils. In any case the ten-year-old cried a lot, and was afraid to go to school for several months. The Woods tried hard not to judge, and aware of the possibility of doing more harm than good for the child if they attempted to intervene with the teacher, insisted on waiting to see if things would work out.

Finally, there was loneliness for Mrs Wood. She had more time than she was used to with the children both in school for the first time. Although she had been very active on the circuits of teas and wives clubs, and also with the church and the neighbours, she had no good friends in Geneva yet. Geography was a complicating factor: the Woods lived in a different neighbourhood from most of the other 'company' families, and school hours and traffic patterns imposed severe limits on the informal visits with other company wives that helped many other newcomers begin to feel attached. When I saw the family four months after their arrival Mrs Wood talked quite a bit about one new friend, but I sensed the evening I was there that having company was an unusual event. Her tearful comments about loneliness, and about having to restructure were cited in Chapter 3, and the conjugal tensions raised, and the ambivalent support of a first friend, analysed in Chapter 4. The interview was tense, but Mr Wood commented about participating in the study:

THE EFFECT OF THE MOVE: TWO CASE STUDIES

H: If it helps other people then fine. [But] I don't think we've shared anything with you tonight that we haven't already shared with each other.

(Wood/1)

Follow-up

When I phoned them some six months later things were much better. Mrs Wood commented that she didn't know if Geneva would ever feel like home, but things were becoming more familiar, especially since she had: 'A bit of French under my belt, and I don't feel like people are hitting me in the face with it any more'. The family was about to make their first visit back to North America, and she said she was anticipating finding it difficult to talk to people about the things they were doing in Europe since people might think they were boasting.

I interviewed them again after this trip, 14 months after the move. The situation was radically better than at the previous interview. They had made friends. They had deliberately decided not to limit their contacts to the North American company-related community (they had made their original choice of housing with this in mind, avoiding a neighbourhood with a large concentration of company houses). By year two they had constructed a network of three different sets of friends; those made through neighbours, through church, and through work. They commented that they enjoyed putting people from different environments and different countries together, and laughed about doubling the number of people they invited for the North American celebration of Thanksgiving each year. Mrs Wood had gently broken away from the friend who had been important in sharing her misery at the beginning: the friend had remained unhappy, and after a while had become too much of a negative influence (Chapter 6).

Both of the children were happier. Problems at school had resolved themselves with the end of the year and a change of teachers. In fact the child's difficulties had coincided with problems his parents were having, and they all cleared up about the same time. Whatever the relations of cause and effect, certainly the mother was more at ease when her children were happier. Each of the family members was involved in several sports, Mrs Wood was studying French and taking music lessons, the family had travelled a bit around Europe, and Mrs Wood, especially, was simply feeling more at ease, more like her old self:

W: I had a lot of bad things happen to me right at the beginning, like people cutting in on me in a line ... a lot of little things. There's just no way to prepare for them. When I was in North America there's no way I would have buzzed back at anybody,

> that's not my nature. But I got to the point where I was tired of being shoved around. I'd get up to the cash register and I'd stick my elbows out: 'Just try and get in front of me!' ...
>
> M: Last time we talked you felt you were expecting people to criticise you.
>
> W: I still think they do. This sounds tacky, but it's really the way I feel: I think a lot of times Europeans make fun of North American people. I've watched people from behind sometimes, and seen the way they mock the way people talk. They kind of swing the way people are moving. I've heard them chatter behind my heels sometimes. So I don't think I've dreamt it up: I've seen it. But I think you find it in North America, when you have a Japanese come and try to talk English. People don't understand each other ...
>
> H: ... It's not paranoia, it's real, but it's just like it is in North America ...
>
> W: ... It's just people not understanding each other and their cultures, and not trying to be considerate of each other.
>
> M: But it was really bothering you when we last talked.
>
> W: I've thickened up (laugh) – there's something in me that's changed, drastically.

It was not just a new assertiveness in public places that was growing in Mrs Wood. There was an important element of life stage in the equation. The family was now complete: the couple had finished having their children. Mrs Wood had stayed home while the children were young, but now that they were in school, and she was nearing the age of 40, she was starting to think about what she would be doing next:

> W: I was a secretary before we were married. I wanted to be with the children when they were small, but planned to go back when they were older. But I got to a point with myself after ten years out of the work force that I thought I just couldn't go back to work. Who'd want me? With all these new computers, and new things they're doing today, I'm not up with any of that. Inside of me it was like: 'I'm too old to go to school, that's for the young people.'

Having just discovered that she could cope with learning to live in a new culture, and taken music lessons, learned some French, and how to ski, however:

> W: I have a new self-confidence I didn't have before. There's something that wasn't there before. Going back to North

America it was very evident to me. I thought I was just doing these things because I enjoyed them, trying to fill my time, restructure my life in a way that was pleasant to me in a new environment. But when I went back home for a visit I realised my attitude had changed.

H: I'm going to have her parasailing when we go back, jumping off Mont Blanc!

As she said, the visit back 'home' had been an important turning point, highlighting the changes the family had been going through without quite realising it. The change process involved a good deal of stress, as the couple had indicated in the first interview, and as reflected in their responses to the questionnaire concerning the stressful aspects of adapting to a new culture. Mrs Wood, especially, after an initial period of being in better health than usual after they moved, developed several problems. She had two or three long-standing medical conditions known to be made worse by stress, one of which required extensive treatment during the family's second year in Geneva. The process also did not occur without mourning. Especially to be mourned by these people who did not like to say negative things about other people, or to feel 'arrogant', were the relationships with people they had outgrown. Perhaps, in fact, Mrs Wood's initial feeling of being menaced when she moved was not so unrealistic after all: certainly an old self was shed ...

What are the effects on the family of these changes? The Woods said they were closer as a family, and did more things together in Geneva, but other than this they could not see any ways the move had affected their family. They thought any changes that might have occurred would have been because the children were growing up. Just as they did not realise the changes that were occurring during their first year after the move, however, until they returned to North America for a visit and saw the contrast with what they had been, it is probably too early, and too close, for the Woods to realise the family changes set in motion. Theirs had been a traditional division of roles, with husband working while wife stayed at home with the children, fishing in his leisure as she took courses in flower arranging. He chose a new car; she did most of the food shopping, the cooking, and the laundry. When fruit juices were offered during an interview it was he who went to get them, but fumbled a bit with exactly where the glasses and bottle openers were, and, as in one or two similar instances with other families, I could not help wondering if it was not something of an exception that he was doing the serving that evening. In North America it had been Mr Wood's role to negotiate ordinary exchanges with neighbours, officials, sales people and the like, but since she had learned more French it was increasingly Mrs Wood who took care of this sort of thing in Geneva.

THE EFFECT OF THE MOVE: TWO CASE STUDIES

In matters large and small, Mr and Mrs Wood will have to work out a new relationship with each other, and perhaps with the children, as Mrs Wood becomes increasingly assertive. We have seen how she was beginning to stand up for her rights in ordinary exchanges such as those with sales people. Mr Wood maintained that he was proud of his wife, encouraging her new growth, and was unmistakably so in the interviews we had together. Whatever forms Mrs Wood's new assertiveness takes, whether or not it begins to impinge on what had been Mr Wood's territory, requiring a fundamental renegotiating in the couple, the promising sign is that the Woods continuously talked to each other. The first interview had been tearful and tense, but, as noted above, difficult as the reproaches were, they said nothing to the researcher that they had not already said to each other. At my request they filled out separately the various questionnaires I gave them, but then asked me to wait as they compared and discussed their answers together.

The Woods eventually adjusted to living in a new culture to the point of not really wanting to go back, although this was merely hypothetical since Mr Wood's was a time-limited assignment to the company's overseas offices. Never having really thought about living abroad, and in retrospect having accepted the move largely for career reasons, Mr Wood said at the last interview that, had he known in the beginning what he now knew, he would have accepted it even without the career factor. Certainly the family would gladly take another overseas assignment.

In sum, coming at a critical moment of transition in the family life stage, as the children entered full-time school, the move precipitated major changes in at least one member of the family. Adapting to the new culture put a good deal of stress on the marriage and on the family, and becoming more cosmopolitan brought significant regret for what had been left behind. But in contrast with the Fosters, the Woods constructed a social network around themselves on which they could rely for support in addition to each other. They recognised problems, and, although the process was at times painful, continuously talked with each other about them. Although they were not yet aware of all the changes this may entail for the family, it seems reasonable to postulate that, in addition to whatever they acquired in knowledge of other cultures and other ways of being, having weathered stressful times together, the Wood family will have come out strengthened.

Discussion

The two case histories demonstrate the complex interplay of factors external to the family that both helped and hindered coping in the early stages of living in a new culture. Such factors include Mr Foster's great professional opportunity that brought the entire family, but that Mrs Foster felt entailed significant sacrifice. They also include the support of the employer, which was significant for the Woods but lacking for the Fosters, and – along with their own misjudgement – put them in a situation of deprivation relative to the families they encountered after they had moved. Social isolation – and social support – interacted in a particularly significant way with unhappiness in both families. Removal from their usual social supports started the Foster family on their downward spiral of adaptation. It was loneliness that drove Mrs Wood to close friendship with someone equally needy, and something else that allowed her to extricate herself when she realised the relationship was destructive. This brings us to the factors that have formed the backbone of the book family. One of these is sense of coherence.

As measured by questionnaire, the Foster family SOC was average (and both Mr and Mrs Foster had the same score). The Wood family SOC was high (this was because Mrs Wood showed a very high score at the first interview; Mr Wood's score was slightly below average: see Table A.8 in Appendix). It is in the interviews, however, that the rather subtle SOC-related differences between the two families could best be perceived. The sense of coherence meaningfulness element takes the form in the Wood family of deeply held religious and ethical commitments. As with several of the other families, the Woods did not talk a great deal about their religious beliefs: they merely mentioned going to church as though this were taken for granted (in contrast with the Fosters, who talked quite a bit about going to church for an essentially different reason – in order to meet people). Mr and Mrs Wood did talk at some length about values, especially as the encounter with other cultures and other systems of values made them examine their own beliefs. Mr and Mrs Foster lacked such a sense of engagement, commitment and questioning. Their acts had a more superficial quality about them, as they rushed into an international move uniquely because of a job opportunity (although the job opportunity was admittedly an excellent one), then, with little real reflection, into their separation and the acts that were related to it, and finally to Mrs Foster's return to North America with the children.

Somewhat similarly, the Fosters were to some extent lacking in both comprehensibility and manageability aspects of sense of coherence. They had more children than they wanted. After they moved they did not understand the new environment, and jumped to conclusions that it was hostile (the new rules were 'stupid', the employer lied, the neighbours did not want to have their children play with North Americans). Their attempts to put some order and control in the family's life were somewhat inappropriate and extreme (imposing strict rules from one day to the next, moving precipitately out of the house [Mr Foster] and back to North America [Mrs Foster and the children]) or even lacking (not being able to unpack for over a year, not managing to put order in the new space by such symbolic acts as acquiring a family dining table, not managing to have meals together). In the Wood family manageability shifted: along with comprehensibility, manageability was severely challenged at first when the family moved away from the known. In a critical difference with some of the other families studied, the Woods had not actively sought the move. The offer even came as something of a surprise. In accepting it they left a situation in which they felt confident and protected for one that was unknown, and in which they felt slightly threatened. They did not understand the new customs, rhythms and rules, and at first felt as though the people around them were watching and criticising them. For the first several months Mrs Wood let herself be 'shoved around' by sales people: she did not know how to react properly, or perhaps even feel capable of doing so. After this first difficult period, however, Mrs Wood, especially, showing signs of a high SOC, swung into a more active mode. She defined what to do (for example overcoming loneliness by attending courses that interested her and thereby making new friends, deciding it might *not* be helpful to intervene when one of the children had problems with a teacher) and gradually worked through the difficulties.

Closely related to comprehensibility is the rapidity with which one draws conclusions about the new environment, and here the two families differed quite considerably: the Foster family jumped rather quickly to conclusions, whereas in the face of the unknown the Woods waited until much later before deciding. The Fosters brought unrealistic expectations (e.g. finding an urban apartment which would suit their family, travelling around Europe by train with five small children) and reconstructed a North American way of life (e.g. two cars, a North American-style house and ways of eating). Partly because the weight of their own problems interfered with understanding others, the Fosters, in addition, showed little cultural sensitivity. Having decided the outside environment was hostile, they somehow seemed to portray an equally hostile attitude that failed to attract the friendly assistance encountered by some of the other families, and they even attracted some decidedly unhelpful interventions.

The Woods were equally inexperienced with international moving yet they delayed making judgements about the new place. Mrs Wood, especially, was even less secure about breaking rules and about handling ordinary encounters (perhaps in fact precisely because she postponed making judgements), but in this case such insecurity led to trying to find out. It also led to the wait and see attitude portrayed with the child's problem with his teacher. After an initial uncomfortable period the Woods' refusal to stereotype eventually led to appreciation and to evaluation of cultural differences. They came to better understand the culture in which they were living, their own culture, and also phenomena such as misunderstandings and criticism of strangers that may be found everywhere.

THE EFFECT OF THE MOVE: TWO CASE STUDIES

Finally, on 'co-ordination' (a sense of operating together as a group), the two families were rated similarly at the beginning of the study. Both, at least so it seemed, were functioning from approximately the same experiential world or emotional space, feeling that what affected one family member affected the entire unit. It is here, obviously, that the most shift occurred for one of the families analysed. Mr and Mrs Wood may each have been having difficulty with their own problems adapting to living in a new culture, but not so much that they were unable to help each other, and especially their children, with their difficulties. They continuously, although sometimes painfully, discussed their difficulties and compared their reactions. Lines of communication remained open throughout. The Fosters may perhaps have begun at the same place, but in retrospect there was a critical difference between the two families in the way they moved. The Woods moved together as a unit into the unknown. The move for the Fosters, on the other hand, was very much driven by Mr Foster's job opportunity. Mrs Foster felt she had sacrificed her own interests for those of her husband (although they both to some extent confused the husband's professional trajectory with what would be good for the entire family). Such a feeling of having sacrificed may well, in fact, have been the wedge that eventually led to the family's splitting. One felt martyred and was having difficulty, the other became impatient with the partner's problems (and perhaps felt some degree of guilt for getting the family into the situation), and eventually sought solace elsewhere, at which point the process of separation became irreversible. In the Foster family, furthermore, in contrast with the Woods, there was little real communication between husband and wife about the difficulties they were having, and since difficulties were not admitted there was little that could be done about them. The couple's problems, finally, were so overwhelming that Mr and Mrs Foster were unable to help their children with the latter's increasingly significant difficulties, difficulties which were undoubtedly in very large part precipitated by those their parents were having.

10
FAMILIES TWO YEARS LATER

This chapter starts with the remainder of the family strains discussed in Chapter 4, describing how families addressed the issue of transporting dual careers. It then goes on to discuss phases of adaptation, then the way the move affected the families studied. Several factors other than sense of coherence and family 'co-ordination' are discussed as they may be related to the effect of the move on the families. The rapidity with which a family draws conclusions about the new environment is discussed at the end of the chapter.

Coping with issues around two careers

A complex problem appears when both spouses have careers about which they care, but when only one of them will be able to pursue the career in the new place. The discussion of dual careers among the families studied starts with those who had in fact already dealt with the issue, then goes on to the strategies used by those for whom it was a very pertinent concern indeed.

Among the families who moved to Geneva the year the study began, it was almost always the husband's career that caused the relocation. Almost half of the families had already dealt with the issue of the wife's career, usually because she had few career aspirations, at least at this particular moment in her life (Table A.3). There were plenty of other things to keep such women busy: helping the rest of the family settle in, meeting new people, learning a language, travelling. Those who had moved extensively because moving comes with their husband's job had addressed the problem of dual careers long ago. Most agreed that maintaining two serious careers is incompatible with extensive geographical mobility. Mr and Mrs Kennedy, who had lived together on four continents, stated the position very clearly:

> W: It's impossible to juggle two full-time careers if you are abroad. Every time the family moves one of them has to look for work, so if you're very ambitious and professional, overseas is not

the place to be ... Stability at home is very important when one has an erratic lifestyle. Dual careers are OK in North America where there are support systems like day care, churches and after-school activities, but you don't have that here.

H: If both parents are trying to satisfy their own careers in that crucial period when you're trying to settle in, the children get neglected (he gives a series of examples he has observed among colleagues).

(Kennedy/1)

Mrs Kennedy returned to the theme at the final interview some two years later. She had in fact found a part-time job in the international sector in the meantime, but had not changed her mind about dual careers for couples who must change cultures frequently:

W: You cannot possibly have a career if you have a rotational lifestyle. You only get frustrated: it doesn't match. People try to *pretend* they have a career, but in fact they don't ... There are people who pick up work, as teachers or in international organisations, but it's not a career, it's a job, a job you are going to leave eventually because you are going to be transferred back.

(Kennedy/3)

What about the families for whom dual careers *were* a major issue when they moved?

Families currently coping with dual career issues

Three of the women among the 28 core families who participated in the study were able to fully pursue their careers after they moved to Geneva. One was, of course, Mrs Quincy, the career 'government' employee. Another, Mrs Ogbourne, a professional musician, started by giving lessons and working on the fringes of the regular job market, but by two years later had become successful enough to be able to choose between the most interesting offers. The third wife who was able to pursue her career was Mrs Thomas (Chapter 4). She experienced a great deal more difficulty, however.

The Thomas family

At the end of a very frustrating year of searching Mrs Thomas accepted the job that 'sounded good on paper', but, as she had in fact sensed from the beginning, several structural factors made the post unsatisfactory:

W: It has not been a happy experience for me ... There are some limitations that will keep the job from being very satisfying. I could hide out there for a long time and not do much, but it's not been my experience either in my work or in my life to not love what I'm doing.

(Thomas/3)

Mrs Thomas's professional situation and that of the rest of the family were highly interrelated. For one thing, her professional situation affected the family's integration into the local community. One of the family's goals when they moved to Geneva had been to integrate as much as possible into Swiss life, and it was with this in mind that they enrolled their children in the local neighbourhood school. But Mrs Thomas's depression before she started working, compounded by her lack of ease in French, interfered with her resolution to meet other mothers in the neighbourhood. Partly because of their handicap with the language, neither Mr nor Mrs Thomas was comfortable with the school. One of the children, in addition, had a great deal of difficulty with the transition to being educated entirely in French. One of the benefits that came with Mrs Thomas's job in Geneva was that tuition at the International School was paid, and because of the child's difficulties – although not without regret since it was against the family's policy of trying to integrate – both of the children were transferred there at the beginning of the following school year. The child's problems cleared up rapidly with the change of environment, but the change of school removed yet another possible point of contact with the local community.

Not a couple to dwell on problems, Mr and Mrs Thomas talked at the last interview about the pleasure they experienced in discovering the international community, but also admitted that having had to relinquish one of their cherished goals had been 'a blow to our family self image'. As for the professional situation, at the last interview Mrs Thomas was looking for another job. Although the family had originally thought they would be moving to Geneva for a relatively long stay, Mr Thomas was talking about the possibility of looking for a post in North America if his wife did not find something more satisfying in Geneva.

The Renton family

The other family discussed in Chapter 4 was the Rentons, who by living on one side of Geneva and driving the children to and from school on the other found themselves in a style of life almost as hectic as when they had been juggling parenthood with two serious careers. They had begun to sort themselves out a year later. First of all, much as they loved both their house and the school, they decided they could not maintain each on opposite sides of the city, and changed the former, moving to a more convenient location. Second, although Mrs Renton was still not able to pursue a serious career, she had found a part-time job in her field. She laughed that the job as a consultant involved 'easy stuff', things her staff would have done before, but: 'it's wonderful to be working again'. Finally, since the job involved a small amount of travel, and it was difficult to find somebody to stay with the children for several days at a time while she was away, they had also found a student to live with the family (an au pair).

Other families

What about the other families in which the women had career frustrations with which to cope? Mrs Bateson and Mrs Friedson both went through very similar processes: Mrs Bateson, who had commented at length about losing an important part of her identity when she left behind her role as a teacher, at first did volunteer work at the school and tried various activities and women's clubs, including assuming leadership of an important 'company wives' committee. This phase lasted about a year. By the second year she had found, then eventually completed, a degree programme that should help her career when the family returned to North America. Mrs Friedson, similarly, had talked at length at the first interview about her frustration on the professional front. In common with Mrs Renton and Mrs Thomas, she had not really believed she would not be able to find a position in her field once she arrived. She spent her first year in Geneva intensively studying French, and in fact was one of the few people in the study to become proficient within a year. By the second interview she had also found work to do, work which would help her keep up with changes in her rapidly changing professional field, but for which she did not receive a salary. In her various searches for something else to do she discovered a specialised educational programme, and by the third interview was working on a degree that may well reorient her career in an interesting new direction.

One further solution to the dilemma of 'his career versus her career' was that of working as a team. One variant was that of a 'two-person single career'. Mrs Collins, for example, had been working full-time to further her husband's aggressive advancement through a number of companies across several continents. In the other variant the families had also lived in several different countries and were coming to posts for which they had striven, but the husbands worked for 'the organisation'. The collaborative functioning of Mr and Mrs Davidson was discussed in Chapter 7. In two other such families the wives worked as volunteers beside their husbands. One did so successfully and gratifyingly in a section of 'the organisation' where volunteer work was the norm, organising receptions, taking notes at meetings, and organising files. The volunteer's role in Geneva was more difficult for the other wife, a highly qualified and experienced professional in her own right. She had worked beside her husband for many years, at one point being promoted into his post when he went on to a higher level of responsibilities. The couple had hoped to continue working as a team in Geneva, and she worked beside him without pay throughout their first year. Volunteer work was not the norm in this section of 'the organisation', however, and the lack of a clearly structured and recognised professional role became increasingly uncomfortable. She eventually withdrew, and at the time of the last interview was taking university courses simply for her own pleasure. The waste of her talents, however, was one of several factors that was leading her husband towards what he termed a major re-evaluation of his priorities. Among other things, he was wondering whether or not to remain in his post in Geneva.

The discussion of one of the most difficult dilemmas with which several of the families had to cope in moving abroad serves as a reminder of the complexity of coping. Not all of the problems with which the families had to cope were amenable to their control, and some involved true dilemmas. For example, conflicting needs were impossible to reconcile in families such as the Rentons, where husband and wife would not both be able to pursue their careers because of the demands involved in that of one of them. Families such as the one just discussed, and also the Thomases, could not alter the characteristics of the organisations in which they were able to find jobs. Being able to maintain a career obviously depends on such external factors as the kind of work involved (some careers, such as those of musician or author, are relatively easy to transport, whereas others require a patient building up of local contacts that is impossible to move elsewhere) or the rules in the country to which the families were moving (strict Swiss legislation concerning work permits meant that it was difficult at best for an accompanying spouse to find a professional-level position). Other factors that affect coping, both external and internal to families, are discussed later in this chapter. First, however, the discussion turns to stages through which families may pass as they learn to live in a new culture.

Phases of adaptation

A theme in the literature about moving abroad, which is often taken up by courses and sessions meant to prepare families for such an event, is that of 'phases of adaptation' through which people are said to typically pass during the first year or so after a transcultural move. Three stages are typically described:

> First, a *honeymoon*, or excitement phase: for the first few months the person who has just arrived tends to be enchanted, full of the

joy of discovering a new place, of meeting new people, of settling into a new home, arranging possessions and starting a new chapter in life.

Second, *depression*: The excitement phase wears off after two to six months, leaving the way open for the newly arrived person to pay more attention to various problems and hassles which had been pushed aside in the beginning. What had been charming cultural differences become annoying and/or incomprehensible quirks, loneliness surfaces as old friends are missed and have not yet been replaced with new ones, doubts surface about the wisdom of the move and about how long one may be staying in the new place.

Third, *levelling out*: The depression phase may last for several months, but eventually wears off as the individual or the family settles in. Cultural differences are evaluated more objectively, social networks are reconstructed as new friends are made, and the individual begins to function adequately, no longer giving a great deal of thought to the fact that this is a new culture. By this point those who have moved for a limited stay may already begin to think about going back.

These stages of adaptation were discussed in the second and sometimes also in the third interview, well after the presumed 'depression' phase, in the midst of which I had, in fact, first interviewed several of the families. Virtually all had learned about such phases, from courses about moving abroad, from reading, or from discussions with others who were well aware of them:

W: Our neighbours read four books. If I have a bad day she asks me if I know what stage I'm in!

(Renton/1)

Seven families reported experiencing the stages of adaptation just as described in the literature. The Vances' description is classical:

W: I loved it from the beginning. All those very commonplace things – the doctor, the grocery store, the cleaners, the hardware store – are an adventure. You get a feeling of being a pioneer, of conquering. It's a good feeling: it makes you feel strong. It makes you feel euphoric, the honeymoon.

And then it hits the skids. I remember very well. It was Stephen's birthday. I had just had a rough time: it was in the Fall, and I don't like the Fall; I was tired of fighting with the language; I wasn't comfortable with the lack of communication with the school; I was tired of the Swiss; I liked this new house, but was lonely. That day two things happened that were very minor in the long run: I couldn't get the icing right on the cake – *Swiss* ingredients (laugh), and Stephen [had just very carelessly lost a significant sum of money]. It was pouring rain, and in front of Stephen and his friends I just sat down on the floor and cried.

At the end of that day we decided we'd pretend the day had never happened. I baked another cake, we re-celebrated his birthday the next day, and things began to look up from there.

M: This all happened at once, suddenly.
W: Well it had been slowly building up. You let it fester until it just comes pouring out. Then the loneliness began to dissipate. I became more comfortable with the friends I was making, and began to get involved more in a women's group. I finally accepted that you're not going to change the Swiss, you're the one who has to adapt, and it begins to slowly turn around. It's not a constant up, life never is.
M: That's a classical case.
W: That was the absolute worst. Then lately with [several family problems having nothing to do with the move but more difficult to deal with over long distances, see Chapter 6] I've gone through another phase, not against the Swiss this time, but a period of thinking I'm not sure I like living in a foreign country ... Life would just be so much *easier* ... Because you're still between two worlds: you've got things going on back there, and you've got things here, so sometimes the straddling gets a little tiresome. That's really what it is.
M: ... What about [Mr Vance]?
H: After the first four or five months of adventure there were frustrations. I've always been a very social person, and there was nobody to do things with, like go to a baseball game. Not having that escape made me realise I was in a place where I didn't have any roots and probably wasn't going to develop any. Once I accepted that, it was a bit easier to deal with ... Once you're thrown in this different environment and recognise after six months that you can survive and function, then you think you can probably handle anything. I get back to North America often, but that hinders forming roots here. I'm a North American. Displaced, but North American. I don't like feeling like a minority.
W: We had to come to grips with that. Last year [our country] had an election. We'd always been politically very aware, and enjoyed that. It made us really feel isolated over here. That's

when I started reading [a home country newspaper]. It was a lifeline. It was a little touch of home that made you feel you're still plugged in.

H: I don't miss the habit of watching football all day Saturday and Sunday, but I had the bends at first! (laugh) But after not doing it for a while, who cares?

(Vance/2)

As well as beautifully describing the stages of euphoria, depression, then levelling out, with all of its ambivalence, the Vances recall another important point already made in Chapter 6: the families did not simply drop all and adapt to a new situation. The old ties were still present – family members left behind were very often objects of concern, former interests and attachments maintained. In their thoughts the families were still living in the old place as they simultaneously adapted to the new.

If seven of the families experienced the stages of adaptation just as described in the literature, what about the other three-quarters? Some who were experienced in transcultural moves said they simply settled in, going through no phases. They may have experienced such feelings at other times, but this time their attention was elsewhere: they simply moved in and picked up their lives in the new place. Others seemed to have maintained a 'honeymoon' feeling all the way through the two to three years I followed them. They all said by the end of the study that they felt they could happily settle down to live permanently in Geneva, but such was merely hypothetical: all but one in fact were to be staying for a relatively limited sojourn. They described their experience as 'like a long vacation' or 'like a four-year sabbatical', and spoke enthusiastically of new experiences and of travel. It is noteworthy about this group that, although they were manifestly enthusiastic about their experiences, they also spoke in some detail of encountering a fair amount of stress in adapting.

Five families, on the other hand, reported no 'honeymoon period' of joy or excitement, either immediately after arriving or later. They remained in a depression 'phase' all the way through. The move itself was problematical for all of these families. Among them are the Foster, Zelig, Gibbs and Smithers families who have been discussed at some length. Finally, eight families started out similarly, without enthusiasm, feeling depressed and overwhelmed with problems after they moved, but then went on to feel they had made satisfactory, good, or even excellent adjustments to living in the new place. For them a series of other factors, which may or may not have been related to the move, were perhaps more important than the expatriation itself. Examples are the Allen family surprised to find themselves expecting another child, the Newtons who were fed up with moving in general, or Mrs Renton who was very unhappy about giving up her career.

Having read about such phases, many, if not most, of the people interviewed for this study had already reflected on their own 'stages of adaptation'. Most said that even if they did not go through them, it helped to know about them. Some even mentioned taking perverse pleasure in not feeling what they had heard they should be feeling! For those who did experience a phase of depression and negative feelings about having moved, being prepared for a difficult period made it easier to cope with. Several commented: 'it's nice to know it's not just me'. Stages of adaptation, though, may happen 'all other things being equal'. It is the 'other things' that form the subject matter of the rest of this chapter.

Families' reflections on the effects of migration

Everyone who participated in the study was abundantly aware that it was about the effects on families of moving to a new culture: this had been announced in an initial letter, discussed when I phoned for a first appointment, and discussed again at the beginning of each of the interviews. Most of those interviewed, having already given a good deal of thought to the question, were not only willing, but often even eager to discuss the subject with a neutral outsider. Many had been through employee preparation programmes and most, if not all, had read about moving families abroad, and were well aware of the various problems discussed in the literature.

Most said the main effect of moving on families was to 'bring them closer together'. Several said they now carried out more of their leisure activities together. What most meant, though, was that they had been obliged to cope together, and in relative isolation, with the strains that have been discussed throughout this book. Another way it was often put was: 'moving can make or break a marriage', or 'moving can make or break a family': removed from their usual social supports, couples or families were far more vulnerable to external strains. Since they had only themselves on whom to rely, small strains and cracks were magnified. The Fosters' story in Chapter 9 showed how such cracks may become rifts that in the end separate an entire family. As for '*making*' a family or a marriage, on the other hand, what interviewees meant was that the very process of having weathered such strains, or successfully coped together, reinforces a family who has done so.

Effects of the move for 28 core families

With each of the families we tried to assess what this particular move might have meant not individually, professionally, socially, or educationally, but for the family as a whole. In other words, did the overall experience seem to have a positive, beneficial effect on the family? Or was it negative, or even destructive? Or did the move, in fact, really not have much effect on the family one way or the other? What was evaluated was the upward or downward spiral of consequences that seemed to have been set in motion within each family as the members coped with the relatively moderate stress of an expatriation: change was assessed after two years, after this *particular* adaptation, but it is assumed that families will continue to evolve long after the specific incident that was examined here. Evaluations of the outcome of the move were based on data gathered throughout the study, and especially at the final interview. For example, each family was asked to evaluate the experience on a scale of 1 to 10. (Most people looked surprised when asked to rate their experience, then immediately responded: 'I don't know why, an 8 – or a 3 ... or a 10 – just jumped into my head'. The mean was 8.) Outcome was far more complex than that, however. Professional successes and frustrations were taken into account, but only as they affected the family. I looked at the social relationships the family had sought and been able to establish in Geneva, and their satisfaction with such relationships; what they said about the phrase: 'moving making or breaking marriages'; the worries they expressed connected with moving, and whether or not the problems they had worried about seemed to be occurring; whether family members seemed to be moving closer together (in the sense of voluntarily coming together, not out of fear of the outside world, but out of a wish to be together), or away from one another (apart from the normal letting go of older children). I tried to evaluate for the family as a whole and not for individual members, paying attention to problems and tensions that had arisen, especially marital difficulties and problems with children, or tensions not talked about but which could be perceived. Problems and tensions were not considered in and of themselves to be negative: I tried to see how they were dealt with, and successful resolution of problems was seen to be positive, an indicator of growth and of improved functioning in a sort of tempering process. What was evaluated was the effect of this particular move: thus, for instance, a family such as the Davidsons, whose coping skills had already been tested under more trying conditions than those they found in Geneva, and in which members were already extremely supportive of one other, were rated as not having been affected by this particular move. They simply went on functioning well.

Seen in this way, just over half of the 28 core families seemed to have been positively affected by expatriation to a new culture. These families felt they had grown together through the experience. They felt they had increased control over the family's life course, increased mastery, and a sense of accomplishment. They talked of learning and discovery and of now, having mastered the last one, being more willing to take additional reasonable risks. All of these families (Allen, Elm, Graham, Hill, Renton, Exon, Bateson, Collins, Friedson, Jackson, Kennedy, Ogbourne, Rodgers, Vance and Wood) reported stress, and indeed had a rather large variety of problems, but they felt they had coped successfully with them. Not all were by any means euphoric about moving, but they talked of discovery, of personal growth from learning to cope with stress, of increasing sophistication, and of increased independence for family members. All of these families reported that they had grown closer together since the move. The example of the Wood family was discussed in Chapter 9. Another rather striking example is the Vance family, for whom a move described as a high-risk one with a somewhat troubled adolescent seemed to be turning out not only adequately, but extremely well. Mr and Mrs Vance felt strongly that the move had forced the family to work out certain problems. Removed from their habitual sources of support, they were thrown together to learn to live in a very different environment, handled it, and in the process discovered many things to admire about each other (Chapter 8).

Just over one-third of the families seemed to have been somewhat negatively affected. Most said that they thought this particular move had not been good for the family, or portrayed a feeling of depression when they talked about the subject. Family members felt they were drifting apart, in separate directions, against their will. In contrast with those who were proud of the way they had coped, their feelings of mastery and control were diminished. They felt they had not accomplished their goals, were not living up to expectations of how they would like their family to be. They talked of feeling overburdened, and were rather reluctant to take further risks. The example of the Foster family, the most negatively affected, was discussed in Chapter 9. Other examples that have been discussed throughout the chapters are: the Thomases, suffering from 'a blow to our family self-image' when they were not able to integrate into the local society as much as they had wished (Chapter 10); the Zeligs, with half the family still ill-at-ease with living in Geneva after two years, and where unresolved tensions were apparent between husband and wife, who seemed to be drifting slowly apart (Chapter 4); the Gibbs, for whom this was one of a long series of vaguely regretted moves outside the family's control, and about which Mrs Gibbs remarked: 'you can't help but make some mistakes about moving. If you'd stayed in North America maybe it wouldn't have worked out that way' (Chapter 5); the Madisons, for whom increasingly divisive strains between family and work were also putting them at risk of growing apart (Chapter 7); and the Smithers, whose unthinking rush towards living abroad, denial of problems and stresses, and removal from the social supports important to them before they left, caused tensions between husband and wife and problems with the children that were largely unresolved when the family was forced to return prematurely to North America.[9]

9 A neutral evaluation was given to three families: in one, the effects of this particular move were not yet apparent (the Newtons). In another, potential changes in the realm of the family were due far more to dual-career considerations than to this particular

Towards explaining the effects of the move on families

Analysis throughout this book has focused on sense of coherence and family 'co-ordination' as major factors through which to explain how families coped with learning to live in a new culture. The way families experience themselves as a group in relation to the external world ('co-ordination') was discussed in Chapter 7. Sense of coherence was the principal theme of Chapter 5, has been discussed in most of the other chapters and will come up again in Chapter 11. The remainder of this chapter focuses on the *other* factors that may be correlated with the outcome of the move for families – or that may fail to be correlated. A number of factors raised in Chapter 2, factors which might have been expected to affect the way the move affected the families studied, are discussed first.

Factors that might have been expected to affect families' adaptation

Previous experience with geographical mobility might have been expected to facilitate the transition to living in a new place. As already discussed (Chapter 2) the families who participated in this study were on the whole experienced in changing locations, and several mentioned at the first interview that they thought such experience would help them with the current move. It quickly became apparent, however, that this was not the case. Some of the families who, objectively, had hardly ever moved seemed to be having very little difficulty, whereas some who had moved many times were having a great deal. Contrasting examples are the Batesons, who, although they had never moved before, felt that in coming to Switzerland they were returning to their family roots. That it was several generations ago that their ancestors had moved from Switzerland to North America was relatively unimportant to them: what was far more important was an almost mythical feeling of homecoming and of identification with the society to which they were coming. This feeling of returning to their roots helped all three family members cope with the stresses they nevertheless experienced. At the other end of the continuum were the Newtons, whose experience had been the opposite: having lived in four very different places in the four previous years they were hoping to be able to settle down at last, but in the meantime feeling depressed and angry about this latest disruption. With them, as with several others who felt they were

move (the Quincys). The third family had already gone through a great many previous moves requiring substantial adaptation. This particular one simply reinforced patterns that were already very well established (the Davidsons, see Chapter 7). The effect of the move could not be evaluated for two families (the Cadys and the Kents) who were inconsistent in what they said about themselves.

too far away from their older children, it was this very experience with geographical mobility that was felt to be a problem. In sum, far more important than the simple number of previous moves for helping a family cope was their feeling about this particular move in relation to previous ones.

As for *push and pull factors*, the latter had clearly predominated for those who participated in this study. What, then, of the two families who had mentioned specific push factors among their reasons for moving? Both the Fosters and the Madisons had talked of being glad to get away from drugs and crime, and both were negatively affected by the move. As it turned out, both later revealed that they were also distancing themselves from problems in their extended families. The problems had come back by two years later, however (see Chapter 8 on the Foster family's reconstruction of problems with their neighbours, and Chapter 7 on the difficulties of the Madison family), and it is not impossible that in talking of escaping drugs and crime these families had in fact been talking about escaping problems that were far closer to them. If so, since the problems *were* closer to home they simply moved with the families.

As for the families who talked of the rather nebulous push factors of getting away from a previous place of residence or style of life, or of a simple *desire for change*, the relation was less clear-cut. Some settled into a more compatible way of life in Geneva far more easily than they themselves had expected. What proved to be important was having attempted to think through the implications of the decision. Families such as the Zeligs, who had not adequately thought through the decision, ended up finding themselves in situations that were far more complex than they had bargained for, and were negatively affected by the move (Chapter 4). Perhaps equally important among families who said they were moving partly out of desire for change was the ability to adjust their hopes in the light of the conditions they encountered once they arrived in the new place. The Thomas family are an example. Their extremely ambitious goals for their stay could not be met: they did not revise their goals, but instead were disappointed with themselves for not attaining them.

Other factors were perhaps more surprising. The *length of the projected stay* in Geneva proved to be highly related to the effect the move had on the families studied. Effects of the move were generally positive for the families who had moved for limited stays (typically of three to five years). It is interesting to note that several of these families said by the end of the study that they wished they could stay longer, or even forever (the Woods are an excellent example), and that several indeed later changed their plans, staying longer or leaving earlier than they had anticipated. On the other hand the move proved to be particularly difficult for those who had envisaged open-ended stays from the outset. It may be the ambiguity of their situations that created more stress for these families (see the discussions of the Zelig family for example, Chapters 3 and 4). While changing plans implies flexibility, not having a clear and limited time frame for a stay creates ambiguity that may impede coping.

The possible influence of the *employment setting* for effect of the move on families raises a good many questions. As discussed in Chapter 2, it was the employer, or the new job, that determined the meaning of the move ('an opportunity', 'a transfer' 'a challenge', etc.) and that structured the characteristics of the decision (a routine matter, an extraordinary event, a source of stress, etc.). Some employers also provided a goodly amount of support in the form of help around the move itself as well as facilitating the formation of a social environment that would support a newly arriving family. Effects of the move after two to three years turned out to be mostly positive for the 14 families who moved so that one of their members could work for a company (of these only the Zeligs and the Smithers were negatively affected). The tendency was quite the opposite among the seven families attached to 'the organisation', however, among whom only one was *positively* affected. Were the 'company' families formally or informally screened before they were offered an opportunity to sojourn abroad? Was the positive effect for these families due to the fact that they came for time-limited stays? Or did the employer support just mentioned smooth over some of the practical difficulties, thus allowing families to get on with more fundamental processes of learning to cope with the changes required? What about the families attached to 'the organisation' then? Are these families different from the others? They do not differ on any of the measures or instruments used in this study. Do international organisations, many of which are oriented towards humanitarian efforts, actually aid the families of their own incoming personnel less well than do international companies? Is a general climate of demoralisation within the United Nations system that has been brewing for many years (Ghebali, 1988; Kanninen, 1995) having repercussions on families of employees? Or may the extensive commitment shown by some employees have a negative impact on their families (as for the Madisons, for example, Chapter 7)? The relationship between the family, the specific type of employer, and moving abroad is obviously one that needs to be examined far more extensively.

The final section of this chapter returns to a family characteristic that was introduced in Chapter 1, but that has not yet been discussed.

Accepting stereotypes (family 'closure')

The word 'closure' is often used to denote a process of coming to terms with an event, such as a death in the family. It is used differently here. The concept of 'closure' used here comes from the work of D. Reiss, and is defined as 'a family's proclivity for suspending or applying order and coherent concepts to raw sensory experience'. At one extreme 'early closure families' rapidly apply structured explanations to all incoming stimuli. They struggle to apply past explanations to new data, or, failing that, apply new explanations as quickly as possible, and avoid periods or episodes where stimuli seem uncanny or inexplicable. At the other extreme, 'delayed closure families' for the most part experience stimuli as continuously novel and, at times, chaotic. They cannot utilise or cannot remember the family's previous approaches or solutions to similar problems. Their sense of the present is very intense (Reiss, 1981, p. 75). In sum, 'early closure' families make rapid judgements and impose previously existing paradigms to all new experiences and sensations. At the other extreme, families whose closure was greatly delayed would be unable to impose any at all. Both very early and very late closure would be expected to impede adaptation to a new culture. An example of early closure concerns a 'company' employee who in fact, on the basis of an orientation visit, wisely decided not to move his family abroad after all:

> H: We had a guy who was offered a job in Kenya and accepted. He had never been out of [a small North American city] before. On the way in from the Nairobi airport for his orientation visit he commented that the potholes were even worse than in [his home town]. He was surprised there was no American TV: 'What will my kids watch?' He had accepted the job, and came out to be introduced, and only then did it dawn on him that his kids couldn't watch television. He declined the assignment.
>
> (PP/1)

At the other extreme, and among families such as those studied here, would be an exaggerated cultural relativity, a tendency to continuously collect morsels of information that were never inserted into a framework of interpretation. Closure that was more than moderately delayed could well lead, among other things, to the adoption of 'crummy values' referred to in Chapter 4.

The study focused only on the first few years of a sojourn, however, and only early closure was examined. The indicator was the rapidity with which people made up their minds about the place to which they were coming, in other words the degree to which families were willing to accept stereotypes about Swiss culture and people. This was evaluated by means of responses to a simple question asked at the first interview: 'Did you have any ideas about the Swiss when you came?' Virtually everybody had heard stereotypes about the Swiss as being punctual, serious, hard-working, precise, orderly, and rich, as well as reserved and difficult to get to know. These ideas were practically always nuanced when people talked about them: nobody was either entirely neutral or entirely hostile. Only one study participant, Mrs Bateson, claimed she had not heard any stereotypes at all, only to be contradicted by her daughter, who implied that her mother had forgotten the stereotypes she had heard as a matter of policy. Thus it was not having heard about the stereotypes that was an indicator of closure, but what the respondent then said about them. The families who exhibited 'early' and 'delayed' closure are listed on Table A.9 in the Appendix.

Mr and Mrs Vance demonstrate the attitudes typical of delayed closure. Four months after they arrived they were beginning to formulate their own observations, not only about the Swiss, but about other cultures, including their own:

M: Did you have any ideas about the Swiss when you came?
W: Only what other people told us: efficient, private, stand-offish, hard to be friends with.
H: So far we can't judge. I've met them only through work, where I'm their boss so it's hard to measure. I've noticed that Swiss and Italians don't necessarily mix well, but haven't been here long enough to judge.
W: I've learned to redefine efficient. North American efficient is quick. Swiss efficient is steady, on time, and a job well done, but not necessarily quick. Most of the Swiss I have run into (in stores, people who come to do repairs, etc.) are pleasant and eager to help. Those who seem to look down their noses at the expatriates are more the ex-expats themselves. They were born and raised in a different country, but have been here for many years and gone into the society themselves – they define themselves as Swiss now. The Swiss are not overly friendly, that's their way, but they certainly do not snub you. They put up with my meagre attempts at French and try to be as helpful as possible. (She tells of waiting in a doctor's office, and of having one of the other patients waiting *encourage* her to carry on a conversation in her halting French.)

(Vance/1)

Mr and Mrs Vance report the stereotype they have heard ('Only what other people told us . . .'), but withhold judgement so that they can form their own ideas ('So far we can't judge'). They then proceed to elaborate in some detail, advancing explanations and applying conceptual order to the rather fine observations they have made.

In contrast are couples who reported the stereotypes they had heard about their hosts without further comment, apparently not disagreeing with the ideas they were reporting. The Fosters' hasty conclusions about their neighbours were analysed in Chapter 9. Other examples help understand why early closure at best hinders, and at worst actually prevents, satisfactory adaptation to living in the new culture:

M: Did you know anything about the Swiss?
W: No, actually.
H: (laughs) ... gnomes, eat cheese, make watches ...
W: ... The ones we have dealt with are arrogant, adamant.
H: I think that's a special feature of Geneva. The biggest industry is taking money away from foreigners. The United Nations, and all these American companies setting up their headquarters send money, and the Swiss expect to get it.

He goes on to complain about various charges such as that for having the car converted to Swiss standards, and about a lack of work ethic, giving examples. Mrs Allen takes up the theme, complaining about poor service in stores, restaurants, and so forth. Later he comments:

H: There are irritating things, but they're interesting to watch as an outsider. I think one of the hobbies of the Genevois, as well as taking money from foreigners, is sneering at us, especially North Americans. That's fine: we can chuckle at the Swiss too.

(Allen/1)

It should not be surprising that people portraying such attitudes had trouble making friends with the people about whom they held such opinions. It should also be noted, in all fairness, that such hostile attitudes had largely disappeared among the families who remained in Geneva for at least a year or two. They have their importance, however, in leaving the door open for major misunderstandings, discomfort, fears and feelings of insecurity about the society in which the family is living. They provide a fertile ground for hostile rumours and stereotypes, creating wedges between 'the locals' and 'the foreigners'.

Closure clearly affects adjusting to living in a new culture in other ways as well. Delayed closure permits maximising opportunities to gain new experiences. Geographically, for example, delayed closure was linked to mentions of extensive exploring of Geneva and of its surroundings: families able to 'suspend applying order to raw sensory experience' were undaunted by the risk of boarding a wrong bus or train. They were able to simply wander and explore, ending up somewhere unexpected:

W: I like going places with the kids. We have 'jolly holidays' together. Sometimes we go for drives and let the kids take turns saying whether to turn left or right. We discover all sorts of interesting places that way.

(Elm/2)

Delayed closure families are also more likely to be comfortable with ambiguity, with not quite yet knowing the cultural rules that prevail:

W: It doesn't bother me that I don't understand everything yet ... There were certain situations I didn't understand when we arrived, but by the second time that happens you know what to do. It's not the language, it's knowing how things work here. I always stand back and observe ... We don't try to act like North Americans, we try to pretend we might be Europeans.

(Kennedy/2)

Putting off establishing mind sets allows people to note proxemics (Hall, 1966), in other words to appreciate the culturally determined distances at which people feel comfortable interacting with one another, to get used to functioning in smaller spaces, to being physically closer to strangers, whether living in apartments, sitting in restaurants, walking down a sidewalk or shopping for groceries. Delayed closure, by allowing ambiguity, and thus nuance, also leaves people free to notice and to analyse cultural differences. Refusal to espouse stereotypes is not necessarily equivalent to liking the style of life, or even to feeling comfortable in the new country, but not being afraid to encounter the unknown allows families to make choices which will promote whatever integration they may be able to achieve. It allows them to choose, for example, to live in a neighbourhood that is not primarily North American in hopes of meeting people from other countries or Swiss nationals.

A final point needs to be made in this section about closure. This is that if moderately delayed closure helps a family come to understand where they are living, the opposite, moderately early closure, would not necessarily be negative. In the case of families who move through many cultures, for example, early closure might well be necessary to provide the conceptual structuring that will give continuity in the face of shifting external environments. Reiss writes that for early closure families: 'Not only may the world be experienced as ordered; it may be experienced as derived from the past in an uninterrupted way. Each individual has a clear experience of how his family has responded to similar input in the recent or remote past. This remembrance of things past forms a central basis for the structuring of current experience.' Stability was what some families, such as the all-too-mobile Newton family mentioned above, were seeking in moving to Geneva for the long term. Several of those who had moved extensively spoke of the necessity of maintaining a stable, structured family environment when the external one changed every two or three years:

> M: The impression you give of your family is one of quite a bit of negotiation in the margins, but of a fairly structured routine of bedtime, mealtimes etc. for the security of it ...
>
> W: Yes ... We need that – some people don't ... I think when you move around you have to carry on certain traditions. We don't change the rules and regulations because of where we live.
>
> (Kennedy/3)

The next, and final, chapter summarises and concludes, returning to the possible long-term effects of geographical mobility for families.

11

SUMMARY AND CONCLUSIONS

H: ... getting the car washed, getting gas, going to a supermarket and getting that coin into the slot to get a cart then getting it back. We avoided it for a couple of weeks because we didn't know how to do it. But pretty soon you start saying that's stupid of me to be afraid. Like going through the tunnel to Italy: how do you tell the man 'I'm coming back today'? Then you have the experience and you say hey, why haven't we done this before? Why haven't we taken the train down to the other side of the lake? Each experience builds and you get more experience.

M: Pushing back the limits.

H: You're pushing back the limits every time you do something else.

(Davidson/2)

The 28 core families who participated in the study reported on in this book tell 28 different stories about the effects of learning to live in a different culture, yet raise many common themes. This chapter summarises: it briefly presents the people who participated in the study, the stresses they reported, and the short-term effects of the move. The two main concepts used to analyse such effects are then discussed: these are sense of coherence and the way a family operates together in relation to the external world. The chapter ends with some questions concerning the long-term effects of the move, then with brief sections on moving and families, and on stress and families.

Summary

The families studied were all at one stage of the family life cycle, and of the same culture. They were – the point bears repeating – relatively privileged migrants. Most felt they had a great deal of choice as to whether to migrate, and were coming towards something they valued, sometimes greatly. The culture to which they moved, in addition, was in many ways similar to their own. The study was longitudinal: families were interviewed three to four months after they moved, after about a year, and after about two years. Data analysis took place as interviewing was going on, and themes that emerged from one round of interviews were discussed in the next. The focus has thus been on process, examining the ways in which families cope with the relatively moderate stress involved in learning to live in a new culture. The outcome, also, was judged in terms of process, the upward or downward spiral of consequences that seemed to have been set in motion within each family as they coped with such stress.

Those who were studied and why they moved

All of the American and Canadian families with school-aged children who moved to Geneva during the course of one calendar year in the late 1980s were asked to participate in a study of families moving abroad. Just over 80 per cent of the families approached agreed to do so. They were upper middle-class families, moving because one of their members (almost always the husband) worked for a large multinational corporation or for a smaller firm, for an international organisation, or for their government. A minority moved independently, as professionals or artists for example, and five were university professors on sabbatical years. Forty-five families were seen during the first round of interviews, 30 for the second, and 26 for the third, with extra interviews performed as necessary. Most of the analysis and discussion here concerns a core group of 28 dual-parent families who remained in Geneva for two full years. Pseudonyms are used in all cases. Details concerning the families have been changed to maintain confidentiality.

Ages of parents ranged from 27 to 53 years. In the youngest families the first child was just starting kindergarten and careers were in early stages, while the oldest families were already thinking about the empty nest and about retirement. The families had from one to six children: the youngest were born during the study, the eldest was 25 years of age. Some of the wives had careers, and some pursued their careers or found jobs after they moved to Geneva. About one-third of the wives, on the other hand, felt their job at the moment was to stay home to provide a stable point for their families. Almost all of the families had previous experience with geographical mobility, some a great deal of experience. Most expected to stay in Geneva for three to five years, although almost one-third expected to stay longer. These were on the whole 'normal' well-functioning families, many of whom had been selected by their employers, or selected themselves, in relation to their aptitude to move abroad. They were more traditional than their compatriots in their ideas about marital relationships, and also placed more emphasis on sharing, harmony and companionship.

SUMMARY AND CONCLUSIONS

Although about half described the decision to migrate, or to sojourn, as having been difficult to make, most also spoke of new professional challenges, discovery of another culture, exploration, widening horizons, gaining a new perspective on the world, personal growth. The move had a somewhat different meaning for the families attached to each of the three major employment settings. For the four families who moved with 'the government' this was for the most part a routine affair in a series of stays in several countries. These families had signed on for a mobile style of life quite some time ago: the decision to move from the previous place was thus not one about which they had to think a great deal. Geneva was not a particularly challenging post, but rather chosen for its pleasant style of life, and hopes for the sojourn tended to be relatively low-key, for example to see some of the country, get to know the local culture. For the majority of those who moved with 'the organisation' (seven families), in contrast, the specific city of Geneva and its style of life were of secondary importance. Of primary importance was the chance to work internationally, to have a chance to put ideas to work on a global level. Several described the new job as 'the summit of my career'. 'Organisation' families arrived for unlimited or long-term stays. Most of those working for 'the company' (14 families), finally, talked about the move in terms of their careers. Those who are to rise to positions of power, especially, may be expected to spend some time 'seeing how the rest of the world does business': rewards were financial, and also a potential for advancement in the company. Most also talked at some length of having the experience of living in a different culture, an experience they thought would be especially good for their children. All but one initially moved for limited stays of two to five years, and all had in mind that they would return to North America.

Stresses, strains on families

In spite of the relatively favourable circumstances in which they emigrated, the families who participated in the study reported many stresses. Some of the accompanying family members had simply been feeling comfortable where they were living, and dreaded uprooting. In some cases the move coincided poorly with other family events such as children starting or leaving school, illnesses, or needs of extended families. Some felt pressured to make significant decisions, but without having adequate information. Most worried about being able to afford the high cost of living in the city to which they had moved.

Particularly unnerving during the first few months were hassles, trivial annoyances with problems of everyday life that are minor, but that at length challenge feelings of adult competence. Many also described feeling frustrated, incompetent and even humiliated when they did not understand the language spoken around them. More fundamentally, some study participants found that what they normally took for granted had suddenly shifted, that they did not quite master what was going on around them. Some felt they were being criticised for infringing rules they could not even perceive. Finally, having left their usual sources of support, having made new acquaintances but not yet friends, those who moved were exposed to loneliness.

Study participants also described numerous sources of potential strain for families. Expectations and experiences of husbands and wives sometimes differed considerably, creating a potential for jealousy. Small irritations in relationships could inflate into major problems under such circumstances, especially since, away from their usual routines and structures, family members had, for the most part, to rely on each other. One of the most problematic issues for these families was that it is extremely difficult to transport two serious careers across an intercultural move. Several of the accompanying spouses had careers in which they were highly invested, careers they were obliged to put aside for the duration, usually with no guarantee that they would be able to return to them. Another source of potentially serious strain occurred around blame and guilt, when one spouse was seen to be responsible for displacing the entire family, and when one or more of the other members of the family were 'not adjusting well'. Another strain was the rather extensive travel often required for work. Repeated absences and homecomings often caused difficulties around rule-setting and discipline with children, and feelings of abandonment and jealousy on the part of the spouse who remained home to cope in the new place. A final source of potential strain was that of managing encounters with values often quite different from those with which the family was familiar. All study participants had anticipated encountering different values among people from other cultures, but many were less prepared for encounters with other expatriates who were perhaps of the same nationality, but of quite different backgrounds and experiences. The availability of more money, especially, as well as encounters with different norms concerning the use of alcohol, could create situations of risk for adolescents as well as for some adults. Finally, respondents often talked at length of people they had left behind. Many described a feeling of living between two worlds, especially when they were dealing with children left across oceans, or with family crises such as the ill health and death of parents.

Coping and social support

Case histories focused on how several of the families defined and dealt with the strains that have just been sketched. The discussion of coping was organised around sense of coherence, as will be summarised below. Mobilisation of social support was examined in some detail. Immediately

SUMMARY AND CONCLUSIONS

after a move significant practical and emotional support came from old friends, from employers, and also from networks of people of the same nationality already living in the new place. In addition, families just arriving found important social support both from people they barely knew (for example from friends of friends) and from those geographically much more distant than the social support literature usually takes into account (exchanges with people living on other continents were often of significant support).

An obvious coping resource, available in varying degrees to the families in this study, was the informational, practical and also emotional support provided by many of the employers. Another early form of social support came from newcomers and spouse groups. Several of the women, especially, reported significant early support from 'first friends' made shortly after they arrived, during a period that several had found difficult. A common thread of criticism ran through families' discussions of such first friends and newcomers groups however. Primarily frequented by people who share a common series of difficulties and frustrations, such groups may shift a delicate balance away from 'letting off steam' towards 'complaining' or 'whining'. Although several people mentioned that complaining in moderate doses to trusted old friends could be very good for the soul, trusted old friends, of course, were what they did not necessarily have right after they moved. At times when they may have been feeling vulnerable, people were thus obliged to maintain a critical balance between revealing impressions enough to construct a new friendship, letting off accumulated frustrations, and 'keeping a positive attitude'.

Several study participants had difficulty negotiating themselves through the new relationships. Some attached themselves to the first people or groups that came along. Others waited, weeded out and chose. A paradox was noted concerning need for other people: individuals or families who did not urgently feel they needed to form new relationships were those who generally made many new friends anyway. One possible reason is that receiving social support may have a subjective element: the same gesture might be taken for granted – or not even perceived – by one person, whereas another may see it as extraordinarily helpful. Another aspect is certainly that those who reported receiving social support also liberally gave it, and because they were more oriented towards giving help, did not expect it for themselves. Some of those who participated in the study were able to exercise active control over their social environments, limiting hospitality that had been overextended, or tactfully extracting themselves from unsatisfying and unhealthy relationships that had been formed during a time of need and vulnerability.

SUMMARY AND CONCLUSIONS

Effects of the move on families

Outcome was seen as movement and as process rather than as a final state, in other words as something that would be better captured with a film than with a snapshot. The results of the move were looked at from two different points of view, that of children, and that of families. There were some surprises concerning children. One was the disorientation of some of the very young children. Their parents had simply not realised the extent to which they would be confused by the repeated changes of temporary 'home' as families left one place, visited friends or relatives, travelled, and lived in temporary housing until their more permanent residences were ready. Another surprise was that the move proved to be particularly difficult for school-aged children who were described as 'bright' or had been leaders where they lived before. Perhaps less surprising was the finding that the time of the school year during which families moved had considerable importance for their children: adaptation was easier when children arrived during the break in the academic year. A major decision concerning school-aged children was whether they should attend local schools (in a foreign language) or one of the International Schools (either in French or in their own language). Most of the families who participated in the study took the latter course for various reasons, but all of the children whose parents insisted that they learn French had done so by the end of the study.

As for older children, none of the families who participated in the study moved adolescents without giving the matter considerable thought. To the surprise of all concerned, it was the adolescents who perhaps had the least difficulty adapting to the move, and among whom several very positive changes took place. Only one adolescent was seen to have been clearly and unambiguously negatively affected by this particular move, one in a long series of repeated and undesired uprootings. A final surprise was the reaction to the move of older children left at home in North America. If some gained independence and maturity, several had far more difficulty than anyone had envisaged when it was the family who moved away from the 'child' rather than the more usual situation of the adult 'child' moving away from the family.

The strains of adapting to living in a new culture caused repercussions that were clearly damaging for at least one of the families studied, whereas several others seemed to be headed in the opposite, positive, direction. Case histories discussed the series of interrelated factors that severely damaged the first family, and the very significant strain, and even mourning, that occurred, but as a precursor to major growth for another. In all, and as they stated themselves, the move would seem to have had rather negative short-term effects for just over one-third of the families who participated in the study. They were suffering, at least temporarily, from the strains of feeling that they were growing apart from some of their family members, or that they were not living up to the goals and images they had set for themselves. In some of these families vaguely defined regrets seemed to predominate: the underlying feeling was one of dissatisfaction and of regret, but the feelings remained mostly unformulated. Others were in the midst of more overt – and unresolved – tensions, tensions that were putting the nuclear family at risk of growing apart.

Effects were noted as being positive for about half of the families studied. They all reported stress, and indeed experienced a rather large variety of problems, but they felt they had coped successfully. They all rather strikingly talked about being convinced that one learns through successful resolution of problems, about growth from learning to deal with stress, from learning to cope with strains. They talked of discovery, of increasing sophistication, of an expanded world view, and of increased independence. All reported that they had grown closer together. Removed from their usual social supports, they had been forced to cope together with the strains of learning to live in a new culture, and doing so successfully had made them more united. In some cases relations between parents and children had been challenged, renegotiated, and strengthened.

The influence of SOC and of family 'co-ordination'

Although factors external to families, such as the conditions provided by the employer, are obviously important in affecting the results of a move (see Chapter 10), much of the focus of this book has been on factors within families themselves. Of these, sense of coherence (SOC) and family 'co-ordination' have been emphasised.

'Sense of coherence'

Coping with the strains of adapting to a new culture has been discussed throughout the book largely in terms of sense of coherence (SOC) or a: 'global orientation that expresses the extent to which one has a pervasive, enduring though dynamic feeling of confidence that (1) the stimuli deriving from one's internal and external environments in the course of living are structured, predictable, and explicable; (2) the resources are available to one to meet the demands posed by these stimuli; and (3) these demands are challenges, worthy of investment and engagement' (Antonovsky, 1987). SOC has been found, in numerous studies over the past decade, to affect the way individuals cope with stress (see Geyer, 1997, for a review). Most of the discussion involving SOC in this book has been oriented around its three components. Of the three interrelated elements (comprehensibility, manageability, and meaningfulness), the last has been stressed. Other things being equal, and among people such as those studied here, meaningfulness, or commitment as opposed to alienation, may underpin the choice of professional field in which one of the family members works, and the way in which the rest of the family aligns itself around this work. Meaning and comprehensibility allow a family to determine and chart its course, manageability to navigate it. Sense of coherence influences decisions to move abroad, how stressful such a move is felt to be, and what is done about the stress. It also very clearly affects what the positive aspects of the decision are felt to be.

The sense of coherence elements of meaningfulness, manageability and comprehensibility underlie the answers to the question 'why move?'. Families who scored high on SOC portrayed a clear sense that they were taking a particular action for a specific reason, be it because one of them might thus have better chances of becoming vice-president of a corporation, or because they wished to see in some depth what life is like in another part of the world. The sense of meaningfulness, especially, leads to engagement, to willingness to cope, to being able to decide whether a stressor matters or not.

High SOC families did not describe the decision to move as being either easier or more difficult, but portrayed the impression of having thought out their priorities: moving required giving up certain things, but the choices had been clearly thought through. The factors to be taken into account in making the decision to move abroad differed according to whether someone in the family worked for 'the government', 'the organisation' or 'the company', but across the three employment settings the high sense of coherence families transmitted an impression of doing, at least to some extent, what they wanted to do, of feeling relatively in charge of what happens to them. They all rather strikingly talked about 'challenge'. Low SOC families, on the other hand, basically followed what the employer had decided for them. They were less likely to take into account complexity, and to think through the ramifications of their decisions. High SOC families expressed a wider range of hopes for themselves and their children in moving, whereas low SOC families generally took a more modest, passive stance. Their expectations were of being able to settle down, or 'enjoying it' and they also spoke less of seeking broadening experiences for their children in moving.

The families interviewed varied in the amount of information they would need about living in the new place, but those higher on SOC took it for granted that faced with a new situation they did not understand they would be able to define what they needed to know and take the steps required to learn it. They thus prepared more appropriately for the move. Low SOC families were more likely to simply jump into a new situation, thus to later find themselves dealing with more than they had bargained for. They were also more likely to find themselves in situations that would

SUMMARY AND CONCLUSIONS

force them to make necessarily unsatisfying choices, such as that of one partner having to give up a highly invested career so that the other could relocate.

Once they arrived, families high or low on SOC coped quite differently. High SOC families were more able than the low SOC families to *see* the difficulties that would require to be coped with in the first place. Those lower on SOC were less likely to admit to themselves when things were going just slightly wrong. They were more likely to deny difficulties, to let matters simply slide along. Less likely to define problems, they were thus quite obviously less in a position to do something about them. On the other hand when a family high on SOC determined that they had made a mistake they most certainly talked of stress, but took steps to correct the problems, inconvenient as such steps often were. The opposite attitude of the lower SOC families is more difficult to put into words. It implies more passively following whatever currents life brings, experiencing disappointments, becoming frustrated. It involves not tackling problems since family members simply do not feel they will be able to do anything about them, and feeling influenced by not-quite-understood forces. If SOC affected a family's definition of the problems that can be tackled or coped with, it also affected the definition of what is beyond the range of coping efforts, either because family members have determined they are not a priority, or because they simply cannot be helped, and are thus not worth regret. Thus the high SOC families avoided the wistful regret that marked the low SOC families. Very far from finding that life was 'using up our only long-term goal', as one low SOC family put it, the high SOC families were more likely to take on new challenges, to expand limits in ever-widening circles.

SOC also affected the way in which families mobilised social support. In low SOC families the accompanying spouses, especially, were more likely to fight loneliness right after they moved by becoming prematurely busy and active. They joined groups in order to meet people rather than out of interest for whatever the group's function was. They ran the risk of becoming too dependent on a limited number of sources of support and thus of making implicit or explicit demands that others might find exaggerated. Finding their social environments less comprehensible than those with a high SOC, they were perhaps less at ease, less able to make realistic assessments of the people they were meeting, more liable to be just slightly on guard, thus to elicit similar reactions in return. Less likely to define problems in relations, they were less likely to be able to take early steps to correct them, and thus more liable to find themselves in difficulty. Similarly, they were less able to impose limits, thus more liable to find themselves overrun with demands from others. High SOC families, in contrast, may have needed less formal external support. They also tended to form their sources of support around interests beyond those based solely on need for contact with other people. If they joined groups they did so because they were interested in the goal around which the group was formed, not simply to meet people. They took precautions in approaching other people, but those precautions taken, assumed most people would be reliable, and, perhaps, expecting the best from people, tended to elicit it. High SOC families were also able to modify their relationships if necessary, for example by putting limits on demands, or by extracting themselves from relationships that were destructive.

'Co-ordination'

The other main theme of analysis used was that of 'co-ordination', defined as the family's belief that they, in fact, occupy the same experiential world (Reiss, 1981). Families high on this characteristic share common principles and patterns of the universe. They function as a group, very much more than the sum of its parts. The world of husband and of wife, as well as those of the children, comprise 'our world', as opposed to the separate worlds of members of lower co-ordination families, who tend to approach the environment as unrelated individuals. Several indicators of family co-ordination were used, including indications that family members deliberately arranged to share most activities and to spend time together, and felt that significant events that happened to one family member affected all.

In moving abroad, a family high on co-ordination was more likely than a low co-ordination family to have taken a decision together in the first place. They were also more likely to have attempted to balance the needs of all family members in making the decision, and to have done what they could to ensure that conditions of the move were as favourable as possible for each family member. Older children, especially, thus felt less as though leaving one place and arriving in another had been imposed upon them, and more as though they were equal participants. Joint family ownership was especially important where there were difficult decisions to be made, such as that for children to attend local schools in a foreign language, or to separate from close family members in pursuit of a goal felt to be important.

Once they arrived in the new culture, and removed from their usual social supports, families who 'lived in the same experiential world', who 'came from the same place', who operated *together* rather than as a collection of individuals, were clearly at an advantage. High co-ordination families had difficulty comprehending how families (as opposed to individuals) could be lonely just after they moved, and had less difficulty than low co-ordination families with the initial period of isolation. Less likely to rush off into the first group or friendship offered, they were thus less likely to later find themselves entangled in relationships that had been

SUMMARY AND CONCLUSIONS

based mainly on mutual need for company. Since they needed other people less, they paradoxically had less difficulty meeting new people, or creating new social networks. High co-ordination families, also paradoxically, were less afraid of the absences of family members that were another major source of distress for some families after the move. Spouses 'living in the same experiential world' could, at least to a degree, share an experience that only one of them had.

Low co-ordination families, on the other hand, portrayed a feeling that between husband and wife was a separate 'his world', and 'her world'. The two worlds did not necessarily have a great deal to do with each other. A very high degree of commitment of one family member was not necessarily shared by the rest of the family. Each family member coped relatively independently with whatever came along. In case of problems adapting to the new culture, members of low co-ordination families kept their difficulties to themselves: they coped alone, and tried to keep a brave face for the rest of the family. In families 'living in the same experiential world', on the other hand, it was simply taken for granted that the difficulties of one family member would require action on the part of the others. When a child in a lower co-ordination family had trouble, efforts were made to address the difficulty, but the feeling was of attempting to cope as individuals or as dyads (mother and child, especially) rather than as a larger family unit. The feeling was quite different in high co-ordination families, who described coming together to help when one member was having difficulties. One family member would, moreover, help another formulate, recognise, and bring out the difficulties another was experiencing. The entire family was more able to remain relatively sanguine in the face of fairly severe stress, as well as provide a sort of safety net, or refuge.

It is quite possible that it is through co-ordination that moving to a new culture will have its primary effect on a family. When asked how they thought moving may affect families in general, the families interviewed for this study most frequently cited that of 'bringing them closer together'. What most meant was that families were forced to cope together in an unknown environment and without those who usually helped them. Another way it was often put was 'moving can make or break a marriage', or 'moving can make or break a family': removed from their usual social supports, couples or families were far more vulnerable to external strains. In the face of such vulnerability, working through the subtle shifts in relations between parents and children that may be involved as family members adapt differently to the new culture, weathering the different preoccupations of each family member when they have just moved, families that could hold together in the first place were nudged in the direction of living in the same emotional space, of greater sharing.

SUMMARY AND CONCLUSIONS

Long-term effects?

The study concerns short-term effects of moving abroad for families. As was discussed in the previous chapter, by two years after they moved many families will have seen changes set in motion. It is, however, far too soon to perceive the possible long-term effects. There are two ways in which such long-term effects should be examined: those of perhaps just one sojourn, and those of repeated moves across cultures.

For the effects of just one sojourn in another culture, some of the families studied seemed to have been negatively affected in the short- and medium-term, whereas others seemed to be positively affected. For all, however, it may take a great deal more time for the full effects of the move to become apparent. Some effects may run their full course over generations, for example if older children decide to stay in Europe after the rest of the family returns home. To examine the medium-term effects it would be interesting, to say the least, to return to the same families a decade or so later to see what they had to say about the effects of the particular move to Geneva. What will be the eventual fate of the shifts in roles among family members that were precipitated by the move? Will some have lost their footing amid the different values they encountered, and ended up without any values of their own? Will their national identity have been reinforced as a consequence of encountering people from other nations? Will they have maintained the French they learned? Will their newly acquired sophistication have lasted? Will they remain more cosmopolitan? Which among the new ideas planted will remain? How will they handle the return home, a step that some authors have described as being the most difficult in the cycle of international life (Werkman, 1980; Austin, 1986)? What will happen to the new career directions discovered? What will be the ultimate repercussions of even apparently trivial changes, such as heretofore very North American children who begin to insist that 'our family traditions' at Christmas now include preparation of a typical Swiss dish?

As for the effects of repeated moves across cultures, most of those whose careers required extensive moving across cultures had given a great deal of thought to how migration had created special needs within their families, such as that for extra structure and stability. They were almost unanimously convinced that successful transcultural moves, especially when they are repeated, bring families closer together. This is particularly the case when the moves are to places where they must cope with relatively difficult conditions of daily life. On the other hand, families who had moved extensively were worried about rootlessness. When they were asked at the last interview what place they considered 'home' many said: 'wherever the family is'. Five couples, though, could not say. Especially disconcerting are the two couples in which husband and wife considered different places to be their 'home'. Some of the families who had moved extensively worried that their children would lack cultural identity. They worried about growing apart, and about eventually finding their children scattered over several different continents.

The long-term effects of extensive geographical mobility also need to be studied. Will the problems worried about by the parents who participated in this study be tempered in an age of e-mails, mobile telephones and easily affordable airfares? Do repeated moves lead to increased sophistication, mastery, ease in the world and with meeting people – or may they lead to alienation, rootlessness, superficiality, lack of attachment, inability to fit anywhere and inability to deal with other than short-term relationships (Haour-Knipe, 1989)? Do the children who have grown up in several places in turn choose professions that will involve living in many different places (Useem and Useem, 1967; Useem and Downie, 1976)? What are the effects of mobility on family unity: are very mobile families indeed closer than others over the long term? If so, may such closeness, when fed by feelings of guilt and anxiety, paradoxically lead to exaggerated concerns about the health and well-being of the family's offspring – or will children's early difficulties and culture shock soon be coped with, and in fact *insulate* them against further problems (Öry et al., 1991; Tamura and Furnham, 1993). What happens in 'close' families as children leave the nest and become independent? What about sense of coherence: a stable, predictable world in childhood is thought to be linked to the development of a strong sense of coherence (Antonovsky, 1987) – does rapid change of cultures weaken it?

Expatriation, stress, coping and families

As discussed in the preface, three professional literatures underlie this book, those on migration, on stress, and on families. What the book hopes to have shown is the way in which families who are relatively healthy and well-functioning interact both together and with their environment to cope with a series of stresses they themselves had sought, in a process of seeking change and growth. The next two sections briefly sketch some of the implications of the study, concerning migration and families, and concerning stress and families.

Migration and families

Family migration is often seen in terms of permanent relocation, the adaptation to which may precipitate a stormy period of decompensation and crisis. Such a period may be plagued with conflicts, symptoms, and difficulties as a family learns to reshape its new reality, to find ways to become compatible with the new environment and at the same time to preserve

SUMMARY AND CONCLUSIONS

its identity (cf. Taboada Leonetti and Lévy, 1978; Sluzki, 1979). Those called to live *temporarily* abroad may also experience unhappiness, distress and poor adjustment (Furnham and Bochner, 1986). Most of the people studied here were well aware of their relatively privileged status. Accompanying spouses, especially, very often said they felt: 'you're not supposed to be unhappy'. The message was rarely stated so bluntly, but it was implied from several directions. It came from people back home who may have thought their friends were leading a glamorous life abroad, from other groups of migrants in the host country whose living conditions were substantially less comfortable, and even from fellow expatriates whose own initial difficulties were long past and who may not have wanted to be reminded of them in the form of the difficulties of others. Yet what the people who participated in this study have shown is that, even under relatively ideal conditions, migration with families has many stressful aspects, which may go so far as to threaten identity and feelings of competence, as well as many potential sources of strain for family relations.

Their advantages notwithstanding, failure rates (premature repatriation) among expatriate families are often cited as being as high as 25 per cent to 70 per cent (depending on the study, the year, and the country to which the employee had gone). Problems of family members – particularly of the accompanying spouse – are one of the main factors cited for such failures (Hiltrop and Janssens, 1990). The study has underlined the importance of a number of factors for influencing these families' experiences. Perhaps the most important among such factors is a feeling of having had a choice about making the move. A related factor is that of coming towards something positive – rather than going away from something negative – when a family changes locations. Few readers will be surprised, moreover, to be informed of the importance of the economic context in which a move takes place, or of that of the support provided, both of a practical and of an emotional nature. Nor is it surprising that dual careers are extremely difficult to transport (cf. Cooper, 1996), and that this is a principal problem for a significant proportion of the families such as those studied here. Devising an adequate solution will go far beyond the measures a single family will be able to exercise: it will involve changes both in legislation concerning work permits and in personnel policies of the companies and organisations that do the hiring.

Not new either is the importance of shared family goals in moving: the study has shown the destructive impact of a move when some family members feel they have unfairly sacrificed to the interests of others. The study has also shown the importance of keeping lines of communication open within families, of discussing together throughout the entire process of moving to a new culture, from before the decision is actually made, through the difficulties and achievements of various family members as they learn to live in the new place, to deciding to return home, to remain

SUMMARY AND CONCLUSIONS

in the new place, or to move on somewhere else. It has also shown that the strains of displacement may introduce wedges that may drive families apart, and also the contrary, that families may come closer together through coping together. The end result can be learning, widening horizons, and increased competence, although even positive change may involve a degree of mourning of old selves and ways of being.

The study has shown several things that are less obvious. One is that there are many different patterns of, and routes to, adaptation to a new culture. Generalisations, such as those concerning phases of adaptation or children's reactions, should certainly be considered, but only with a degree of scepticism: they should not be treated as though they were universal processes. Migration literature tends to stress integration, but those studied here have shown that integration may not be the only path to adaptation: some families live quite happily on the margins of the society to which they have moved. The study has also shown that migrants do not simply drop all when they move to a new place: they often 'live between two worlds', dividing attention between life in the new place and concerns from the old place that are still very pertinent. Relations with family, friends, acquaintances, and even friends of friends, are maintained across long distances. Similarly, those studied here have shown that social support of informational, practical, and emotional sorts does not necessarily come from people in the immediate vicinity: significant social support may come from people who are geographically very far away. Finally, the study has shown the importance of sense of coherence, for influencing coping. This brings us to what the study has shown about stress.

Stress and families

The book has talked much of social support. Social support affects how individuals cope with stressful events, and how individuals cope, in turn, may influence their use of social support in the future (Pierce et al., 1996). The book has shown how some of these mechanisms work for families and also how community members may decide how social support is to be distributed (Reiss and Oliveri, 1983). The study has also shown the importance of hassles (Kanner et al., 1981; Perrez and Reicherts, 1992), the small annoyances or grains of sand that can end up seriously damaging both self-confidence and family relations. The principal contributions of the study, however, are to see family stress as having potentially quite positive repercussions, and to examine family sense of coherence in action.

The families who participated in this study all deliberately chose to do something they knew would be stressful. The stance of the book has been to see the individual as a psychological activist (Thoits, 1994), to see people as conscious, active agents in their own lives, acting deliberately to resolve acute and chronic stressors, and affected by the results of their own efforts to resolve their own problems. (cf. Holahan, Moos and Schaefer, 1996). Pauline Boss (1988), in particular, has argued that stress is normal in families, and even desirable at times: it becomes problematic only when the degree of stress in the family system reaches a level at which family members and/or family systems become dissatisfied or show symptoms of disturbance. More recently, and in a current in which this author most certainly joins, others have turned to examination of family resilience (cf. Haggerty et al., 1994; and Walsh, 1996). Such authors have pointed out that if life conditions must offer predictable and achievable rewards in order for resilience to develop, it is around crisis and challenge that a coherent life story may be organised. In other words, resilience is forged *through* adversity, not *despite* it. What has been argued here is that sense of coherence serves as an important key for understanding how such resilience comes to be.

The discussion has attempted to demonstrate the way in which seeing the world as being meaningful, comprehensible and manageable encourages individuals, and thus the families in which individuals are grouped, to find out about their surroundings. High sense of coherence leads to willingness to grapple with a new situation, and also to the ability to more clearly assess a given situation and its possible repercussions. Clear assessment, in turn, increases the chances that the outcome of such tackling of a new situation will be positive. In other words, a strong SOC family will choose experiences which may well be stressful in the medium term (judiciously, choosing stresses and risks that have chances of succeeding), but which, through successful coping, will ultimately lead to learning, to even better coping. Also discussed has been the way in which SOC influences the mobilisation of the social support that will aid coping.

Such behaviour reinforces the original paradigm. In other words, if defeat leads to feeling depleted and defeated, successful coping leads to greater capacities. This gives the first inkling of how the ability to cope with and to learn from stress may be transmitted from generation to generation. A parent's sense of caring deeply about something that is at the core of sense of coherence will be obvious to the children in a family – meaningfulness may be transmitted as children watch their parents live out a sense of commitment and engagement.

More generally, what the study suggests is that moderate doses of stress are necessary and beneficial for growth and for the development of resilience. Stress, thus, the necessary preliminary to coping, cannot be entirely negative. Choice of challenges and successful coping occur in a circular process of tempering. In other words, as suggested by the study participant quoted at the beginning of this chapter: 'You're pushing back the limits every time you do something else'.

REFERENCES

Antonovsky, A. (1979) *Health, Stress, and Coping*, San Francisco: Jossey-Bass.
Antonovsky, A. (1987) *Unravelling the Mystery of Health: How People Manage Stress and Stay Well*, San Francisco: Jossey-Bass.
Austin, C. (ed.) (1986) *Cross-Cultural Re-entry: A Book of Readings*, Abilene, Texas: Abilene Christian University Press.
Boss, P. (1988) *Family Stress Management*, London: Sage.
Cooper, C. (1996) 'Corporate relocation policies', in Lewis, S. and Lewis, J. (eds) *The Work–Family Challenge*, London: Sage, pp. 93–102.
Datan, N., Antonovsky, A. and Maoz, B. (1981) *A Time to Reap: The Middle Age of Women in Five Israeli Subcultures*, Baltimore: Johns Hopkins University Press.
Fitzpatrick, M. A. (1988) *Between Husbands and Wives: Communication in Marriage*, London: Sage.
Furnham, A. and Bochner, S. (1986) *Culture Shock: Psychological Reactions to Unfamiliar Environments*, London: Routledge.
Geyer, S. (1997) 'Some conceptual considerations on the sense of coherence', *Social Science and Medicine*, 44/12, pp. 1771–9.
Ghebali, V.-Y. (1988) *La crise du système des Nations Unies*, Paris: La Documentation française.
Granovetter, M. (1973) 'The strength of the weak ties', *American Journal of Sociology*, 78, pp. 1360–80.
Haggerty, R., Sherrod, L., Garmezy, N. and Rutter, M. (eds) (1994) *Stress, Risk, and Resilience in Children and Adolescents: Processes, Mechanisms, and Interventions*, Cambridge: Cambridge University Press.
Hall, E. T. (1966) *The Hidden Dimension*, New York: Doubleday.
Haour-Knipe, M. (1989) 'International employment and children: geographical mobility and mental health among children of professionals', *Social Science and Medicine*, 23, pp. 197–205.
Haour-Knipe, M. (1997) 'Continuités et changements chez les familles de cadres internationaux', in Bolzman, C. and Béday-Hauser, P. (eds) *On est né quelque part mais on peut vivre ailleurs: Familles, cultures, migrations, travail social*, Geneva: Les éditions I.E.S.
Haour-Knipe, M. (1999) 'Moving families: migration, stress and coping'. Thesis presented to the Faculty of Social and Economic Sciences, University of Geneva, September 1999.
Haour-Knipe, M. (2000) 'Family SOC and adapting to a new culture: a case study', *Polish Psychological Bulletin*, 30/4, pp. 311–21.
Hiltrop, J. M. and Janssens, M. (1990) 'Expatriation: challenges and recommendations', *European Management Journal*, 8/1, pp. 19–26.

REFERENCES

Holahan, C., Moos, R. and Schaefer, J. (1996) 'Coping, stress resistance, and growth: conceptualizing adaptive functioning', in Zeidner M. and Endler N. (eds) *Handbook of Coping: Theory, Research, Applications*, Chichester: John Wiley & Sons, pp. 24–43.

Holmes, T. and Rahe, R. (1967) 'The social readjustment rating scale', *Journal of Psychosomatic Research*, 11, pp. 213–18.

House, J. and Kahn, R. (1985) 'Measures and Concepts of Social Support', in Cohen, S. and Syme, S. (eds) *Social Support and Health*, Orlando, Fla.: Academic Press.

Kanner, A., Coyne, J., Schaefer, C. and Lazarus, R. (1981) 'Comparison of two modes of stress measurement: daily hassles and uplifts versus major life events', *Journal of Behavioral Medicine*, 4, pp. 1–39.

Kanninen, T. (1995) *Leadership and Reform: The Secretary-General and the UN Financial Crisis of the Late 1980s*, The Hague: Kluwer Law International.

Lavee, Y. and Olsen, D. (1993) 'Seven types of marriage: empirical typology based on ENRICH', *Journal of Marital and Family Therapy*, 19/4, pp. 325–40.

Lazarus, R. and Folkman, S. (1984) *Stress, Appraisal, and Coping*, New York: Springer.

Oliveri, M. E. and Reiss, D. (1984) 'Family concepts and their measurement: things are seldom what they seem', *Family Process*, 23, pp. 33–48.

Öry, F., Simons, M., Verhulst, F., Leenders, F. and Wolters, W. (1991) 'Children who cross cultures', *Social Science and Medicine*, 32/1, pp. 29–34.

Perrez, M. and Reicherts, M. (1992) *Stress, Coping, and Health*, Bern: Hogrefe & Huber.

Pierce, G., Sarason, I. and Sarason, B. (1996) 'Coping and social support', in Zeidner, M. and Endler, M. (eds) *Handbook of Coping*, New York: John Wiley & Sons, pp. 434–51.

Reiss, D. (1981) *The Family's Construction of Reality*, Cambridge, Mass.: Harvard University Press.

Reiss, D. and Oliveri, M. E. (1983) 'Family stress as community frame', *Marriage and Family Review*, 6, pp. 61–83.

Sluzki, C. (1979) 'Migration and family conflict', *Family Process*, 18/4, pp. 379–90.

Taboada Leonetti I. and Lévy, F. (1978) *Femmes et immigrées: L'insertion des femmes immigrées en France*, Paris: La documentation française.

Tamura, T. and Furnham, A. (1993) 'Re-adjustment of Japanese returnee children from an overseas sojourn', *Social Science and Medicine*, 36/9, pp. 1181–6.

Thoits, P. (1994) 'Stressors and problem-solving: the individual as psychological activist', *Journal of Health and Social Behavior*, 32, pp. 143–59.

Useem, J. and Useem, R. (1967) 'The interfaces of a binational third culture: a study of the American community in India', *Journal of Social Issues*, 23/1, pp. 130–43.

Useem, R. and Downie, R. (1976) 'Third-culture kids', reprinted in Austin, C. (ed) (1986) *Cross-Cultural Re-entry: A Book of Readings*, Abilene, Texas: Abilene Christian University Press.

Walsh, F. (1996) 'The concept of family resilience: crisis and challenge', *Family Process*, 35/3, pp. 261–81.

Werkman, S. (1980) 'Coming home: adjustment of Americans to the United States after living abroad', in Coelho G. and Ahmed, P. (eds) *Uprooting and Development: Dilemmas of Coping with Modernization*, New York: Plenum.

Some books about moving abroad

Albright, S., Chu, A. and Austin, L. (1986) *Moving and Living Abroad: A Complete Handbook for Families*, New York: Hippocrene Books.

Cleveland, H., Mangone, G. and Adams, J. (1960) *The Overseas Americans*, New York: McGraw-Hill.

REFERENCES

Gordon, E. and Jones, M. (1988) *Portable Roots: Voices of Expatriate Wives*, Maastricht: Presses Interuniversitaires Européennes.
Hampshire, D. (1989) *Living and Working in Switzerland: A Survival Handbook*, Zurzach: Survival Books.
Kalb, R. and Welch, P. (1992) *Moving Your Family Overseas*, Yarmouth, Maine: Intercultural Press.
Kohls, L. R. (1979) *Survival Kit for Overseas Living: For Americans Planning to Live and Work Abroad*, Chicago: Intercultural Press.
McCollum, A. (1990) *The Trauma of Moving: Psychological Issues for Women*, London: Sage.
Piet-Pelon, N. and Hornby, B. (1985) *Women's Guide to Overseas Living*, 2nd edn, Yarmouth, Maine: Intercultural Press.
Seidenberg, R. (1973) *Corporate Wives – Corporate Casualties?* New York: Amacom.

APPENDIX

Tables A.1–A.5 summarise information concerning the families studied. Most of the tables refer to the 28 core families retained for most of the analysis.

The families *not* retained for the study are a rather mixed group. Five were single mothers, some of whom were professionals coming to challenging positions. Eight of the families originally interviewed were in Geneva for short stays, usually of less than a year (five of these were families of professors on sabbatical). Three families were eliminated because they did not meet sample limitations.

All tables exclude one family which withdrew from the study.

Table A.1 Family composition and age

Marriage		
Mixed-culture	8	(29%)
Second	8	(29%)

Age	range	mean
Men	34–53	42
Women	27–49	38
Children		
Number	1–6	2.6
Ages	0–25 years	

Family life stage *(by age of oldest child)*		
Pre school (< 6)	1	(4%)
School age (6–11)	13	(46%)
Early adolescent (12–14)	4	(14%)
Adolescent (> 15)	2	(7%)
Left nest (> 18)	8	(29%)
Total	28	(100%)

APPENDIX

Table A.2 Characteristics of previous and present moves

Previous moves as a family		
none	10	(36%)
1–2 moves, North America	4	(14%)
3–4 moves, North America	3	(11%)
1 international move	6	(21%)
3–4 international moves	3	(11%)
5+ international moves	2	(7%)
Total	28	(100%)

Came to Geneva from		
North America	23	(82%)
Other	5	(18%)
Total	28	(100%)

French spoken on arrival (subjective estimation, family member most fluent)		
mother tongue French (entire family)	1	(4%)
mother tongue French (part of family) all speak	1	(4%)
fluent	6	(21%)
'manage OK'	5	(18%)
'halting'	10	(36%)
none	5	(18%)
Total	28	(101%)

Expected length of stay		
less than 1 year	0	–
1 year	0	–
2–3 years	5	(18%)
3–5 years	13	(46%)
more than 5 years but to return	7	(25%)
perhaps permanent	3	(11%)
Total	28	(100%)

Table A.3 Education and careers

Education (years)	range	mean
Husbands	13–22	17.3
Wives	12–22	15.1

Where men work		
Business: large companies	8	(29%)
Business: small companies	8	(29%)
Government	4	(14%)
International organisation, NGO	5	(18%)
Independents	3	(11%)
Total	28	(101%)

Women's careers (a few months after the move)		
'Wife and mother'	11	(39%)
Plan career when children older	1	(4%)
Job (as opposed to career)	4	(14%)
Able to pursue career	3	(11%)
Pause, established career	0	–
Serious volunteer work	2	(7%)
'Two person single career'	2	(7%)
Move causes career problem	5	(18%)
Total	28	(100%)

Table A.4 Push and pull factors in decision to move

Push factors		
none	16	(57%)
drugs, crime	2	(7%)
previous place of residence, style of life	6	(21%)
routine, desire for change	6	(21%)

Pull factors		
job-related	12	(43%)
travel, see Europe	15	(54%)
experience another culture	6	(21%)
learn language	8	(29%)
personal growth	3	(11%)
make Swiss friends	3	(11%)
settle down	3	(11%)
extended family	7	(25%)

Note
Families were invited to discuss as many push or pull factors as they wished. Some listed one or two, most listed several. Percentages are thus not cumulative.

Table A.5 Decision to move and preparation

Decision		
difficult	12	(43%)
sense of crisis or pressure concerning decision	4	(14%)
easy	13	(46%)
no real decision involved	3	(11%)

Who decides		
couple together	19	(68%)
wife	0	—
husband	5	(18%)
family together	3	(11%)
the company	1	(4%)
Total	28	(101%)

To prepare		
talk to others	13	(46%)
read	13	(46%)
stock up on food and supplies	10	(36%)
study French	9	(32%)
visit Geneva	8	(29%)
nothing necessary	5	(18%)

Note

These were open-ended questions and families may have given several different responses. Percentages are cumulative in the middle segment only, concerning who in the family made the decision to move.

APPENDIX

Table A.6 Positive aspects of living overseas as reported by North American parents (3–4 months after arrival)

	Men (N = 36)[a]	Women (N = 43)[a]
(score 0–3)[b]		
professional challenge	2.5	1.1
travel	2.5	2.5
broader world view	2.2	2.5
discovering new culture	2.2	2.4
new ways of looking at things	2.1	2.3
meeting new people	2.0	2.3
getting to know Swiss	1.7	1.4
increased family togetherness	2.2	2.1
personal growth	2.2	2.1
learning new language	1.9	2.1
self testing	1.3	2.0
educational opportunities	1.5	1.7
financial gains	1.2	0.8
starting over again	1.2	1.7
freedom from interpersonal responsibilities	0.7	0.8
freedom from practical responsibilities	0.6	0.7
freedom from constraints	0.5	0.7

Notes
a All families studied are included in this table.
b 0 = does not apply to me at all; 1 = applies to me a little bit; 2 = applies to me moderately; 3 = very much applies to me.

APPENDIX

Table A.7 Stressful aspects of living overseas as reported by North American parents (3–4 months after arrival)

	Men (N = 36)[a]	Women (N = 43)[a]
Overall stressfulness of moving (Score 0–3)[b]	1.9	1.8
Specific stressful aspects		
language	1.5	1.8
housing	1.2	1.3
daily shopping	1.2	1.3
difficulties getting to know the locals	1.1	1.2
contacts with locals	1.0	1.1
family far away	1.0	1.3
no close friends nearby	0.9	1.2
loneliness	0.6	1.1
problems with schools	1.1	1.0
work problems	0.9	0.7
financial problems	0.9	0.9
daily schedules	0.6	0.7
rootlessness	0.5	0.9
people moving away	0.4	0.8
different moral values	0.4	0.7
lack of community roles	0.4	0.7
lack of control over decision to move	0.4	0.6
not having own possessions around	0.6	0.5
boredom	0.3	0.6
other people, your nationality	0.3	0.2

Notes
a All families studied are included in this table.
b 0 = not at all stressful; 1 = a little bit; 2 = moderately; 3 = very stressful.

Table A.8 Sense of coherence scores, approximately 3 months after moving, in descending order[a]

Family	High SOC			Family	Medium SOC			Family	Low SOC		
	H	W	Fam		H	W	Fam		H	W	Fam
Kent	–	195	[b]	Hummell	151	161	159	Madison	148	141	143
Graham	175	135	183	Renton	159	156	157	Exon	131	146	142
Cady	174	172	173	Thomas	159	155	156	Kennedy	154	138	142
Hill	–	169	[b]	Collins	171	150	155	Smithers	156	130	137
Jackson	152	175	169	Bateson	143	158	154	Ogbourne	118	142	136
Allen	167	168	168	Quincy	122	161	151	Zelig	156	128	135
Wood	144	172	165	Foster	148	148	148	Rodgers	145	131	135
Elm	134	173	163	Friedson	141	150	148	Gibbs	110	135	129
Davidson	163	163	163	Nathanson	145	148	147	Newton	150	112	122
				Vance	159	143	147				

	Mean		Range		Standard deviation
Husbands	149		110–175		16
Wives	154		112–195		19
Families	151		122–183		15

$$\text{Family SOC} = \frac{H+W}{2} - \frac{H-W}{4}$$

Notes

[a] Family sense of coherence was calculated using a formulation developed by Lavee and Olson (1993) for use with another self-report instrument. One quarter of the difference between the husband's score and the wife's score is subtracted from the couple's mean score:

In families in which scores of husband and wife differed, the formula was thus biased in favour of the wife. Such weighting makes sense in families such as those studied here, in which it was almost always the wives who had more daily contact with the new culture, and also who stayed home to be with the children after the family moved, and thus had a great deal of potential influence on shaping family members' perceptions of the new environment (see Haour-Knipe 1999 and 2000 for more extensive discussions of ways of measuring family SOC).

[b] Scores for both husband and wife were measured at the last interview only in these families.

APPENDIX

Table A.9 Family characteristics: 'co-ordination' and 'closure'

Co-ordination	
High	Thomas, Exon, Bateson, Davidson, Hummell, Jackson, Kennedy, Nathanson, Ogbourne
Medium high	Elm, Foster, Graham, Hill, Quincy, Wood, Collins
Medium low	Allen, Renton, Gibbs, Rodgers, Smithers
Low	Cady, Kent, Newton, Vance, Zelig, Friedson, Madison

Closure	
Delayed, both husband and wife	Graham, Hill, Kent, Newton, Renton, Thomas, Vance, Wood, Bateson, Collins, Davidson, Friedson, Jackson, Kennedy, Madison, Nathanson, Ogbourne, Rodgers
Delayed, one spouse only	Mr Cady, Mrs Elm, Mr Quincy, Mr Exon
Early closure	Allen, Foster, Zelig, Gibbs, Hummell, Smithers

INDEX

accidents 57–8, 104, 120
activities 122, 127, 130; dual careers 193; reflections 198; social support 139, 141
adaptation 8, 99, 194–9; migration 201
adjustments 78–81, 111, 125–6; case studies 182; conclusions 212; social support 128, 136, 152
adolescents 94, 120, 132, 161–2; conclusions 214; effects 164–8; family support 144, 147; reflections 200
alcohol 103–4, 114, 212
alienation 51, 146, 216
Allen family 13, 35, 143–4, 161–2
American Women's Club 3, 56
Americans 1, 8, 12–13, 210
anger 78–9, 81, 86, 201
annoyances 58–60
Antonovsky, A. 4–5, 6–8, 9–10, 96, 98
apartments 2, 58, 72, 100, 131, 179
au pairs 170–1, 174, 193
authority 145–54

babies 162, 169, 171
Bateson family 35–6, 74–5, 142, 164–5
boarding school 161

Cady family 36, 81–3
Canadians 1, 8, 12, 13, 210
challenges 106, 109, 114–15; case studies 174; conclusions 216, 217; family support 152

children 7–9, 11, 14; age ranges 15; alcohol 103–4; bedtimes 139; case studies 175–6, 181–3, 187–8; co-ordination 218–19; conclusions 212, 214; coping 104–5; decision-making 31; dual careers 192; duty travel 82–5, 89–90; effects 156–69; extended families 116; family support 141, 143–5, 148, 150; hopes 18; language 63; leaving 23, 25–6; long-term effects 220–1; neighbours 171–2; peers 16; school-aged 54, 59, 68–9, 109; social support 112, 122, 132, 151–2; values 91–4
Christmas 120, 148, 152, 220
church 1, 151, 173, 182, 187
closure 4, 203–8
co-ordination 4, 10, 138–45; case studies 189; children 168, 169; conclusions 218–19; effects of moving 201
coherence 4–5; *see also* sense of coherence
cohesion, family *see* co-ordination
Collins family, sketch 36–7
company (as employment setting) 12, 14, 25–8; case studies 172, 180–1; closure 204; conclusions 211, 216, 222; coping 96–7, 99, 106; dual careers 74; duty travel 81; effects of moving 203; family support 146; newcomers groups 126–7; support 121–3, 178
complaining 127–9, 144, 149; case studies 170–3; conclusions 213; family support 150

237

INDEX

comprehensibility 5–6, 9–10, 34; case studies 187–8; conclusions 215–18; coping 96–8, 100, 105–6, 114; social support 133
conclusions 209–24
confidentiality 11–13, 180, 210
conformity 156, 167
control 53–4, 59–60, 62; conclusions 213; coping 98, 99–100, 102, 108, 110–12; dual careers 194; social relations 123–9; strains 89; support 116, 133
coping 96–115, 212–13, 221
core families 198–200, 210–11, 228–36
crime 16, 24, 53, 202
culture 5, 64–7, 86; case studies 174, 181, 186, 188–9; children 157; co-ordination 219; conclusions 214; coping 90–5; limits to help 128–9; long-term effects 220–1; migration 198; stereotypes 204–56; stress 99–112

Davidson family 22–3, 37; family support 138, 145–6, 151–4; social support 131–2
death 117–18, 121, 203
decision-making 14–15, 28–32, 56; case studies 178; children 158–9; conclusions 216; coping 111–12; effects of moving 202
delayed closure families 204–7
denial 114, 200
depression 59, 75, 110; case studies 173–5, 177; coping 113; dual careers 78, 192; effects of moving 201; phase 195–8; reflections 200
developing countries 133–7, 151, 165
disintegration of families 176–80
divorce 11, 176–8
doctors 56, 58, 121
driving 65, 76, 162, 182, 192
drugs 16, 94, 171, 202
dual careers 28–9, 34, 74–8, 145, 190–4, 222
duty travel 73, 81–90, 142

early closure families 204–7
effects of moving 201–8, 214–15
Elm family 31–2, 38

emergencies 116, 120–1
emotional support 116–17, 122, 151, 154, 179
employee preparation programmes 198
employers 121, 128–9, 187, 203; *see also* company; government; organisation
English language 1, 61–2, 103; children 172; coping 109; school 159–60; social support 130
excitement phase 194–5
Exon family 49
expatriates 1, 7, 91–2; case studies 178; coping 221; social support 126; stereotypes 205; stress 199; support comparison 134–6
extended families 18, 116–19, 171, 176, 179

families 4, 15–16; closure 203–8; effects of moving 201–8, 214–15; migration 221–3; openness 130–1; sketches 35–50; SOC 98–9; strains 71–95; stress 223–4; support 138–55; two years on 190–208
finance 57, 123, 150; case studies 173, 178; family support 152
first friends 123–7, 160, 182, 213
food 31–2, 58, 63; case studies 172, 178; children 157; social support 126, 148, 151
Foster family 11, 38, 170–9
French language 27, 31–3, 53–4; careers 193; case studies 183, 184, 185; children 156–7, 158, 168, 172; conclusions 214; coping 100, 103–4, 106–7, 109, 111, 115; dual careers 192; family support 145; school 159; social support 130; stereotypes 205; stress 60, 61
Friedson family 38–9
friendships 68–70, 112, 119–23; case studies 182; children 159–60, 165–6; conclusions 213; support 133, 136, 140; *see also* first friends
frustration 59, 61, 74–5; adjustment 80; case studies 175, 177; conclusions 211–13; coping 102–3, 106, 114; dual careers 78; extended families 118–19; family support 153–4; limits to help 128; newcomers groups 127; reflections 199; strains 88

INDEX

frustrations: career 193; phases of adaptation 195

Geneva 1–3, 7–8, 11–13, 133–7
Gibbs family 20–1, 39, 102–6, 165
gifted children 161–2, 166
goals 202, 215, 217–18
government (as employment setting) 12–14, 18–22; children 165; conclusions 210–11, 216; coping 96–7, 99, 104, 106; duty travel 81; social support 121
Graham family 25–6, 39–40, 106–9
grandparents 117–18, 163

hardship posts 20, 101, 133–7
hassles 52, 58–60, 62; conclusions 211–12; coping 97, 99–100, 102, 106; family support 144–5; strains 71, 73
helplessness 62–3, 66, 98, 117
hidden expenses 172, 178
high family co-ordination 138–43, 151–4, 218–19
Hill family 40
home leave 162
homesickness 128, 166
honeymoon phase 194–5, 197
housing 2, 51, 56; case studies 170, 179; conclusions 214; coping 100, 109, 111–12; support 131–2, 151–2
humiliation 62, 113, 182
Hummel family 40–1
husbands 71–3, 122; adjustment 79–81; case studies 174–5, 177–8; co-ordination 154–5, 218–19; dual careers 74–8, 190–4; duty travel 82–5, 142; family support 143–5; limits to help 128–9; long-term effects 220–1

identity 65–8, 74
ill-health 56–7, 59, 76; case studies 185; extended families 117, 119; support 116, 118, 143, 152; younger children 163
imbalances of authority 145–54
insecurity 53, 104, 161, 171, 188
integration 17
international organisations 1, 3, 13; *see also* organisation

International School 7, 91, 94; conclusions 214; dual careers 192; social support 151, 159; tuition fees 192
interviews 8–10, 51–2
isolation 68–70, 88, 127; case studies 177, 179–80; children 167; phases of adaptation 196; reflections 198

Jackson family 18–20, 22, 41–2; coping 99–102; extended families 119; support 140–1

Kennedy family 42, 190–1
Kent family 42–3

language 1, 51–2, 109; case studies 181; children 156–7, 159–60; conclusions 214; coping 97; dual careers 192; family support 145; stress 52–3, 60–3
learning difficulties 110–11
length of stay 202–3
levelling-out phase 195, 197
limits to help 128–9
local schools 159, 168, 192
loneliness 51–2, 54, 56; case studies 182, 188; coping 109; family support 138–9, 140, 142, 154; privacy 131; strain 79; stress 68–70
long-distance support 119–21
long-term effects 220–1
low family co-ordination 138, 143–5, 147–50, 219

Madison family 23–4, 43, 138, 147–50
manageability 6, 9–10, 34; case studies 187–8; conclusions 215–18; coping 96–8, 100, 105, 107, 111, 114; social support 133
marriages 9, 15, 131; case studies 173; co-ordination 219; reflections 198–9; social support 140
meaningfulness 6, 9–10, 34; case studies 187; conclusions 215–18, 224; coping 96–8; social support 133
methodology 7–10
migrants 1, 7, 198–200, 221–3
mobilisation of support 130–3
money 91–5, 146–7
mourning 118, 185

239

INDEX

multinational corporations 1–3, 12, 210; see also company

Nathanson family 44
negativity 172, 177, 183; case studies 185; conclusions 214; effects of moving 202; reflections 200
neighbours 171–4, 177–9, 182, 187, 195
networks 7, 9, 119, 131, 139, 151
newcomers groups 125–7
Newton family 44–5, 120
non-government organisations see organisation
North Americans 1–3, 7, 12–13
nursery school 171, 173

Ogbourne family 45, 131
older children 164–8, 214, 218
organisation (as employment setting) 1, 3, 13–14; conclusions 210–11, 216, 222; coping 96–7, 99; duty travel 81; effects of moving 203; family support 138, 147–51, 153; social support 121; volunteer work 193–4; work 22–5

paradigm 4, 106, 204, 224
parents 94, 117, 122
phases of adaptation 194–8
police 104, 151, 172
politics 1, 156, 165
practical support 116, 151, 179
pre-school children 162–4
pregnancy 143, 162, 173
preparations for moving 31–2
privacy 130–1
psychiatry 11, 175–6
psychology 166, 175, 223–4
public transport 2, 103, 161–2, 164
pull factors 17–18, 25, 28, 202; stress 51
push factors 16–17, 28, 51, 202

Quincy family 21, 46

Reiss, D. 4–5, 7, 10; closure 203–4, 207; family support 138
relationships 16, 68, 111; case studies 173, 177; co-ordination 218–19; conclusions 210, 212–13, 217–18; extended families 116–19; strains 88

religion 151, 187
Renton family 29–30, 46–7, 59, 75–6, 192–3
risk 199–200, 224
Rodgers family 47
role reversal 145–6, 153
roots 14, 17, 24, 165, 201
rules 65–8, 98, 104; case studies 172, 187–8; conclusions 212; coping 114; social support 128, 151; stereotypes 208

sacrifice 187, 189
salaries 57, 178
school year 158, 169
school-aged children 157–62
schools 7–8, 54, 59; case studies 175, 182–3, 188; coping 109, 112; dual careers 192; social support 132, 151–2; stress 68–9, 214; values 91–2; volunteer work 122, 193
sense of coherence (SOC) 5–6, 9–10, 32–3; case studies 187–8; children 168; conclusions 212, 215–18, 224; coping 97–9, 111, 114–15; effects of moving 201; families 105–6; questionnaires 51–2, 61
shopping 51, 67, 106; case studies 185; coping 111; hassles 58; social support 122, 126, 144
shyness 120, 156, 160
siblings 117, 119, 157, 163, 168
single parents 8, 83, 152, 167
Smithers family 47–8, 88–90, 109–12
SOC see sense of coherence
social support 116–37, 212–13; family 138–55
spouses 9, 14, 28–9; co-ordination 218–19; conclusions 212; decision-making 31; dual careers 34, 74–8, 190–4; migration 222; strains 71–95
stereotypes 203–8
strains 71–95, 198, 211–12
stress 4–5, 6, 9; case studies 185; children 166; co-ordination 219; conclusions 211–12; coping 108; culture 99–112; effects of moving 202–3; expatriates 199, 200, 221; families 223–4; family support 138, 143–5, 147–54; language 60; types 51–70

240

INDEX

stressors 51, 112, 216, 223
support 116–37, 138–55; case studies 187; company 178; conclusions 217; social 212–13

telephones 119, 120, 221
terrorism 108, 113
Thomas family 48, 77–8, 191–2
transport *see* driving, public transport

United Nations 203, 206
university 1, 15, 105; children 157, 161, 166–7; coping 109, 112; extended families 116
uplifts 52

vacations 148–9, 163, 166
values 73, 90–5, 138; authority 145–54; case studies 187; children 164–5; closure 204
Vance family 48–9, 117–19, 165–8

visitors 109, 120–1, 123–4, 131
volunteer work 193–4
vulnerability 90, 98, 127, 133, 219

wills 171
wives 1, 71–8, 82–5; adjustment 79–81; careers 193–4; case studies 170–1, 173–5, 177–8; co-ordination 154–5, 218–19; dual careers 190–4; family support 143–5; groups 141; limits to help 128–9; long-term effects 220–1; social support 122, 130
women 68–9, 78–81, 122; careers 193–4; duty travel 142; family support 150; friendships 213; groups 141; social support 130; spouse groups 126
Wood family 11, 49, 52–5, 180–6
work permits 74, 194, 222

Zelig family 50, 66–7, 85–8